CULTURE AND CUISINE

Books in English by Jean-François Revel

CULTURE AND CUISINE

THE TOTALITARIAN TEMPTATION

WITHOUT MARX OR JESUS

THE FRENCH

AS FOR ITALY

ON PROUST

CULTURE
AND
CUISINE

A JOURNEY THROUGH THE
HISTORY OF FOOD

by JEAN-FRANÇOIS REVEL

TRANSLATED FROM THE FRENCH
by HELEN R. LANE

DOUBLEDAY & COMPANY, INC.
GARDEN CITY, NEW YORK
1982

Library of Congress Cataloging in Publication Data
Revel, Jean-François.
Culture and cuisine.
Translation of: Un festin en paroles.
1. Gastronomy.   I. Title.
TX641.R4813   641'.01'3
AACR2
ISBN: 0-385-15107-1
Library of Congress Catalog Card Number 78–22645

DESIGNED BY LAURENCE ALEXANDER

Originally published as UN FESTIN EN PAROLES
© Société Nouvelle des Éditions Jean-Jacques Pauvert, 1979

to my mother

CONTENTS

CULTURE AND CUISINE

PROLOGUE

ON
GASTRONOMICAL
SENSIBILITY OR
THE MARRIAGE
OF THE
CORDON BLEU
AND THE
THINKING CHEF

Sensibility and History: a new subject. I know of no book that deals with it," Lucien Febvre wrote in *Combats pour l'Histoire* (*Battles for History*).[1] And the founding father of the *Annales* school of historiography continued: "I do not even see a formulation anywhere of the multiple problems that it involves. And so (may a mere historian be forgiven this cry of an artist) here is a splendid subject." Yet, paradoxically, earlier twentieth-century historians long kept psychology and the study of mentalities at a distance in order to allow the naked truth of "quantitative" history to speak, with exciting results. But later they returned to the study of mentalities, and the labors of the last decade have demonstrated that psychology, sensibility or sensibilities, collective representations, and ideologies are also part of that "enduring" history that Fernand Braudel was the first to conceive of and prove to be a reality. Any observer of the Third World today can attest that sensibilities are more influential and sometimes persist far longer than the material bases of a given society.

After this solemn exordium, I hasten to add that writing this book has been above all a diversion for me. Since cookbooks aroused my curiosity, I ended up collecting a number of them, because they are the unconscious reflection of everyday life and a crossroads where different manners and customs meet down through the centuries. But as I studied them, I noted that the majority have two defects in common. The first is that the historical or retrospective introduction, in books that have one, is generally superficial and false. For the most part, the authors are content in this section of the book to copy each other without troubling to go back to the sources, and hence they perpetuate legends and prejudices concerning the past. The second defect is that the older these treatises are, the less they lend themselves to any sort of concrete representation in the mind of today's reader. The methods for cooking various dishes—the cooking time, for example—were presumed to be already known to contemporary users of these manuals. Cooking time might vary by so much as a factor of three. Flavors, aromas, dishes, condiments once used universally—Roman *garum* or medieval *cameline* sauce, for instance—no longer evoke

---

[1] Paris, Armand Colin, 1953.

anything at all for our minds or palates. The terminology of cuisine and the methods of serving food at table (I shall give a few examples farther on) have constantly changed. With the evolution of cattle-raising, agriculture, and horticulture, even the raw materials have changed, and not always for the worse. A mere three or four centuries ago beef in Europe was barely edible: at the beginning of *Don Quixote*, Cervantes offers as proof of the extreme material straits of his hero, who is about to become a knight, the fact that he "ate beef more often than mutton." Leaving aside the potato, whose introduction into Europe and whose consumption even in America are of recent date, we find it hard to realize that two vegetables as intimately linked in our minds to the idea of Mediterranean cuisine as the tomato and the eggplant did not in fact begin to be widely consumed everyday foods until the nineteenth century. The very popular *ratatouille* of today, variously referred to as "Nice style" or "Bohemian style," is not included in J. B. Reboul's classic *La Cuisinière provençale* (*The Provençal Family Cook*), which appeared at the end of the nineteenth century. The white bean, the basic ingredient of the *cassoulet occitan* of southwest France or of *fagioli all'uccelletto* of Tuscany, dishes that many people would swear derive from a peasant tradition dating back to Neolithic times, in fact arrived in Europe from Mexico at the end of the sixteenth century, when it almost completely replaced the chick-pea and the broad bean. It is also false that the consumption of meat, for example, was restricted to the affluent classes until very recently. Meat consumption depended, rather, on the period and the region. Dante's Florentine contemporaries of all estates raised pigs and poultry in the city itself, and had the right to hunt for the then-abundant game on the hills round about. In his *Monsieur Nicolas*, Restif de la Bretonne provides evidence that during his childhood, on the eve of the French Revolution, young peasants in northern Burgundy trapped partridges and thrushes and hunted them with slingshots. He notes, too, that the raising of cattle and poultry on farms was a relatively flourishing enterprise.

Even more than the history of various foods, it is the history of *taste* that is the question here—in the primary meaning of the word or, rather, in both senses of the word. That is to say: What did a meal, a wine *taste like* in the third century before or after Christ?

And *what sort of taste* did the guests have? What did they like, what was particularly sought after? What sort of wine was in one of the old bottles that Horace took out of his cellar on any and every occasion? For that matter, what were the Sabine wines like, of which he was not particularly fond? And what about the floods of ordinary wine that flowed into the cups of Agathon's guests at Plato's *Symposium?* To readers of the time, reconstructing the exact taste of these things in their minds presented no problem.

Gastronomical imagination, in fact, precedes experience itself, accompanies it, and in part substitutes for it. To speak today of being served a dozen oysters washed down with a Chablis or a Pouilly immediately evokes a very precise, characteristic marriage of tastes. But in a thousand years it will mean nothing to a reader who will doubtless have no notion as to what Chablis was, just as it will mean nothing to him that around the year 1900, oysters, above all the type known as *belons,* were traditionally served with Sauterne (a fact that is forgotten today, and would strike seafood lovers in these closing years of the twentieth century as monstrous). This future reader may have no way of knowing that Sauternes were sweet white wines and Chablis and Pouilly dry white wines. He would also have to know that "dry" in this context meant "not sweet" rather than "with a high alcohol content." We do not know what taste experience Horace is referring to when he writes, in an invitation to Maecenas, "you will drink bad Sabine wine," adding that he himself put it up and sealed it in "a clay amphora once filled with Greek wine." Why? What Greek wine? The poet then mentions several growths of wine: Cecubo, Cales, wine of Formies, hinting that he is too poor to offer them to his guests.[2] These names, for us, evoke little or nothing. Habit is everything, and what is habitual is never precisely defined for those to whom it is so familiar as to be self-explanatory, for those who take it completely for granted, so that it is almost impossible to reconstruct it once it is lost. Tourists consider it picturesque and amusing to drink wine with resin in Greece because this preparation is something they know about, but they would be horrified if they were served wine diluted with sea water. Yet this mixture was the general rule in certain regions of ancient Greece, just as

---

[2] *Odes,* Book I, 20.

wines were later almost universally mixed not only with pure
water (a custom that was to persist down to the seventeenth century A.D.) but also with all sorts of liquids or solids (soluble or
not) with a strong scent, a practice that would naturally scandal-
ize a modern oenologist—except, once again, when such a combination resembles one of our own habits, such as the drinking of
hot wine with cinnamon in France or sangría in Spain, or champagne with orange juice, and so on . . . To compound the
difficulty of reconstructing what is remote from us, let us add that
cuisine travels as badly in space as in time, and the same is true of
information about cuisine: the Hungarian goulash to be found in
Hungary is not a stew but a soup, the *paella valenciana* that is
eaten in Valencia is based not on seafood but on rabbit, and so
on . . .

It is literary texts, as much as and indeed perhaps even more
than cookbooks properly speaking, that have served as the warp
and woof of the present book. From Aristophanes to Zola, from
Juvenal to Gogol, passing by way of Fielding or Goldoni, poetry,
the novel, or the theater offer us a reflection of the contemporary
gastronomical sensibility of a given society that is all the more be-
lievable in that it is usually involuntary and peripheral. Here too it
is necessary, certainly, to make allowances for "pantagruelian" exaggeration, a *literary* device, as well as for its opposite, exaggerated "hunger pangs," which are particularly frequent in the pic-
aresque novel, beginning with the first of them, *Lazarillo de
Tormes*, and, even earlier, with their Latin ancestor, Apuleius'
The Golden Ass. The "ridiculous repast," as portrayed by Nicolas
Boileau or others, in verse or in prose, is also a frequent theme;
thanks to the satirical treatment of bad cuisine that it involves, the
reader can deduce what was considered to be good cuisine in a
given time and place.

There is hardly a single literary genre that does not provide
similar information. In the course of each of the ten days of the
Decameron, for instance, the elegant company of young ladies and
handsome gentlemen who have fled to the countryside to escape
the plague in Florence are served sweets, preserves, and jams as
light repasts. The reason was doubtless that it would have been
unseemly to show these arbiters of wit and good taste soiling their

fingers and garments by downing cold cuts and meats with sauces. Sugar, moreover, was rare and costly at the time. It was, indeed, a condiment—used principally in sauces—rather than a "food," and did not become a staple until the end of the seventeenth century. Hence, when Boccaccio portrays the ruling aristocracy of the day, he shows it eating sweets, just as today he would show it eating caviar and smoked salmon. So as not to spoil the charm of his portrait, he would take care not to show young women of the "jet set" stuffing themselves with cream puffs and *babas au rhum*. When Baudelaire writes *Pauvre Belgique* (*Poor Belgium*), an admittedly mad indictment of that country (but for that very reason a revealing reflection of certain fixed ideas), he complains several times, rightly or wrongly, of the absence of ragouts in Belgian cuisine. From this we can deduce that meats in a sauce represented, for a Frenchman of the Second Empire, the main dish par excellence, whereas for today's Western man it is grilled meat. Baudelaire also deplores what he considers to be the bad quality of vegetables in Belgium, made even worse by what he calls the "rancid butter" used to prepare them—an indication that cooked vegetables played a greater role than they do today in gastronomical expectations. There is no history of cuisine that is not also a history of prevailing appetite, habits, and taste.

This is a literary history then, as I have said, a history by way of texts, one that sometimes even becomes a sort of anthology; for I have felt it my duty to quote at length from works that are difficult to come by or that are too classic to be omitted. I, nonetheless, make no claim to being exhaustive. I have made soundings, exploratory diggings in certain periods, certain geographical areas, certain social classes. I composed this book little by little, during vacations that afforded me the opportunity to read and reread texts that took me far afield from my usual preoccupations. It was my recreation, and I hope that the reader will find it one too.

Such a pastime in the history of gastronomical sensibility, as glimpsed in cookbooks and other texts, is particularly justified from a literary point of view. For this is a domain in which sublimation through language is one of the factors that constitutes a feast, when it is not a substitute for one, as it was for Baudelaire when he wrote, again in *Pauvre Belgique:* "No restaurants. The means of consoling oneself: reading cookbooks."[3] To as great a degree as sexuality, food is inseparable from imagination.

❧

Every menu is an exercise in rhetoric, every gastronomical criticism tends to be couched in the noble, or heroicomic, style, as though the fortuitous and transitory nature of its object had to be redeemed by the grandiloquence of the praise or blame being heaped upon it. Cuisine has always moved forward, like Descartes,[4] masked behind a superabundant, high-flown terminology, whose lack of rigor as regards the names, the composition, and the preparation of dishes is one of the principal causes of the well-nigh impenetrable mystery that always surrounds the gastronomy of the past and often paves the way for the disappointments of the present. It is also an ever-changing terminology. A mere 100 to 130 years ago, entrées were the main dish of a meal rather than the ones served at the beginning of it. The French word has kept this meaning in the United States, where on all hotel and restaurant menus it designates the main dish. But the entrées of the last century did not include either roasts or *relevés*, a term that has since disappeared as a noun, by which was meant the boiled meat served immediately after the soup, whence the complete expression *relevé de potage*. As for *entremets*, they were not at all the synonym for desserts that they have since become. Most *entremets* were salted dishes—meats, pâtés, eggs; only a few of them were sweets. But all of this was by no means the invariable rule, and though entrées (of meat or fish) designated in principle dishes served in the *middle* of a meal, and in a sauce, one also finds dishes that would normally figure in the list of roasts cited in this category. This lack of precision, characteristic of cookbooks in every era, extends to the recipes themselves, for often they are as prodigal of flowery flights of eloquence as they are silent as to the essential steps in preparation and cooking. Moreover, gastronomical revolutions are also revolutions in terminology. We must consider

---

[3] Immediately following this phrase, Baudelaire writes: "No mistress, read a book on love." With regard to Belgian cuisine, I solemnly affirm that in my opinion either bitterness misled the great poet or Belgian cuisine has improved enormously in a hundred years.

[4] *Larvatus prodeo* (Cartesius).

ourselves fortunate when they are not limited to being that. Honoré Bostel, a former journalist who is now a restaurateur, penned in 1978 a witty spoof of the rhetorical innovations of the "New French Cuisine":

"Here is a list of dishes taken from the menus of Paris restaurants in this beginning of the end of the [twentieth] century:

Aiguillette of guinea hen with compote of watercress petals (36 francs)
Rillettes of tuna with avocado mousse and lime (24 francs)
Suprême de Saint-Pierre with currants (48 francs)
Strawberry soup . . . Etc., etc., etc.

"Hence it is language more than cuisine that has its fashions. It is more the word than the content that sustains cuisine, even if it is new.

"Here is how to proceed in order to exploit this latest fashion if you wish to establish an 'in' menu:

1) Baptize the entrees with the name of desserts; as an example, begin with a 'head cheese sherbet.'

2) Do not forget that terrines can be made only of fish or vegetables (preferably small ones).

3) For the main dish, reverse the name of the traditional content, especially as regards meat and fish. Example: 'rumpsteak of sole.'

4) Reconvert the names of desserts into names of entrees; for example: 'fig soup' or 'strawberry soup.'

"Thus it will not be the dish that will prove tempting so much as the subtlety of the syntax.

"There are very few creations in cuisine, so let recreations amuse us!"[5]

Indeed, the function of this toplofty jargon is to disconcert and thereby create the illusion of originality, a more facile solution than the honest execution of tried and tested recipes. But there is another function, which we might call (if we are being nasty) that of intimidating or (if we are being kind) that of spellbinding.

---

[5] "*Le nouveau langage de la cuisine*" ("*The New Language of Cuisine*") in the weekly *Paris-Poche*, 1978.

"This influence of language on sensation," Bergson writes, "is more profound than is generally thought. Language not only makes us believe in the invariability of our sensations; it also sometimes deceives us as to the very nature of the sensation experienced. Thus when I eat a dish reputed to be exquisite, the name that it bears, freighted with the approbation given it, interposes itself between my sensation and my consciousness. I can persuade myself that the taste pleases me, whereas a slight effort of attention would prove the contrary to me."[6]

Bergson has chosen the instance where the "dish reputed to be exquisite" has an indifferent taste or no taste at all. In this case, for lack of anything better, it is the dish's "delicacy" and "lightness" that is praised.

Masking error or banality is fortunately not the only function of gastronomical literature. But the difficulty when one explores the past (and even the present) lies in appreciating the difference between silent cuisine and cuisine that talks too much, between the cuisine that exists on the plate and the one that exists only in gastronomical chronicles. Or else, to state the matter in a different way, the difficulty lies in discovering, behind the verbal façade of fancy cuisines, the popular, anonymous, peasant or "bourgeois" cuisine, made up of tricks and little secrets that only evolve very slowly, in silence, and that no individual in particular has invented. It is above all this latter cuisine, the average cuisine, the gastronomical art of the "depths," that is responsible for there being countries where one "eats well" and others where one "eats badly." But by itself, cuisine that is merely practical, traditional family cooking does not suffice either. If it is not stimulated by the innovation, the reflection, and indeed the extravagance of a handful of artists, popular cuisine itself becomes atrophied, dull and uninteresting. The gastronomical serial written by the centuries has as its "plot" the constant battle between the good amateur cook and the thinking chef, a lover's quarrel that, as in all good adventure novels, ends, after many a stormy scene, with a marriage.

---

[6] Henri Bergson, *Essai sur les données immédiates de la conscience* (*Essay on the Immediate Data of Consciousness*), Paris, 1888, chapter II.

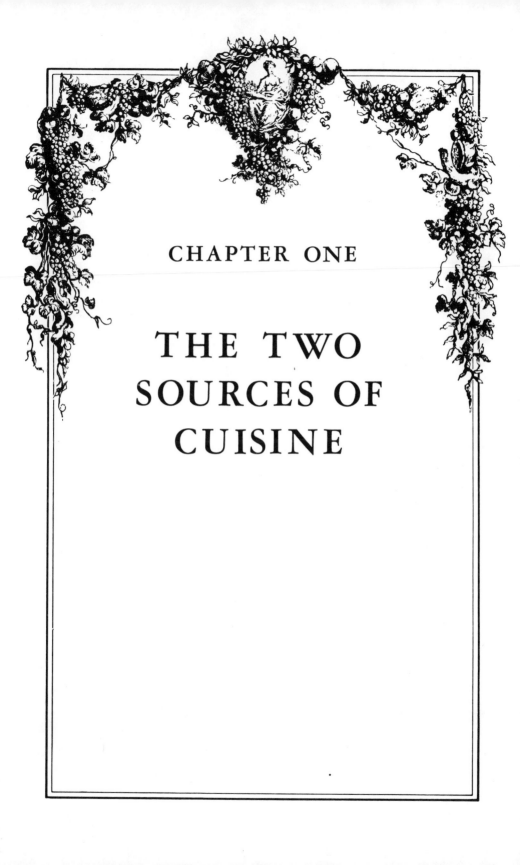

CHAPTER ONE

THE TWO
SOURCES OF
CUISINE

How to eat well without really taking nourishment? This might well be the question that gastronomy seeks to answer. Being hungry is not always a state favorable to the appreciation of food, because at such a time any dish seems delicious. Conversely, satiety, the permanent state of semirepletion in which people in prosperous countries live, may make them sensitive to the exploits of their chefs, but it also limits the extent and the frequency of the use that can be made of their chefs' talents and the legacy of tradition.

It is unfortunately a fact, however, that gastronomical pleasure can really be experienced to the fullest only if a variety, a contrast, and hence a multiplicity of dishes and wines is offered. Therefore the summits of this art are reached in precisely those periods when the refinement of recipes allies complexity of conception with lightness of touch in execution. This is a basic principle that should never be forgotten while reading these pages: expert cuisine is not a matter of accumulation alone; mixing is not the same as combining; the most barbarous dishes may be very heavy without being any more flavorful. Conversely, the most simple preparations may be *haute cuisine* when the association of two or three foods, which may be quite ordinary, results in an original flavor, a flavor that only the proper skill can produce.

Periodically in the course of this history we see a return to the natural product being preached as a reaction against an excessively heavy and complicated cuisine. But the real art lies neither in products in their natural state nor in heaviness and complexity: a great chef glorifies natural elements, uses them in ways that enhance their essence, knows how to extract their aromas and flavors and set off their consistencies—but he does so by transposing them into a new register, where they disappear only to be reborn as a whole that owes its existence to intelligence. In this respect, the knowledge of flavorful associations (what are the foodstuffs that can set each other off best and how should they be cooked?) is as important as the knowledge of the quantities, the proportions that must guide their marriage. There were entire centuries, for example, in which every dish was bombarded with spices and smelled only of cinnamon, nutmeg, saffron, or hot pepper. At other times and places, everything was drowned in cream or olive oil, two culinary adjuvants that have a particularly negative effect when used heavy-handedly. In tourist restaurants today, one sees the incorrect, theatrical use of herbs becoming the general rule: thyme for grilled meats, branches of fennel for sea perch (*loup*), that fish called sea bass (*bar*) in the North of France. Steaks are served smothered in thyme, an herb never meant to be eaten—does one eat the tea leaves that remain in the bottom of the teapot? The sole value of thyme is the aroma it gives a sauce, a stew, or possibly a grilled mutton chop, but only if one tosses a few bits of it *under* the grill to burn on the coals. As for branches of fennel, it is a veritable farce that we witness in the so-called "great fish restaurants" of Paris every time we see uniformed maîtres d'hôtel making desperate efforts to control a fire that they themselves have just lighted by putting a match to a heap of hay piled up under the wrinkled flanks of some hapless sea-creature whose skin thus chars to a cinder while its flesh remains ice-cold. No, Mr. Swallow-Tails! When one bakes a sea perch in the oven, in a white wine sauce or a lemon sauce, one delicately places two or three bits of fennel in the belly, so that the aroma will impregnate it, after which one puts them aside as one detaches the filets.

This leads us to note that only very rarely does good cuisine take place in the dining room. The little ballet round crêpes suzette, a flaming omelette, a pepper steak soaked with cognac, in the hollow of a silver platter beneath which a dangerous and evil-smelling alcohol lamp is burning, may be mindful of a traveling show and of the vigilance of a fire department, but not of gastronomy.

Let us say it once and for all: regional cuisine does not travel well. This is a basic truth that experience confirms, and before grouping it with certain principles that I shall set forth in the following pages, I shall here provide a few illustrative examples.

Let us take *bouillabaisse marseillaise*. In every seaside region there exists a fisherman's dish that consists of putting various kinds of fish into a pot and putting this pot on the fire, adding to the fish condiments that vary with the region and may be cream, hot pepper, saffron, white wine, onion, etc. . . . The result of this *pot-au-feu* made with fish (which need not necessarily be salt-water fish since there exists a *bouillabaisse* of fresh-water fish in white wine, called *pochouse* or *pauchouse*) is first of all a soup with bits of vegetables, bread, and fish (more or less softened by boiling) floating in it. In *cacciucco livornese*, mussels are added, and *moules marinières* (mussels fisherman-style), for which there are many recipes, depending on the region, are nothing but a *bouillabaisse* made exclusively of mussels. The *baudroie en bourride* (Provençal fish soup) of Sète is a *bouillabaisse* in which the sole ingredient is anglerfish (*baudroie*), the stock of which is particularly spicy and refined. Moreover, this anglerfish must come from the Mediterranean and not the Atlantic: the two are not the same. The anglerfish of the Atlantic, otherwise known as *lotte*, whose head has a different shape from that of the Mediterranean *baudroie*, is an excellent fish, but it is not the traditional ingredient of *bourride sétoise*. The *bourride* of Marseille in turn is a *bouillabaisse* consisting of only three species of fish—anglerfish, sea perch, and whiting (*merlan*)—and is characterized above all by the fact that one mixes garlic-flavored *aïoli* into the stock before serving. Aside from these variations, there are certain skillful touches to improve the dish that depend not on the recipe but on its execution: in particular knowing how to measure the cooking time so that one ends up with both a flavorful stock and edible fish; that is, fish not overcooked to the point that they fall apart. This is achieved in some instances by learning to put the fish with the most delicate flesh in the pot last. If *bouillabaisse marseillaise* has become famous all over the world, it is because the fish of the Golfe du Lion, called rockfish (*poisson de roche*), happens to be particularly tasty and firm. Into the making of a classic *bouillabaisse* go not only fish that are to be eaten but also fish included solely for their aroma, principally scorpion fish (*rascasse*). On the other hand, lobster in a *bouillabaisse marseillaise* is merely a tourist "frill": its flesh becomes flabby in the cooking and its flavor is lost, adding nothing to the dish. But this dish is indissolubly linked to local conditions, in the sense that its merits are due less to the recipe, which is actually quite ordinary, than to the nature and the origins of the products that go into it. Already very difficult to make well on the spot (since rockfish are rare and saffron that has not lost its flavor is hard to come by), and almost always adulterated even in Provençal restaurants (which use already-prepared stocks or, more precisely, *leftovers*, for real stocks are meat juices that are very costly to make and that have their role to play in Grand Cuisine) real *bouillabaisse* can be had only in private homes

or on special order, that is to say, in the precise circumstances in which it came into being—after the day's fishing, at the water's edge—and it becomes tasteless when attempts are made to reconstitute it in the abstract, in Paris, for example.

In such cases, culinary genius is the genius of a particular place. Unfortunately, an immense majority of the clientele of restaurants around the world confuse gastronomy with exoticism. In their eyes, the dish that is special is an exotic dish. But it is precisely this sort of dish that has the least chance of being prepared successfully. That is why the restaurateur makes up for it by "flaming" his grilled sea perch, or, in the case of *bouillabaisse,* by serving it with a *rouille,* an overrated sauce made with hot peppers or mayonnaise with garlic whose link with classic *bouillabaisse* is as extrinsic as that of mustard with meat. As for grilled fish, I merely point out that of all fish sea perch is the least fit to be grilled, being one with very dry flesh. No Provençal cookbook prior to 1914 gives a recipe for grilled sea perch. When it is grilled, the flesh of sea perch loses its flavor and dries out. Only "fat" fish—sardines, mackerel—gain by such treatment. But ours is the era of "grilling"; this method of cooking is its predominant bias, just as other eras had a veritable obsession for boiling, and subjected every sort of meat to this treatment, even that destined to be subsequently fried or roasted.

I have here sought only to give a few examples of the misdeeds of the *picturesque* in gastronomy; for usually, instead of making an effort to prepare what can be well prepared in their region, too many people imagine that they are improving their menu by introducing into it supposed exotic concoctions that for material reasons have no chance of success. It is not true of course that all local traditions are incapable of being exported, but Provençal cuisine is one of those that is the least capable of being reproduced elsewhere. I have chosen it as my example because of the current fad for cuisine from the South of France. But I might well have chosen examples from other parts of France: how, for instance, to make a successful *potée franc-comtoise* (a sort of *pot-au-feu* with bacon and Morteau sausages scented with cumin) without the marvelous, irreplaceable aroma of bacon and sausages that have hung in the fireplace for months before being placed in the stew-pot? *Potée* is basically the same sort of sturdy peasant dish that turns up in other slightly different versions as Flemish *hochepot*, as *petit salé* with cabbage, or as the *pot-au-feu* of the Île de France, with or without a marrow bone. The chef's art is precisely the art of knowing what he can borrow from various traditions without betraying them.

≈

You have doubtless already wondered why the author of the present book has adopted the tone of the critic, and why he has assumed from the outset the role of the moralist rather than that of the historian. It is because—fortunately or unfortunately—cuisine is a normative art in which, as with grammar, ethics, and medicine, description and prescription can scarcely be separated. And, second, it is because the history of cuisine cannot be properly understood unless the origin of various types of dishes is understood.

Cuisine stems from two sources: a popular one and an erudite one, this latter necessarily being the appanage of the well-off classes of every era. In the course of history there has been a peasant (or seafarer's) cuisine and a court cuisine; a plebeian cuisine and a family cuisine prepared by the mother (or the humble family cook); and a cuisine of professionals that only chefs fanatically devoted to their art have the time and the knowledge to practice.

The first type of cuisine has the advantage of being linked to the soil, of being able to exploit the products of various regions and different seasons, in close accord with nature, of being based on age-old skills, transmitted unconsciously by way of imitation and habit, of applying methods of cooking patiently tested and associated with certain cooking utensils and recipients prescribed by a long tradition. It is this cuisine that can be said to be unexportable. The second cuisine, the erudite one, is based by contrast on invention, renewal, experimentation. From antiquity to our own day, in Europe and elsewhere, as we shall see, a number of such erudite gastronomic revolutions have taken place, the two most important of which, at least insofar as European cuisine is concerned, occurred at the beginning of the eighteenth century and at the beginning of the nineteenth. As we shall see, certain of these revolutions even represented an unwitting step backward: thus the alliance of sweet and salt, of meat and fruit (duck with peaches for instance), which today is regarded as an eccentric specialty of certain restaurants, was the rule in the Middle Ages and held sway down to the end of the seventeenth century: almost all recipes for meat up to that time contain sugar.[1] But if erudite cuisine for its part innovates, creates, imagines, it also sometimes risks falling into the sort of pointless complication that we spoke of earlier, into a dangerous form of the Baroque, thus impelling amateurs to return periodically to the cuisine whose roots lie in the products of the land. I shall add that a chef who loses all contact with popular cuisine rarely succeeds in putting something really exquisite together. Furthermore, it is a striking fact that truly great erudite cuisine has arisen principally in places where a tasty and varied traditional cuisine already existed, serving it as a sort of basis. Let us point out, finally, that the formation of urban middle classes, in the eighteenth and above all the nineteenth century, brought "marriages" of the two cuisines, the popular and the erudite, the cuisine unconsciously transmitted and the cuisine deliberately created. The result was what is called "bourgeois" cuisine, which was codified in numerous treatises and which retains the heartiness and the savor of peasant cuisine while at the same time introducing into it the subtlety and the "distinction" of *haute gastronomie*, in sauces for instance.

If regional, peasant cuisine has sturdy basic qualities that allow it to be compared to the draft horse or the plow horse, if *haute gastronomie* has the elegant virtues and the fragility of the thoroughbred, bourgeois cuisine is what breeders call a half-bred horse: it trots but it does not gallop. It nonetheless trots faster than its peasant mother, from which it has inherited staying power and resistance, and outlasts its galloping father the purebred, from which it has inherited finesse and the ability to sprint. What is

---

[1] In Pierre de Lune's *Le Cuisinier* (*The Chef*) (1656) we find recipes mixing oranges with meat; preserved fruits and dates with salted fish; raspberry, melon, muscat grape soups . . .

"The Bean-eater." *Painting by Annibale Carracci (1560–1609), c. 1585. Galleria Colonna, Rome.*

more, bourgeois cuisine does not exclude invention, unlike strictly traditional cuisine which is transmitted with the invariability of a genotype. No "cordon bleu" hesitates to incorporate his own personal variations in a recipe, and all of us have seen family recipe books for bourgeois cuisine, stuffed full of yellowed handwritten pages that are precious witnesses to an oral teaching handed down by a forebear or to a little "extra secret" recently discovered.

The history of gastronomy is nothing more nor less than a succession of exchanges, conflicts, quarrels, and reconciliations between everyday cuisine and the high art of cuisine. Art is a personal creation, but this creation is impossible without a base in traditional craftsmanship.

An example will serve to demonstrate what I mean by collaboration between popular cuisine and erudite cuisine. In Tuscany there exists a certain peasant know-how with regard to the preparation of white beans (*fagioli*), which makes them particularly rich and tasty. The process consists of filling a bottle, or better still a flask from which the raffia wrappings have been removed, three quarters full of beans, of covering the beans with water, and then hanging the flask by a string at a slight angle above a continuous slow fire of charcoal and warm ashes. After eight to ten hours or more of very slow evaporation and cooking, the beans, though still whole, are tender enough to melt in one's mouth and can be eaten either *all'uccelletto*, that is to say with a ragout sauce, or with olive oil and raw onions (which in my opinion sets them off better). A painting by Annibale Carracci, "*Il Mangiafagioli*" ("*The Bean-eater*"), attests to how far back in time the fondness for this dish goes in Central Italy and in Tuscany.[2] This is a case of genuine popular cuisine, in which intelligence and experience find the best possible preparation for a foodstuff, which costs nothing outside of the basic ingredient. How could *haute cuisine* be grafted onto this gift from peasant tradition? By incorporating beans cooked in a flask within a master chef's recipe (I leave this task to the reader's imagination, since no such recipe exists in Tuscany).

Cuisine is a perfecting of nutrition. Gastronomy is a perfecting of cuisine itself. A chef who does not begin by cooking or seasoning the basic foodstuffs of cuisine, which for him should be the notes of a more complex symphony, at least as well as a peasant, is an impostor, as would be an orchestra leader who would endeavor to improve his art by gathering together a large number of musicians, each of whom played off-key individually. Such cooks ruin cuisine: they are the plague of modern gastronomy. I do not mean to say that culinary art is always the prolongation of popular cui-

---

2 The recipe obviously does not antedate the sixteenth century, for white beans were imported then from America.

sine, which is a refined way of preparing food but one that never
aims at the unexpected and indeed steers clear of it. Often the
reformers of gastronomy, on the contrary, must know how to
react against family cuisine, which clings to its errors as to its
qualities and can both drown in grease and boil to death things
that ought to be grilled plain or barely poached. These remarks
are intended to demonstrate, however, that great cuisine is not
only the cuisine of the privileged. Rich people, the wealthy classes,
are not necessarily those that eat the best. Since antiquity, a real
connoisseur such as Horace has reacted by deliberately and judiciously embracing rusticity as an antidote to the pretentious mixtures of parvenu gastrophiles who, thanks to their heavy-handed
combinations, worshiped their pride rather than their stomachs. It
is scarcely my intention to contest the legitimacy of great art, but
the sublime marriage of ingredients of an Antonin Carême is no
more within the scope of the first kitchen bungler who comes
along than the *terribilità* of Michelangelo is a model to assign to
the first wielder of a hammer to happen by. There would be something immoral about treating the subject of cuisine as if money
were all it takes to consume good food—it is among the poor peoples of the world that the author of the present book has on occasion eaten exquisite dishes: the *barbacoa* of the Indians of Mexico,
a young goat cooked slowly beneath warm earth, or *mole poblano*
in the same country, or, yet again, *caponata* in Sicily.[3] But it is unfortunately true that even though a high standard of living is not
sufficient in and of itself to call forth great culinary art, a gastronomic tradition nonetheless tends to suffer if poverty is too extreme and too prolonged. Sicily is a good example of this: a country where gastronomy flourished in the classic era of Greece
(since in Athens itself cookbooks written by Sicilians were used,
and Plato, in the *Gorgias*, goes so far as to have Socrates
specifically cite a certain "Mithraicos, the author of the treatise on

---

[3] *Mole* is turkey served with a chocolate sauce. In its natural state chocolate is
not sweet; it is pure cocoa flour. This is a pre-Columbian dish par excellence,
since both turkey and chocolate originated in the New World and were unknown
in Europe before Columbus. *Poblano* may come from the word *pueblo* (meaning
people or *village*), thus indicating that *mole* is a popular dish (on feast days at
least), or from Puebla (a Mexican city), which would point to a regional origin
of this dish. *Mole poblano* is brown, but there is also *mole verde*, with a green
sauce whose principal ingredient is a local hot green pepper (*chile verde*). *Mole*
sauce made with chocolate is also very hot.

Sicilian cuisine"[4]), Sicily would appear to have had a great deal of
difficulty preserving this culinary patrimony in the course of its
long dark age. A tradition cannot be perpetuated unless it is applied daily, and it cannot be applied without a modicum of general
material well-being. If Mexican *tacos*[5] have a flavor and an aroma
alongside which our general run of sandwiches, however numerous the layers, are mere blotting paper embellished with
rubber, let us not underestimate the immensity of the cataclysm
that engulfed pre-Columbian cuisines once the impoverishment of
the Indians in the colonial era set in.

These are the two sources of gastronomic art, which is produced by their subtle and indispensable intermingling. Let us note,
however, that the history of gastronomy is above all that of
erudite gastronomy, for this is the tradition that has left the
greatest number of written traces. The great cookbooks are obviously the fruit of study, of invention, or the reflection of a *change*,
rather than the fruit of the everyday run of things. The meals
which history has recorded are clearly memorable repasts, princely
wedding banquets, the menus served on festive occasions. This is a
drawback when one is attempting to trace the history of societies
and of their everyday life. It is not a drawback, however, when
one is attempting to write the history of gastronomy as art, as it is
in exceptional circumstances that the great masters had the freedom and the material means to give full play to their creative
imagination.

---

[4] *Gorgias*, 518 B. There is also mention in the *Gorgias* of the existence of another gastronomical author, Archestratus of Gela, some of whose texts have come
down to us.

[5] Meat and hot peppers or black beans (*frijoles*), rolled in corn-flour pancakes
(*tortillas*). As a cheap and tasty popular snack we might also mention *tamales*,
small cakes more or less the shape of a European roll made of hot cornmeal and
flavored with ground hot peppers (*chiles*).

CHAPTER TWO

FROM ARISTOPHANES' HARE TO PETRONIUS' BOAR

Aristophanes came from peasant stock. His tastes reflect those of the tillers of the soil of Attica, and his comedies are filled with descriptions of food and drink: he wrote of that popular reflex that makes any occasion, good or bad, a pretext for downing a glass or putting something in the oven to roast. In the *Archanians*, he shows us a landowner, good Diceopolis, who has tired of war and decides to make peace with his enemy on his own. The event calls for a gastronomic celebration, the description of which must have struck the imagination of the Athenian spectators with particular force since in this year, 425 B.C., a famine, brought on by war, had left them cruelly hunger-stricken. "Children, women, haven't you heard? What are you doing . . . ?" Diceopolis cries. "Boil the hare, roast it till it is done, turn it, take it from the fire, hurry."

This is already a precious bit of evidence: meat was boiled before it was roasted. To a cook today this would appear to be disastrous, for the principle behind roasting is that it is a method of cooking through *concentration* of juices inside, whereas, as Reculet judiciously remarks in his *Principes et les lois culinaires* (*Culinary Principles and Laws*), "boiling operates by *insinuation* and not by concentration."

In simpler terms, if you boil a piece of meat before roasting it, you lose all the benefit of the roasting, since the juices escape into the water. But the explanation for this cooking in two steps is to be found in Archestratus: a great many of the world's peoples feel a repulsion for bloody meat, and I think that I may safely state that in no country do peasants of the traditional sort consume rare meat. It is this prejudice that Archestratus is combating when he provides the following recipe: "There are several ways of cooking and preparing a hare for the table; this is the best procedure: roast it, take it from the spit when it is still somewhat rare, simply sprinkle it with salt, and present the flesh of it to each of your hungry guests. Do not make a face at the blood dripping from the flesh; eat quickly. All other manners of preparing hare are absurd in my view." But Archestratus' return to simplicity is in fact a refinement (a development we often witness in the history of cuisine), since boiling at one time had been considered a step forward from grilling: "Homer when he sacrificed oxen made no sauce," we read in Athenaeus, "for him no boiling of meat, not even of the brains; he grilled even the entrails, so primitive was he." Antiquity firmly held that grilling was the most barbarous method of cooking (as though a process of cooking could be barbarous or civilized in and of itself, aside from whether or not it is a suitable way of preparing what is to be cooked). Like a number of antidemocratic authors, Plato attributed the political decadence of his country to, among other things, luxuries at table, and he preaches to citizens of his *Republic*[1] a return to a more virile diet whose charms he sets forth as follows: "It is evident that they will have the salt, olives, cheese, onions, and vegetables that are the fare of country folk; we will even serve them dessert, namely figs, chick-peas, and broad beans, and they will roast myrtle berries and acorns on the coals and nibble on them while drinking in moderation." This primitive fare would not have been to Aristophanes' liking at all, for his theater is steeped in the scent of thyme and oregano and the pleasant smell of wood pigeons toasted a golden brown over the fire and of eels from Lake Copais, and full of such things as pâtés wrapped in fig leaves, cakes made with cheese, and loaves of bread with sesame seeds.

In *The Peace* there is also mention of "toasting chick-peas, roasting beechnuts," but in this comedy the soldier weary of war, "of the helmet, of cheese, and of onions," the fare of the warrior in the field, cries: "Let them bring a thrush and two finches from my house. There was also buttermilk at home and four pieces of hare." There is no good meal without its hare, it would seem, and along with pig this animal is the most prized meat throughout antiquity. Much later, in the heyday of the Roman Empire, Martial still claims: "If the thrush occupies the first rank among birds, the hare occupies that rank among quadrupeds." The Romans, moreover, raised hares in wooded enclosures, along with roe deer and red deer.

Outside of the culinary allusions and descriptions to be found in the literature of antiquity in general, there also existed, as in our day, numerous specialized treatises on cuisine. To these must be added works by physicians, dietitians, and naturalists, which provide information as to the food habits of the Greeks and Romans.

---

[1] Book II.

But since it is gastronomy, the art of the cook, and not simply nutrition that interests us, what we would most like to study would be collections of recipes. Unfortunately no complete treatise on cuisine has come down to us from ancient Greece. The Mithaicos mentioned by Plato is only a name to us, as are Archytas, Erasistratus, the specialist in fish, Hegesippus of Tarentum, the two Heraclides, both from Syracuse, Nereus of Chios, who could cook conger eel in fish stock so elegantly that it was fit to be presented to the gods, Lamprias, the first to conceive of blood stew, and Aphtonitas, the inventor of blood sausage. Certain of their recipes have nonetheless come down to us thanks to an Egyptian compiler, Athenaeus, born at Naucratis, who in the third century A.D. wrote a work entitled the *Deipnosophistai*, that is to say, "The Dinner of the Savants," an anthology of quotations, both from writers and from cooks. The book in fact contains very few recipes with precise technical details, but among them the reader is happy to find preserved a few recipes of the celebrated Archestratus, a contemporary of Pericles.

Archestratus, a native of Gela (in Sicily), was in reality not so much a chef as a wandering gastronome, who told of his experiences in a so-called "gnomic" poem, that is to say, one parodying the ancient poets such as Hesiod who composed "mottoes." Archestratus has been rightly compared to Brillat-Savarin. Indeed, as the author of *La Physiologie du goût* (*The Physiology of Taste*) was later to do, Archestratus traveled far and wide, eager to discover and to record both the intrinsic quality of various natural products and the best way of preparing them, or even of consuming them, for he formulated the precept according to which there must never be more than four, or five at the very most, at table in order really to savor a gastronomic repast. He digested food extremely rapidly, it would appear, and profited little from what he ate, as he was very thin; this permitted him to experiment endlessly.

But in order to plunge us into the atmosphere of Greek cuisine, let us cite a few of the recipes that, thanks to Athenaeus, have come down to us from this famous gourmand globe-trotter.[2]

---

[2] The following is based on the French translation of the *Deipnosophistai* by A. M. Desrousseaux (Paris, "Les Belles Lettres," 1956). (*Translator's note*)

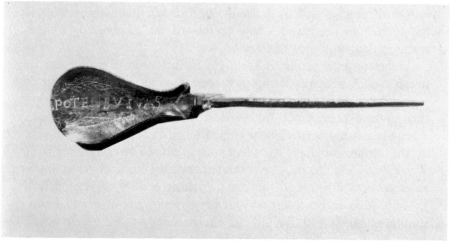

"Funnel in bronze with a lid serving as a strainer." Roman art, sixth or fifth century B.C., *from the Sala Concilina. Musée du Petit Palais, Paris. "Roman silver spoon." Musée du Petit Palais, Paris.*

OPPOSITE:
"Butcher slaughtering a young pig." Terra-cotta figurine, Thebes, last quarter of the sixth century B.C. *Musée du Louvre, Paris.*

"Tuna: In the vast and sacred Samos you will see extremely large tuna called *orcin*, which others call *cete;* buy some promptly, no matter what the price. It is also very good at Byzantium, at Carystus, and in the famous island of the Sicilians. The tuna that Cephalonia and the coast of Tyndarus nourish are also among the best, but if one day you go to Hippona,[3] a city in illustrious Italy, among the Brutians surrounded by water, the tuna there are better than all others, and after them there is nothing comparable. Those that appear in our waters have wandered there from this country, after having traversed a great sea in violently agitated waves, so that we catch them when they are no longer good to take. The hypogastrium or lower belly of this fish is highly praised.

"The *thymnia* or female tuna is found in Byzantium in particular. Take the tail of it, cut it in pieces and roast it until thoroughly done. Sprinkle it with nothing but salt, moisten it with oil, and soak it in a strong brine. If after that you wish to eat it without a sauce, it is an excellent dish which would give the gods an appetite, but if you serve it moistened with vinegar you take away all its merits."

Euthydemus[4] says that "Byzantium is the mother of salted tuna, of mackerel which is a bottom dweller, and of angelfish, which is very nourishing, but that the little town of Pario is the respectable nurse of *cogoils* [large mackerel or hake?]. The merchants of the Abruzzi, of Campania, and of the good city of Tarentum go to Cadiz for marinated *orcin*, stored in large jars in triangular pieces. A chunk of tuna from Sicily that is to be salted in a jar makes me scorn *coracin* that is sought far off in the Pont and those who praise it highly. Few people know that it is a wretched and miserable food, but take a mackerel that has been lightly salted for three days and before it falls apart into brine."

Aphies:[5] These little fish correspond not to smelt, but to young fry such as *blanchaille* or *nonats*. "Scorn any sort of *aphie* save that of Athens, I mean that of the spawning season, which the Ionians call 'sea-foam' and which must be taken very young in the

----

3 Today's Vivonia.

4 The author of a treatise on salted meats and vegetables.

5 The fish called *angulas* in Spain.

depths of the Gulf of Phalerus; there are also good ones on the coasts of the island of Rhodes, provided that they have really been spawned in those waters. If you wish to eat some then, you will add to them sea anemones, of the sort that have hairs all over. Season them together with aromatic flowers of vegetables crushed in oil, and fry the whole in a frying pan. *Aphie* should no more than glimpse the fire; it is cooked in the same time that it takes the oil to crackle." (Chrysippus points out that the abundance of *aphies* causes them to be disdained by Athenians, whereas they are much sought after everywhere else. "It is the same," he says, "as with the hens of the Adriatic, in honor in Athens, though they are less good and smaller than local ones, whereas the inhabitants of this gulf send for theirs from Greece!")

Parrot fish: "Get yourself the parrot fish of Ephesus, but in winter eat the surmullet taken at Trichontus, a hamlet of Miletus, situated in an arid stretch of land, near the Carians who have short stocky arms and legs, or roast a great parrot fish from Chalcedonia which is on the other side of the sea, after having washed it; but you will see very good ones at Byzantium, which as for size have a back as large as a buckler. When you have it, eat it whole; once you have smeared it with cheese and oil, place it in a very hot oven, spread crushed salt mixed with oil and cumin over it, pouring it out with your hand as though you were taking it from a fountain presided over by some deity."

Sar: "When Orion disappears from the sky [in November] and the mother of the grape that bears wine sheds its hair, get yourself a roasted sar, well garnished with cheese. Let it be big and hot, sprinkle it with vinegar (this fish being naturally dry), and remember to prepare in this way any fish that has tough fiber; but as for that which is naturally good, which has fat, tender flesh, simply sprinkle it with salt and then wet it with oil, for it has by itself the quality that makes it tasty."

Mullet: "When you go to Miletus, buy a mullet or a *capiton* from Geson [a pond between Priene and Miletus, communicating with the sea] or a sea perch, that child of the gods, for these fish are excellent there and it is to the place itself that they owe their goodness. There are a number of others in illustrious Calydon, in rich Ambracia, and in the pond of Bolba, but they have a fat which has neither a pleasant odor nor the piquant flavor of the

MARCIO SEMPEREI

"*Roman interior. Activity in a rich household on a day when guests are being received. A banquet scene, and kitchen with oven.*" Bas-relief from the Igel monument, third century A.D. Trier Museum.

others, for in my opinion the first are deliciousness itself because of their good quality. To make them very tender for eating, roast them with the scales on and serve them in a sauce made with brine. To make this dish, take care not to entrust it to a Sicilian or an Italian, for they do not know how to season fish in such a way as to cause them to be eaten with pleasure, but rather they spoil everything by mixing in cheese heavy-handedly or by sprinkling it with vinegar or with their briny infusion of *silphion* [or silphium]; but they are the cleverest at preparing rockfish and a number of little dishes that accompany every course and a great variety of delicious little noodle dishes."

Eels: "I praise every sort of eel, but those that are taken at Reggio, in the strait, are by far to be preferred; those from Lake Copais and Strymon are also highly renowned, however, for their excellent quality. Furthermore, they are very large and prodi-

"*A butcher cutting up a pig's head.*" Detail of the funerary bas-relief of the butcher Titus Julius Vitalis, c. mid-second century A.D. Villa Albani, Rome.

giously fleshy. In any event, the most flattering dish that one can possibly serve is eel, the only naturally sterile fish. One eats them cooked in *poirée* leaves.[6] The strait of Sylla contains, in its waters that bathe wooded Italy, the famous *latos* that is an admirable food; this fish is also found in the Nile."

The reader should note several points with regard to these recipes by Archestratus. First, all of them concern fish. This is doubtless due not only to the sort of chance that presides over the survival of texts, but also to the fact that fish played a much more important role in the cuisine of antiquity than in ours. Second, let us note the interesting mixture of cheese and fish. Let us not forget that butter was unknown to the ancient Greeks and Romans and that the sort of cheese in question was doubtless a fresh white cheese of the same sort as present-day Italian *mozzarella*. The cheeses of antiquity were probably not very much different from many of those that are still made in Mediterranean regions: clabbered milk or white cheese made from the milk of sheep and goasts, which like *mozzarella* are a good vehicle for aromatic herbs and spices. There also existed, naturally, dried cheeses that would keep for longer periods, often mixed with herbs or condiments to flavor them. But what is most striking about Archestratus' advice is the extraordinary attention paid to places and origins. This is a constant preoccupation of the cuisine of antiquity: the place where an animal is caught, the region where a fruit or vegetable is cultivated are the object of observations that are as meticulous, as lengthy as the description as to the ways in which these products are cooked or prepared for the table, and often even more so. It would thus seem that the ancient Greeks and Romans had a more acute sensibility than ours when it came to the native tang of things and the characteristics of different regions. Sturgeon (*galeos*), for instance, was to be eaten principally at Rhodes. And if one chances to see one in the market of this city, it is necessary, if need be, according to Archestratus, "to carry it off by force, even at the price of later having to bear the legal consequences of this kidnapping." This author's remark concerning the mullet in the pond between Priene and Miletus, which are said to be better than mullet caught at sea, may appear to be a hair-splitting obser-

---

[6] A variety of chard or white beet, still widely eaten in Italy, where it is called *bietola*.

"Servants carving meat." Detail of a Corinthian painted wine bowl, seventh century B.C. *Musée du Louvre, Paris.*

vation. Yet a similar phenomenon exists today: anyone from Sète knows that the fish from the waters of Thau, a pond behind the city that communicates with the sea, are superior to those from the open waters offshore. The good bream are those from the pond; in summer, sea perch are thin, except for those from the pond; in the fish market at Sète red mullet from the pond of Thau, which are distinguished by their yellow stripe, are worth twice as much as those taken at sea.[7]

As with wine-lovers today, the gourmets of Imperial Rome were noted for their ability to discern origins. In his Fourth Satire, Juvenal cites a certain Montanus who "from the first mouthful

---

[7] All this was true before the pond of Thau was polluted.

distinguished an oyster from Circeies from those of the Rocks of Lucrin or the depths of Rutupiae, and with one glance could tell on what shore a sea urchin had been gathered."

This discernment was frequently exaggerated to the point of mania. The esteem in which an animal or vegetable product was held depended not only on its place of origin but also on the hour that it had been caught or gathered. Horace[8] has passed on to us a detailed portrait of a host who is a fanatical gastronome: "There was first served a boar from Lucania that had been caught in a light breeze from the south, according to what the table steward told us; all around were hot black radishes, lettuces, ordinary radishes, everything needed to stimulate a languishing stomach, lamb's lettuce, *allec*,[9] tartar of wine of Cos. When these dishes had been taken away and a boy with a girdle tied high above his waist had wiped the maple table with a purple *gausapus*[10] and another had picked up from the floor all manner of debris and things that might have shocked the guests, one saw, advancing at the same pace as a young Athenian girl bearing objects sacred to Ceres, the bronze-complexioned Hydaspus and Alcon, the one bearing Cecuban wines, the other a Chios not mixed with sea water.[11] Then the table steward said: 'If, Maecenas, rather than the wines placed before you, you prefer an Alba or a Falerno, I have both.'

"I was at the head end of the table, having near me Viscus of Thurium; below me, if I remember correctly, were Varius, and then Servilius Balatro and Vidibius, whom Maecenas had brought with him like shadows; our host had above him Nomentanus, and below him Porcius, a jokester capable of downing biscuits whole in a single swallow; if anything escaped attention, it was Nomentanus' role to point to it with his index finger. As for the remainder of the company, that is, the rest of us at table, our dinner consisted of fowl, shellfish, and fish, whose nature was hidden beneath a flavor very different from their usual taste[12] (as became

---

[8] *Satires*, Book II, Satire VIII. The text that follows is based on F. Villeneuve's French translation ("Les Belles Lettres"). (*Translator's note*)

[9] A variety of *garum*, a fish sauce used as a condiment.

[10] A special cloth, smooth on one side and hairy on the other.

[11] Certain Greek wines of mediocre quality were customarily diluted with sea water.

[12] This remark is important: it is one of the reproaches frequently leveled against Roman cuisine.

immediately obvious when Nomentanus had passed to me entrails of plaice and turbot that at first I had not touched. He then apprised me that the apples of paradise were red if one picked them when the moon was waning; why this detail is important he can tell you better than I).

"A *muraena*[13] was brought to the table, lying in the middle of squid swimming in a large platter. Whereupon the steward said: 'It was taken while gestating. After spawning, the flesh of it would have been less good. The sauce was made with the following ingredients: virgin oil from a first pressing, at Venafra; *garum*,[14] made with the juice of fish from Spain, a five-year-old wine, one produced on this side of the sea, added during the cooking (after cooking, Chios wine is more suitable than any other); white pepper, not without vinegar, of the sort produced by allowing the juice of grapes from Methymna[15] to turn. We have been the first to set examples, I of cooking green rocket salad and bitter inula, Curtillus of serving sea urchins without washing them, preferring to brine the juice secreted from the shell of this sea creature.'"

Such refinement, of course, eventually turned into an obsession with the extraordinary, whereby the rarity of a dish and its fancy appearance took the place of skillful, knowledgeable preparation. It is again Horace[16] who apostrophizes in these terms a gourmet corrupted by his predilection for dazzling his guests:

"I shall have difficulty in bringing you to the point where, if a peacock is served you, you will not prefer it to a hen in order to tickle your palate. You are seduced by sheer vanities, since this rare fowl costs its weight in gold and offers the spectacle of a multicolored tail, as though that had anything at all to do with the question. Do you eat this plumage that you praise so highly? Once cooked, does the animal still have its ornamentation? And yet, even though its flesh has no superiority over that of my hen, it makes no difference to me if, misled by an exterior sign, you seek it out: but who made you able to distinguish whether this perch

---

[13] A large sea eel, which from the time of Caesar was a very fashionable delicacy.

[14] A liquid condiment, made from fish entrails broken down in salt.

[15] On the island of Lesbos.

[16] *Satires*, Book II, Satire II. The above version follows the translation of F. Villeneuve.

with its mouth gaping open is from the Tiber or was caught in the open sea? Whether the current drove it between the bridges[17] or to the mouth of the Tuscan river? You praise, madman that you are, a mullet weighing three *librae*[18] that you must serve in a sauce, cut in as many pieces as there are guests. Making an impression is what concerns you, I see."

The strange, the rare, the curious, the colossal excited the culinary imagination. Athenaeus reports how a certain gourmet made a special trip from Italy to Libya after having heard that on this coast the squills—large salt-water crayfish, smaller than spiny lobsters and more tasty than Norway lobsters (these are the real *scampi* of Italy,[19] the *camarones* of the Gulf of Mexico, the Spanish *gambas* that are so delicious grilled)—were larger than anywhere else. Before he disembarked, the local fishermen, excited by his reputation and his wealth, came aboard bringing him the biggest squill. "Don't you have any bigger ones?" he asked them. "No, no finer ones are ever caught than the ones that we are bringing you." On realizing that they were smaller than the squills of Minturno, the city in Campania where he lived, he ordered the pilot to return to Italy, without even setting foot on land.

And it is Juvenal who tells us[20] how the emperor Domitian convoked a sort of council of ministers in order to deliberate the question of how best to prepare a gigantic turbot that had been caught in the Adriatic, off Ancona. If we are to believe Juvenal, the beaches of that day were infested with imperial spies, charged with spotting any unusual catch and making trouble for unfortunate fishermen who did not "spontaneously" conceive the idea of offering it to the emperor.

These preoccupations with dimensions and the unheard-of naturally had only the most tenuous of links with true good taste. Surprise and superabundance were too often the primary concern of newly rich hosts, unless they were, on the contrary, newly

---

17 Perch caught between two bridges of the Tiber (*inter duo pontes capti*) were the ones most appreciated by gourmets (cf. Pliny, *N.H.*, IX, 168; Macrobius, *Sat.* III, 16, 12); but it is not certain which two bridges were meant.

18 The Roman *libra* weighed 327.45 grams; thus the mullet in question weighed almost a kilogram (2.2 pounds).

19 Not to be confused with the tasteless *gamberetti*, often served in their place!

20 Satire IV.

poor, in the process of losing their fortunes by giving sumptuous repasts. It would seem that Roman civilization was intensely "gastric": imaginations worked overtime seeking out new edible products, new preparations. Gluttons abounded: the Emperor Vitellius, for example. Suetonius tells us that Vitellius could not keep himself from devouring the meat being offered on altars as a sacrifice, as I remind my readers below.

Throughout the history of Rome we find "sumptuary laws" being instituted periodically to restrain and control the waste that feasts entailed. There were laws, for instance, forbidding the consumption of animals that were too young or the massacre of certain species (like our laws protecting, just as ineffectively, trout or game). Others were intended to do away with ostentatious and ruinous luxury: "There are great numbers of those whom a creditor who has often been previously shown the door await at the very entrance to a market, and who have no other reason to live than the satisfaction of their palate," Juvenal tells us.[21] "He who serves the choicest and best fare is the deepest in debt among them, and can see ruin already awaiting him . . . Meanwhile, however, cost never stands in the way of their fancy." Certain sumptuary laws even decreed that dinners be given with the doors open so that the police could check on what was served, and a certain consul declared that he was unable to dine out for fear of being obliged to summon his hosts for questioning the next day! The poets, as we have seen, constantly contrast the overpretentious gastronomy of Rome with the frugal and tasty fare of country folk, a classic theme in the history of cuisine. This proves that already there was such a thing as erudite cuisine. What was it like?

The oldest cookbook that has come down to us was compiled between the first and the third century A.D. There seems to have been an abridged edition of it, written in the fourth century, which constitutes, more or less, what remains of it. The first printed edition of it, based on various manuscripts that were handed down and recopied all through the Middle Ages, appeared in Venice at the end of the fifteenth century. It was followed by a second edition, printed in 1498 in Milan. The title of this book varies: sometimes it is given as *Ars magirica*, that is to say, *The Art of the Cook* (*mageiros* was the Greek word for cook), some-

---

[21] Satire XI.

"Persephone receives a rooster and a pomegranate from a nymph." (Against the wall are a water jug and offering plates.) Clay plaque from Locri (Southern Italy), fifth century B.C. Museo di Reggio di Calabria.

"*Roman kitchen.*" *Bronze cooking utensils on iron grills.* A.D. *62–68.* *House of the Vettii, Pompeii.*

"'*Tavern*' *at Herculaneum.*" *Marble counter with sunken receptacles to keep food or drinks hot.*

times as *Apicius culinarius* (*Apicius the Cook*) and, more frequently, as *De re coquinaria libri decem* (*Ten Books on Cuisine*),
or simply *De re coquinaria* (*On Cooking*). Its author is difficult to
identify. His name is Apicius, and the difficulty stems not from
the fact that there is no Apicius to be found in Roman history, but
from the fact that there are too many. There were no fewer than
three persons by this name who could possibly be associated with
gastronomy: the first was alive around 95 B.C. during the reign of
Sulla, the second in the time of the Emperor Tiberius, and the
third in that of Trajan. The most celebrated of the three is unquestionably the second, Gavius Apicius, born in 25 B.C., a gourmet of whom numerous authors of the first rank—Tacitus, Suetonius, Pliny, Seneca—speak in great detail. He is none other than
the traveler mentioned earlier, the one who chartered a boat from
Minturno to Libya in order to go see if the squills there were as
big as they were said to be. Gavius Apicius gave sumptuous banquets and held a free course, so to speak, in *haute cuisine*. There is
mention of young people carefully committing his counsels to
writing, and perhaps these notes taken on the spot are the origin of
the *De re coquinaria*. Seneca taxes Apicius with "infecting the
century with his doctrine," with attracting young people who
twenty years earlier flocked to the schools of the philosophers and
the rhetoricians and now rubbed elbows with each other in his
kitchens as though attending the lessons of a great mentor. "They
watch with inflamed eyes and mouths gaping open," Clement of
Alexandria states. "They mingle cries of tumultuous joy with the
sound of sauces bubbling and boiling on the fire." Apicius had invented the process of force-feeding sows with dried figs and
honeyed wine to fatten their livers, and recipes for preparing
flamingo tongue, camel's heels, and red mullet liver! But these ex-
travagances are not his principal merit in our eyes—what food-
lover does not seek to create a curious or bizarre dish of his very
own? His merit lies, rather, in the intelligent way in which he
codified the cuisine of antiquity, both Greek and Roman, both the
most luxurious and the most popular—providing, that is, that it was
really he who was the author of the treatise attributed to him. Certain critics have in fact concluded that his name is associated with
it only because it had become a sort of symbol of good eating, as
later we have come to speak of a Grimod de La Revnière or a

Brillat-Savarin. In the course of the two centuries that followed his death (a memorable one, in view of the fact that he committed suicide out of fear of dying of hunger after having spent a fortune of a hundred million sesterces on feasts)[22] Apicius is constantly mentioned, sometimes as the ultimate incarnation of the rake (Juvenal), sometimes as the refined connoisseur par excellence (Athenaeus), sometimes as the magnificent host, whom the Emperor Heliogabalus seeks to imitate and who is mentioned later even by such Christian writers as Tertullian and Apollinaris Sidonius. Athenaeus in his *Deipnosophistai* mentions recipes discovered by Apicius, vegetables made fashionable by him, cakes created by him (described, he says, by Chrysippus of Tyanus in his *Treatise on Baking*), yet there is not a single word in the *Deipnosophistai* about his being the author of a cookbook. But what does this really matter? What is of importance to us is that this book does in fact exist, whether it be a compilation placed under Apicius' name as tutelary authority in homage to his memory, or the late fruit of an oral teaching he once propounded (in which case his works have come down to us in the same way as those of Aristotle), or yet again a condensation of a collection of earlier treatises set down in writing by him.[23]

If the reader attempts to deduce through Apicius the fundamental principles of the cuisine of antiquity, what strikes him first of all is the abundance of herbs or spices and the mixture of sweet and salted things. The preparation of every dish inevitably involves seasoning it with *garum*, which is used the way we use salt (though this does not exclude the use of salt itself), and also onion, cumin, coriander, pepper, rue, pennyroyal, sage, chervil, chives, cinnamon, wild celery, mint, oregano, thyme, shallots, calamus root, dill, marjoram, inula, cardamom, spikenard, fennel, juniper berries, and two other plants, silphium, which came from Cyrenaica, and lovage (ligusticum). And the list goes on: horseradish,

---

[22] Twenty-seven million gold francs, or approximately $5,500,000 U.S. in today's money. Seneca describes Apicius' death in his *Consolatio ad Helviam.*

[23] There exist two modern editions that are remarkable for the care and competence with which they are presented: Bertrand Guégan, *Les Dix Livres de la cuisine d'Apicius,* traduits en français et commentés pour la première fois par René Bonnel (1933), and a translation into English by Joseph Vehling (1936), also accompanied by an excellent commentary.

poppy seeds, savory, seseli, ammi . . . These products, almost all of which were very often used together in a single dish, were ground in a mortar and mixed with oil, vinegar, honey, wine, and still more *garum*, if needed to make the mixture go further since it was poured on the dish as a sauce when it was served or else was used to flavor a forcemeat or to reboil a dish. Here is a typical recipe:

"*Sea minutal:* Cook fish in a terra-cotta pot with *garum*, oil, wine, finely chopped bulbous leeks and coriander. Cut the fish apart, chop the flesh fine, and then put the chopped fish in [another] pot with sea nettles that have been well washed, cooked [and chopped]. That being done, grind pepper, lovage, and oregano, mix these spices together, moisten with *garum* and then with the fish sauce, and pour the whole into a pot. Bring to a boil. Stir, thicken with a flour paste, sprinkle with pepper and serve."

A *minutal* is a combination of chopped ingredients. The sea nettles mentioned are our sea anemones, a zoophyte whose scientific name is *actinia*.[24] Dates, figs, raisin wine (made by fermenting grapes, dried in the sun on wicker trays, in must) are frequently added to all these herbs and condiments. (We should point out that most wines commonly used in cooking in antiquity were sweet wines, to which honey was also added. They were often aromatic cooked wines, scented with fruits—quinces, dates, pomegranates—or even flower petals—roses or violets.)

The second characteristic of Apicius' recipes is this: by far the favorite food of the ancient Greeks and Romans, we repeat, was fish (Apicius himself deemed red mullet to be the finest fish of all); as for meat, suckling pig, roe deer, and lamb were prized. Butchered meat (beef and veal) was not of good quality in antiquity. We have already mentioned their decided preference for wild fowl, which were also raised in aviaries: thrushes, grouse, partridge. To this list we must add other birds that are hardly ever eaten nowadays: ostriches, flamingos, parrots, cranes. Barnyard fowl also figured on the menu of course: chicken, duck, capon, guinea fowl. Here is a recipe for partridge, the meat of which doubtless had little taste left after being cooked in this fashion:

---

[24] It is still eaten in Marseille. In his *La Cuisinière provençale*, written at the end of the nineteenth century, Reboul gives a recipe for fried sea anemones (and one for a sea-nettle omelette) that can be found in Apicius.

"Cook the partridge in water, with its feathers on; you will pluck it later. If the partridge is cut up into pieces, it can be boiled in its own juice until it is half-cooked; it is then necessary to finish cooking it in water, and then season it when it has been boiled."

The following will indicate how the creature was to be seasoned: "*For partridge, hazel hen, and turtledoves:* pepper, lovage, rue seed, *garum*, pure wine, and oil. Heat the whole together."

Here is a good recipe for thrushes:

"*Thrushes good for the health:* Grind pepper, silphium, and bayberries with *garum* made with cumin. Stuff the thrushes through the neck and sew them up again. Then cook them with oil, salts, water, dill, and heads of leeks."

Here are two other recipes, one for chicken and the other for suckling pig:

"*Varius Heliogabalus' chicken:* Cook the chicken in a sauce made of *garum*, oil, and wine, seasoned with a bouquet of leek tops, coriander, and savory. When the chicken is done, crush pepper and pine nuts in a mortar; pour over these spices 2 *cyathi* of the cooking juice, from which you have removed the herbs: add milk, blend carefully, and then pour this sauce over the chicken and boil. Thicken with beaten egg whites. Arrange the chicken on a platter and moisten it with its sauce. This sauce is called *white sauce.*"

"*Double-stuffed suckling pig:* Clean it, gut it through the neck, and dress it. Sear it over a hot fire; but first, delicately slit one of its ears, then fill an ox bladder with Terentine stuffing[25] and attach a bird-seller's straw to the neck of this bladder, through which you will introduce into the ear as much stuffing as possible. Wrap in paper, tie with string, and then prepare another stuffing. For this, grind pepper, lovage, and oregano with a little silphium root; moisten the whole with *garum*; add cooked brains, raw eggs, cooked spelt, juice from the preliminary cooking of the animal, little birds if you have some, pine nuts, and whole grains of pepper; blend the whole with *garum*. Fill the animal with this stuffing, wrap it in paper, tie with string, and put it in the oven. When the suckling pig is cooked, remove the paper around it. Sprinkle it [with oil] and serve."

---

[25] A stuffing with almonds, from the name of a type of almond.

These last two recipes are clearly erudite ones; the presence of pine nuts in them will be noted, a condiment to be added to our list, for the Romans liked the taste of them in many dishes, and the use of bulbous plants, for the ancient Greeks and Romans gathered many varieties of them in the fields or grew them in their gardens, and usually prepared them with oil, *garum*, and vinegar. (*We* could eat tulip bulbs then!)

A third remark: the ancient Greeks and Romans were experts at making forcemeats, meatballs, mock meat "birds," fish croquettes, galantines. They were good pork butchers, and made hams, smoked pork knuckles, blood sausage, hard and soft sausages. In Gaul there were already methods of preparing boar's head. The Gauls' pork products had an excellent reputation, and they knew how to make crustacean dumplings and flat sausage cakes encased in a piece of animal intestine. There were not only meat dishes but also seafood ones. As the author of the present book has recently eaten cod sausage in a Paris restaurant, he allows himself to draw the reader's attention to a recipe in Apicius for Spondylus sausage (Spondyli are a bivalve mollusk, known as "spiny oysters," Linnaeus' *Spondylus gaedoropus*).

"*Spondylus sausages:* Boil spondyli, crush them, and remove the sinew. Then grind boiled spelt and eggs with the spondyli. Season this forcemeat with pepper and divide it into balls which you will then wrap in a piece of intestine and grill. Moisten them with wine *garum* and serve them as though they were sausage cakes."

One reason for the Greeks' and Romans' preference for food cut into small bits, reduced to croquettes or forcemeats or meatballs, or even to a purée, stemmed from their position as they ate. It is difficult to cut up food when one dines in a reclining position, resting on one elbow. Everything must be eaten with only one hand. This leads to quite complex mixtures, to which chopped ingredients naturally lend themselves.

"*Galantine:* Pepper, mint, wild celery, dried pennyroyal, cinnamon, pine nuts, honey, vinegar, *garum*, egg yolks. Place together in an earthenware pot fresh bread soaked in vinegar water and then squeezed dry, cheese made from cow's milk, and cucumbers. Alternate layers of these ingredients and pig's feet, dotted here and there with bits of pork and poultry livers. Pour your sauce over the whole, and cook, after which you put it to chill in a recipient containing cold water and then you serve it."

"*A dish with raw asparagus:* Clean stalks of asparagus, crush them in a mortar, sprinkle them with water, grind them very fine and put them through a sieve. Meanwhile, cook warblers after having cleaned and dressed them. Then grind in a mortar 6 scruples[26] of pepper, add *garum*, and grind; thin the whole with a cyathus[27] of raisin wine and 3 ounces of oil; pour this mixture into a small earthenware pot and bring it to a boil. Oil a dish liberally; break into it 6 eggs to which you add *garum* with wine, and then our asparagus preparation. Put the dish over hot ashes, pour over it the sauce that has just been described, and arrange your warblers on top. Cook, sprinkle with pepper, and serve."

"*Dish with roses:* Take roses, remove the petals from them and snip off the white part of them; put them in a mortar and crush them. Pour a cyathus and a half of *garum* over the petals and pass through a sieve. Take 4 brains, remove the sinews, then crush them with 8 scruples of pepper. Spread the rose liquid over them and mix well; then break 8 eggs over this mixture; moisten with a cup of wine, a cup of raisin wine, and a little oil. Oil a dish generously, put it over hot ashes, and garnish it with the preparation just described. When this dish is cooked, sprinkle with ground pepper and serve."

Here is a delicious seafood dish, whose only drawback is the lack of grated cheese on top, and a recipe for sausage.

"*Mixture of chopped seafood:* It is made with shrimp and lobsters, squid, cuttlefish, and rock lobster. The chopped mixture is seasoned with pepper, cumin, and silphium root."

"*Here is how sausages are made:* Roast a pork liver and remove the sinew. You will previously have ground together pepper, rue, and *garum;* spread the whole over the liver, grind and mix together, as for meat. Then make your sausages, rolling each one of them in a bay leaf and suspending them in smoke for as long as you wish. When you want to eat them, remove them from the smoke and roast them."

---

[26] A scruple equals 1.295 grams.

[27] The cyathus was a measure equivalent to .045 liters, therefore very small; today we would say a dessert-spoonful.

Despite their preference for food chopped fine, ground in a mortar, or reduced to a purée, which led to the extensive development of stuffings, the ancient Greeks and Romans naturally employed all the other methods of cooking. They were well acquainted with the use of stock, for Pliny gives a recipe for rockfish which is the ancestor of *bouillabaisse*. They had all sorts of stews, and Apicius is not above pointing out the merits of a simple and succulent roast, though admittedly he recommends moistening it with honey just before it is served! Numerous sauces were prepared on the side and poured over the dish at the last second; this perhaps masked the taste of the food itself, as when today we drown things in tomato ketchup or Worcestershire sauce or pour vinegar-and-shallot sauce over oysters. We should note the mixture of sweet and sour, of sweet and salt, of herbs and fruits, invariably swimming in *garum:*

"*Cumin sauce for oysters and shellfish:* Pepper, lovage, parsley, dried mint, *folium, malobathron,* a little more cumin, honey, vinegar, *garum.*

"*Alternatively:* Pepper, lovage, parsley, dried mint, a little more cumin, honey, vinegar, *garum.*"

"*Silphium sauce:* Dissolve in warm water silphium from Cyrenaica or silphium from Parthia; add to it *garum* mixed with vinegar.

"*Or else:* Pepper, parsley, dried mint, silphium root, honey, vinegar, *garum* (mix everything together).

"*Alternatively:* Pepper, curry, dill, parsley, dried mint, silphium, *folium, malobathron,* Indian nard, a little costus, honey, vinegar, *garum.*"

"*Eleogarum or garum with oil for truffles:* Pepper, lovage, coriander, rue, *garum,* a little honey and oil.

"*Alternatively:* Thyme, savory, pepper, lovage, honey, *garum,* and oil."

"*Oxyporon:* Two ounces of cumin, 1 ounce of ginger, 1 ounce of green rue, 6 scruples of niter, 12 scruples of fleshy dates, 1 ounce of pepper, 9 ounces of honey. Steep in vinegar cumin from Ethiopia, Syria, or Lybia; drain and grind the cumin with the other ingredients, then blend with honey and if necessary with vinegar *garum.*"

These sauces were used principally to season vegetables; among those eaten were cabbages, yellow turnips, kale, lettuce, carrots, white turnips, leeks, pumpkins, winter squash, cucumbers (of which the Emperor Tiberius was so fond that he contrived to have them grown for him the year round and never traveled without having some sent on after him), and artichoke hearts, which the Romans liked very much and cooked in water or wine. Here is a recipe for them that requires a certain amount of work:

"Cook artichoke hearts in water, remove the fibers, then grind the artichoke hearts with boiled spelt, eggs, *garum*, and pepper. Make little balls of the mixture and garnish with pine nuts and pepper. Wrap them in cauls and grill. Moisten with a trickle of wine *garum* and serve as though they were flat sausages."

One last remark: certain dishes are unquestionable evidence of a spirit of experimentation and investigation that characterizes periods in which gastronomy becomes a conscious art. Let us cite a few examples, the first of them in the words of the author of the *Ars magirica* himself:

"*Apicius' dish:* Here is how you prepare it. Take cooked sow's teats and cut into pieces, the flesh of fish, the meat of a chicken, warblers, or the bellies of cooked thrushes and all sorts of excellent things. Chop all of this, except the warblers, and mix this forcemeat with raw eggs and oil. Apart from this, grind pepper and lovage; moisten with *garum*, wine, and raisin wine; heat in an earthenware pot and thicken with starch. But first toss into it your forcemeat and bring it to a boil. When it is cooked, take the pot with its juice off the fire and, using a ladle, transfer the forcemeat, by layers, into a drip pan, after having mixed whole peppercorns and pine nuts into it. Pour a ladleful of the forcemeat onto the bottom, which will have been covered with a rather thick undercrust, and then alternate thin layers of dough and layers of the forcemeat, one ladleful at a time. Cover the whole with a layer of pastry rolled thin with a rolling pin, cook the pie, and then sprinkle it with pepper. The animal flesh will have been thickened with eggs before being placed in the pan."

A great deal has been said about these sow's teats, and about the sow's vulva that figures in another recipe, but these foodstuffs seem extraordinary only because we are not in the habit of consuming them. We, on the other hand, eat calf's head, which the

Greeks and Romans did not. Moreover, teats are still served in Italy, among the boiled meats in a *bollito misto con salsa verde* (mixed boiled meats with green sauce).

Among the elegant, rare, or curious recipes of the time let us cite the following:

"*Stew with cheese:* Prepare it with whatever salted fish you prefer. Cook the fish in oil and remove the bones. Then take cooked pig's brains, the flesh of fish, little livers of fowl, hard-boiled eggs, and soft scalded cheese, heat the whole in a dish that can be put over the fire. Apart from this, grind pepper, lovage, oregano, a clove of rue with wine, honeyed wine, and oil; pour this sauce in the dish and simmer slowly. Thicken with raw eggs; arrange the whole tastefully, dot with little cumin seeds, and serve."

"*Stuffed stomach:* Gut a pig stomach completely, wash it with vinegar to which salt has been added, then rinse it in water and stuff it with the following preparation: mix together pork meat that has been chopped and ground, 3 pig brains with the sinews removed, and raw eggs; add pine nuts and whole peppercorns, then work the whole into a sauce. This sauce will be composed of pepper, lovage, silphium, anise, ginger, and a little rue ground with *garum* of the finest quality and a little oil. Stuff the pig stomach lightly so that it does not burst during cooking. Close it up by tying it with string at its two ends and plunge it into a pot of boiling water. Take it out then and prick it with a needle so that it does not burst. When it is half-cooked, dry it off and suspend it in smoke so that it takes on color. Then boil it in *garum*, undiluted wine, and a little oil until it is completely cooked."

"*Boiling-hot sauce for a roast boar:* Pepper, toasted cumin, wild celery seed, mint, thyme, savory, safflower blossoms, toasted pine nuts or almonds, honey, wine, an acetabulum of *garum*, a little oil."

This latter sauce can be considered to be a more complex and less homogeneous ancestor of a modern *sauce poivrade* (pepper sauce) or of Taillevent's medieval *saupiquet.*

"*Vitellius' suckling pig:* Clean and dress the suckling pig as one does a boar; sprinkle it with salt and roast it in the oven. Grind in a mortar pepper and lovage; add *garum* and mix the whole with wine and raisin wine. Bring this sauce to a boil in an earthenware pot with a very small quantity of oil; pour a liberal amount of it over the roast suckling pig so that the meat will absorb as much of it as possible."

If we have ended this sampler of ancient recipes with the one from Vitellius, it is because this emperor, Suetonius tells us, was a well-known glutton, who not only got himself invited to dinner in five or six houses on the same evening and honored all the invitations, but also, when he attended sacrifices, could not keep from flinging himself upon the roasting animals and devouring them right in the middle of the ceremony! This morbid hunger naturally has little to do with gastronomic art. It nonetheless is indicative of a tendency of the time toward gluttony, superabundance, the pleasure of accumulating, and the desire to dazzle others, a tendency for which Apicius' recipes have often been criticized.

How to judge this cuisine? It has often been held to be too heavy, really indigestible. But as I see it, this objection is based on an optical illusion, so to speak, an illusion that stems from reading: open any book on *haute cuisine* and any recipe will seem too heavy to you, too frightfully complicated, simply because you are reading the *enumeration* of ingredients that end up being *combined*, and of operations whose benefit you will reap without seeing so much as a trace of them when you eat the dish. Moreover, written recipes are necessarily the most subtle ones: an author does not take the trouble to publish a book that teaches what everyone already knows how to do. Hence treatises on cuisine are necessarily an expression of a certain studied refinement, which implies a more ordinary basic practice and aims at putting forth ideas for meals that are more elaborate than everyday ones.

Did antiquity perfect the art of combination, however? It would not appear so. We might say that it knew only the *juxtaposition* and the *superposition* of foods, flavors, and aromas. It did not understand that it is not the quantity of spices and herbs that counts, but their marriage, and that their aromas end up neutralizing each other if every dish is full of them; that the point in the cooking process at which an herb is added to a dish is the important thing if it is to contribute its essential odor, that a very small quantity of pepper, for instance, suffices if it is added just before taking a stew off the fire, for neither pepper nor saffron should ever cook for more than a minute. *Mixing* is not really *combining*, in cuisine any more than in chemistry. But in point of fact, in order to attain the degree of refinement whereby the cook contrives to capture flavors and essences through a whole series of operations, impregnating meats and fish with them instead of overwhelming them, we must wait till the great gastronomic revolution of the eighteenth century, and, indeed, in order for this revolution to be a complete one, until the nineteenth century, with Antonin Carême. Until then, cuisine will often waver between heavy-handedness and the return to rural simplicity periodically extolled by the poets.

It is nonetheless tempting to execute certain of Apicius' recipes, which can be improved by replacing the fatal, universal *garum* with a bit of sea salt. But let us not lose sight of the fact that the interest of these recipes, like those of the Middle Ages and the Renaissance that we shall study in later chapters, stems in great part from the natural flavor of foodstuffs, of fruits and vegetables and animals, a flavor that today is often a thing of the past as a result of the use of non-organic fertilizers by truck gardeners and the more or less universal use of chemical products by cattle-raisers. We will be obliged to discuss this aspect of the problem in the final chapter of this book.

But Apicius apparently did manage to codify one of the constants of gastronomy, for he has been read and studied continually since antiquity. As late as the middle of the nineteenth century he was the object of passionate attacks both by Carême, who had only the most profound scorn for Roman cuisine, as was his privilege, and by an aesthetician and historian of the art such as von Rumohr, one of the authors cited with the most lavish praise by Hegel in his *Aesthetics*. At the beginning of the nineteenth century this great historian of German art attacks Apicius' ideas as being the height of what he calls "destructive cuisine," which reduces everything to stews, jellies, pâtés, inevitably drowned in sauces with a host of ingredients, and admits natural foodstuffs only on condition that they be unrecognizable.[28] This is in part an unjust criticism, as we have seen; indeed, it could be leveled against the very best Chinese cooking.

---

[28] *Geist der Kochkunst*, von Joseph König, überarbeitet und herausgegeben von C. F. von Rumohr (*The Spirit of the Art of Cooking*, by Joseph König, edited and published by C. F. von Rumohr), Stuttgart und Tübingen, 1822. Joseph König was von Rumohr's cook, to whom he attributes his book as a sort of joke.

And why should the desire to disconcert and dazzle, so tirelessly stigmatized by Horace and Juvenal, be necessarily detestable? Is this not one of the forms of hospitality, in a civilization in which the art of entertaining is not confined to the art of providing nourishment but rather extends to the art of distracting, amusing, surprising? Throughout literary history the protagonist of Petronius' *Satyricon*, Trimalchio, has been held up to ridicule as the absolutely typical braggart nouveau-riche. But what trouble Trimalchio has gone to in order to offer his guests a meal that will be a real feast and a celebration, and not just a triple buffet! He has not only long pondered his gastronomical farces and spent hours executing them, but also feigns naïveté, ignorance, and anger so that his guests will believe in his little comedy till the very end, whether he hands out to them peacock eggs with warblers cooked in peppered egg yolk inside the shells—which was doubtless not all that terrible an idea—or else summons a cook before him in order to pretend to scold him for not having gutted a pig: but when it is gutted in the guests' presence a flood of sausages pours out of its slit belly! Or he stages a spectacular stage entrance for his famous boar. Let us reread this famous text:

" 'Admirable!' we shout in chorus, and raising our hands toward the ceiling, we swear that Hipparchus and Aratus could not have been compared to him; meanwhile, servants enter and place on the couches spreads on which were embroidered snares, hunters lying in wait with their boar spears and all sorts of hunting gear. We did not know what to think at that point, when outside the triclinium an enormous clamor was heard, and suddenly Laconian dogs began to run round the table in every direction. Following them came a sideboard on which lay an immense boar with a bonnet on its head; from its tusks hung two baskets woven of palm fibers, one filled with Carian dates and the other with Theban dates. All round it little baby boars made of pastry crusts, seemingly suspended from its teats, indicated that it was a sow that was lying there. They were, moveover, given to us to take home with us. And in order to carve the boar, it was not the *carpus* [carver] who had cut up the hens who came forward, but a tall bearded man with his legs wrapped in strips of cloth and wearing a damask *alicula* [a short hunting cloak]. He took out his hunter's knife and, striking the boar's flank a violent blow, made a hole in it out of which flew thrushes. Bird-sellers were already there, ready and waiting with snares, and they soon caught the birds fluttering about the triclinium. And then, having given each of his guests his bird, Trimalchio added: 'You can see that this wild pig has eaten a delicate harvest of acorns.' Servants immediately went over to the baskets hanging from the beast's tusks and distributed equal portions of the Theban and Carian dates to the diners."

And what, in fact, did the ancient Greeks and Romans drink with Aristophanes' hare or Petronius' boar?

CHAPTER THREE

BREAD AND WINE

Crapulatus a vino . . .
(Dead drunk on wine . . .)
GREGORY OF TOURS

Rinse this glass well, lackey,
So that far brighter it will be
Than all Zeus's thunderbolts,
It will be the scimitar
With which I slit the throat of care.
SAINT-AMAND, La Crevaille

The breakfast of the Greeks consisted of bread soaked in wine or, more accurately perhaps, of crumbled bread moistened in undiluted wine. Moreover, this was the only moment of the day when Greeks took wine in its pure state, for during other meals they always diluted their wine with water. But breakfast was so closely associated with the idea of undiluted wine that the very name of this meal derived from it: it was called *akratismos*, a noun formed on the basis of the adjective *akratos*, meaning "unmixed," "pure," which in turn became a noun designating undiluted wine. An *akratos* was something like a drink downed in one gulp, a "shot." As for the verb from the same root, *akratidzomai* (ἀκρατίζομαι), it meant both "to drink undiluted wine" and "to eat breakfast." The custom is well attested to.

These two products, bread and wine, were to remain the two basic items of consumption in Western civilization down to the twentieth century. Long after the Ancient World was a thing of the past, a French song went: *"Marie, trempe ton pain—Marie, trempe ton pain—Marie, trempe ton pain—dans ton vin"* ("Marie, dip your bread—Marie, dip your bread—Marie, dip your bread—in your wine"). The French expression *tremper la soupe* refers to the custom of pouring the soup on slices of bread, and in several regions (Vosges, Franche-Comté, Gascogne) the peasants mix wine with the soup. Not until the twentieth century will the preponderant place of bread as a basic food in all classes of society be taken over by meat. But as long as meat remained a product that cost too much, a food reserved for feast days for the majority of the populace, and until the time when the consumption of potatoes, brought to Europe from America in the sixteenth century, became widespread, that is to say, no earlier than the very end of the sixteenth century, wheat remained the mainstay of human existence for forty centuries, in a zone that included the Near East and the Middle East, North Africa from Egypt to Morocco, and all of Europe. (We shall examine the case of America later.)

Of all the grains from which bread can be made more or less readily—rice (whose history is quite special), millet, oats, barley, rye, and, later, corn, which originated in America—wheat lends itself best to bread-making. It shares this characteristic with barley and rye, but it is more nourishing due to the fact that it contains a higher proportion of nitrogenous material.[1] This explains why wheat often allowed people to do without meat and fish, which is not true of potatoes. For a long time rye, which is more resistant to disease and grows well even in the poorest soil and in quite cold climates, was the dominant grain in Europe; the progressive retreat of rye in the face of wheat is one of the manifestations of progress in agricultural techniques and the rise of the standard of living in the West. A return to barley and rye took place during periods of famine and bad harvests.

But it was necessary to know how to use this queen of grains properly. It was first consumed in the form of gruel, and then of little toasted or baked cakes, which were merely gruel dehydrated by cooking. *Pulte, non pane, vixisse longo tempore Romanos manifestum*, one reads in Plautus: "It is clear that for a long time the Romans lived not on bread but on gruel." *Pulte*, the ablative case of *puls, pultis,* means gruel or purée in Latin, obviously the word from which Italian, and more particularly Piedmontese, *polenta* derives. *Polenta* is made with corn, as are *gaudes*, a sort of corn bread made in Burgundy and above all in Franche-Comté. But these latter are baked in the oven, whereas *polenta* is air-dried. *Gaudes* doubtless never were considered a very great treat, since in a folk tale from Franche-Comté we note that a peasant says to a passerby: "Would you like some *gaudes?* My pigs refuse to eat any more of them." North African couscous is a use of wheat that also falls outside of actual bread-making: the whole secret of making it well consists of cooking it over steam to the firm consistency of a semolina that is neither wet nor sticky even though thoroughly cooked. As Léon Isnard has so well described it in his *L'Algérie gourmande*, which might be translated as *Good Eating in Algeria*, a classic work published in Oran at the end of the nineteenth century, the right way to make it consists first of all of "rolling" the slightly moist couscous between one's hands so that no lumps form in it, and then going about things in such a way that the water never touches the meal and all the cooking during boiling is done by the steam.

Grains can thus be used to make very delicate dishes that have

---

[1] Wheat contains essentially glucides (starch and sugar), protides, a small quantity of lipides; mineral elements, calcium, phosphorus, and iron; vitamins B_1, B_2, PP, E.

nothing to do with bread-making, and it must not be thought that there is necessarily "progress" in gastronomy, any more than in the other arts. If bread-making is an undoubted technical step forward in the history of human nutrition, this does not imply that gastronomic art was missing from the scene in previous stages of that history. Gruel is not necessarily a crude dish, nor are various sorts of flatbreads primitive fare. These latter should be thought of as a form of nonfermented bread, that is, bread made of kneaded dough without leavening but cooked over a fire, or as a kind of pancake, that is, made of batter cooked over an open fire. We still have today an example of people whose basic food is this sort of pliant flat cake, made in this instance of corn: the Indians of Mexico and Central America. Their *tortillas* (the name the Spanish gave to these corn cakes that served as the bread of the indigenous tribes) possess a nutritional value superior to that of the white bread that is sold on the market in Mexico for the use of Europeans and North Americans, and they are more tasty.

Charred remains of flat grain cakes have been found in prehistoric sites in Western Europe. (It was this charred state that preserved them, as was the case later with the bread of Pompeii.) They were made of various known cereals, from millet to wheat, and the whole grain, including the hull, was used. The phenomenon of fermentation appears to have been discovered in the Near East, by the Hebrews. "The fermentation of bread is an alcoholic fermentation brought on by the action of ferments that transform the sugars present in the dough into alcohol and carbon dioxide."[2] The ferments or yeasts that bring it about are either so-called "wild yeasts" found in leavening for bread dough, or else brewer's yeasts, used in commercial bakeries. Traditional fermentation, due to the first type of leavening, is slower than the second but produces a tastier bread that dries out less rapidly. This is so-called "peasant bread" or "country bread," which, thanks to the completion of one of those cycles of which the history of gastronomy has several times been witness, is making a comeback today in de luxe bakeries.

---

[2] Raymond Calvel (professor at the French national school of flour-milling), *Le Pain*, Paris, 1964. H. E. Jacob's extensive work, *Sechstausend Jahre Brot* (*The Six-Thousand-Year History of Bread*) (Hamburg, 1964; French translation, *Histoire du pain depuis 6,000 ans*, Paris, 1958), is largely a history revolving around bread; the information in it on actual bread-making is minimal.

It would appear, as I have said, that it was the Hebrews who first discovered how to make leavened bread. It is conceivable that a kneaded mixture of flour and water, set aside without being cooked immediately and in contact with ferments in suspension in the air, accidentally began working and increasing in volume with the aid of heat and humidity. Hence the idea was doubtless born of incorporating this yeast transformed by alcoholic fermentation into the bread dough in order to obtain leavened bread, which is less filling and more easily digested than unleavened cakes. Unleavened bread (*azymi*) nonetheless remained the ritual bread, whereas bread properly speaking, that made with leaven (*zymi*), became "ordinary" bread. The Bible attests to the knowledge of bread not only among the Hebrews but also among the Egyptians. Indeed, numerous Egyptian paintings depict wheat being grown, harvested, milled between two stones, kneaded, and baked. The baking was done in earthenware molds, similar to present-day "devils": large porous earthenware pots placed one on top of the other, which permit baking without water, directly over the fire. This utensil is then turned in the middle of the baking process. In short, it is a sort of miniature oven. The Egyptians, whom Hecataeus of Miletus refers to in 500 B.C. as "the bread-eaters," in somewhat the same way that the English and the Germans regarded the French in the nineteenth century A.D., gave their principal staple food all sorts of shapes and forms, and were thus the inventors of fancy baked goods.

But it is with the Greeks that the history of bread enters the history not only of nutrition but also of gastronomy. At the beginning of the first millennium before Christ, all the conditions were present that would permit a progressive refinement in the making of bread, namely: 1) the mastery of milling or bolting: separating the husks and the waste products of wheat from the edible part, thus obtaining at will different types of flour suited for different uses, ranging from the sort that went into the making of heavy black bread to the finest white flour used in making pastry; 2) the adoption and development of large ovens (as opposed to "small ovens"—*petits fours*—which were later to be adapted to the baking of fancy pastry; in fact, the baker's oven of today is still almost the same as it was in antiquity, in the sixth century B.C.); 3) finally, and most importantly, the idea of mixing with the bread all sorts of aromatic herbs or seeds, and oils and fruits with wide varieties of subtle aromas or tastes.

According to Athenaeus, the Greeks of the classical period had seventy-two sorts of bread. Let us cite among others *daraton*, a Thessalian unleavened bread; *phaios*, or "brown" bread; *bromite*, from *bromos*, meaning wild oats; and *syncomiste*, a coarse bread made from by-products of flour. (The word *syncomiste* means "brought from different places and put together." It can also designate a meal in common to which everyone brings something—a picnic—thus attesting to how far back in time picnics go. Applied to bread, *artos*, it designates what we have indicated.) *Crimmitès* was made of coarse barley flour (*crimnos*), while *sémidalitès* was "noble" bread; made with the finest wheat flour. *Cribanitès*, which Aristophanes, partial as always to traditional peasant fare, prefers out of principle to the "fancy bread" in cities, was a bread baked in the old-fashioned way, in a little country oven or a mold. The word comes from *cribanos*, which means an oven to toast barley in, or, more precisely, what in French will later be called a *tourtière*. Every sort of grain, flour, and method of baking thus existed simultaneously. In Athens today, *matza* is still sold, a little flat kneaded cake made of barley flour, which is less expensive than *artos*, bread properly speaking. *Matza* was used in exactly the same way in which a Mexican Indian of today uses corn *tortillas*, as a base for a filling of meat, fish, peppers, and so on . . . Everything that is eaten with *matzas* in Athens is called *opson*, signifying the "inside" of the sandwich, usually fish.

In like manner, in the Middle Ages, in the Renaissance, and up to the beginning of the nineteenth century in Europe a girdle-cake continued to exist, called in France *fouace* or *fougasse*, made of fine white unleavened wheat flour and cooked beneath coals or in a country oven. The famous *fouace*-makers of Lerné, who figure in Rabelais's *Gargantua*, formed a distinct guild. In certain old houses in the town of Lerné *fouace* ovens still exist, at times hollowed out of the living rock; some of them go back to the eleventh century. Rabelais even gives us the recipe: "wheat flour mixed with egg yolks and butter, fine saffron and fine spices and water . . ." Note that it is celestial fare (*viande*) to lunch on raisins with fresh *fouace*. As is well known, *viande* in French long meant not just red meat but any sort of fare. The word thus resembled present-day Italian *vivanda* and English *viands*, both from the same root (Latin *vivanda*), and up until the eighteenth century the expression *vivande de carême* ("Lenten fare") meant fish. Just as the word *viande* in French eventually came to mean *meat*, the Greek word *opson* usually referred to sardines or anchovies. In fact, fish in modern Greek is *psari*, which derives from *opson*. The evolution of vocabulary is often a very clear indication of the evolution of the food habits of a society.

To return to *fouace*, we thus see the survival, or the return, *as a delicacy*, of a way of cooking flour that is prior to the discovery of bread-making and the refinements that the Greeks brought to it.

In effect, the diversity of Greek bread stemmed not only from the continued use of flour coming from all the known sorts of grains (including rice, out of which they made a bread called *orinde*), but also from the very extensive range of milling processes and the mixtures of various flours that they permitted, from the use of all sorts of baking methods (both prehistoric and newly discovered ones), and, finally, from the art of knowing how to flavor bread. We have seen that Rabelais puts saffron in his *fouace;* it was also used in Greek bread. Other sorts of bread included those made with cumin, poppy seeds, fennel, coriander, anise, raisins, fenugreek, nigella, marjoram, rosemary, capers, sage, cabbage leaves, garlic, or onion. In our day, few of these exist, with the exception of cumin bread and raisin bread, and in Paris at least these are no more than curiosities. The Greeks were masters of the art of baking and recognized as such, with the result that the bakers of Rome, even under the Empire and the Late Empire, were almost all Greeks. They had learned how to make excellent bread with milk, with oil, and many other sorts. The introduction of Greek baking arts into Italy toward the end of the Republic was one of the factors leading to a decadence owed to Hellenic influence, according to Cato the Censor, then in his dotage, who exhorted the Romans—in vain—to return to gruel.

The Latin contribution to the baker's art consisted of a single very unusual sort of bread, the celebrated bread of Picenum, a bizarre concoction based on a grain called *zéa*, mixed with an ingredient that boggles the mind: clay, and a particular sort of clay at that—*creta*, collected between Naples and Pozzuoli. It would ap-

"An oven." Gallo-Roman mosaic, first half of the third century A.D.
Detail from a Calendar of Country Life. Musée des antiquités nation-
ales, St.-Germain-en-Laye.

pear that the Emperor Augustus paid the inhabitants of Naples an
annual sum of twenty thousand sesterces to assure himself exclusive ownership of this clay! In short, by mixing *zéa* and *creta*, a
product was obtained that was called *alica* in Latin, the raw material for Picenian bread.[3] This is what Pliny the Elder has to say of
it: "The people of Picenum are still renowned for the bread that
they have invented, which is made with *alica*. The *alica* is soaked
in water for nine days; on the tenth day it is kneaded with raisin
juice into long loaves, then cooked in the oven in earthenware pots
which crack apart. This bread is not eaten without first having
moistened it, ordinarily, in milk with honey" (Pliny, *N.H.*, XVIII,
27). It is clear that Picenian bread is a sort of pastry rather than
bread, properly speaking. As for bread itself, it had become in
Rome, as in Athens, the food eaten at breakfast, the meal called
jentaculum, if one is to believe Martial, among others: "*Surgite!
Jam vendit pueris jentacula pistor.*" ("Out of bed with you!
There's the baker, who has begun to sell breakfast to the children.")

Greek *pistores* had mastered the art of giving their bread the
most extravagant forms, shaping it like mushrooms, braids, cres-
cents, and so on . . . thus illustrating in advance Carême's observa-
tion a thousand years later: "The fine arts are five in number,
namely: painting, sculpture, poetry, music, and architecture, the
principal branch of the latter being pastry."

And since it is not possible for us to discuss flour without
dealing with cakes, the moment has come to pose the question of
what pastry consisted of in antiquity, what it looked like and how
it was made. The regrettable loss of the great *Treatise on Baking*,
by Chrysippus of Tyanus, which included detailed recipes for
more than thirty cakes, each entirely different, leaves us somewhat
short of information on this important subject. But various cross-
checks (not to mention consultation of Apicius) nonetheless give
us a rather good idea of what the ancient Greeks and Romans con-
fected in this domain.

Let us therefore go straight to the facts: the makers of Greco-
Roman pastry had no knowledge of the subtleties of dough, and
thus had nothing like our present-day babas, doughnuts, brioches,
savarins, cream puffs, millefeuille pastry, pastry made from raised

---

[3] Guégan translates *alica* simply as "spelt," which is a variety of wheat.

dough, or shortbreads. The invention of a Middle Eastern equivalent of pudding is attributed to the Greeks. But as a general rule, Greek pastry closely resembled the sort that is still found today in North Africa, the Near East, and the Balkans: the basic mixture was honey, oil, and flour, plus various aromatic substances, notably pepper. The most frequent method of cooking was frying, but pastry was also cooked beneath coals. Other ingredients included pine nuts, walnuts, dates, almonds, and poppy seeds. This mixture was mainly baked in the form of thin round cakes and in the form of doughnuts and fritters.[4] Sometimes sesame flour, sweet wine, and white cheese were kneaded into them. Here is a recipe from Athenaeus:

"Take walnuts from Thasos in the Pont, almonds, and poppy seeds and toast them carefully. Then crush them well in a clean mortar, mix these three fruits together, grind them by adding strained honey to them, and pepper, and blend the whole together well; the mixture will become black because of the pepper. Make a flat square cake of this paste, then grind some white sesame, mix it with flour and strained honey, and make two flat cakes of it, between which you will place the preceding black paste, fastening it securely in the middle."

Roman pastry does not appear to have included many innovations over and above what the Greeks had already invented. Apicius gives us a number of recipes that allow us to imagine what sweets were like in his day:

"*Domestic cakes:* Grind dates, walnuts, or pine nuts with spelt cooked in water. Work fine-ground pepper and honey into this gruel; make little balls of it, salting the outside of them lightly. Fry them in oil and then moisten them with strained honey.

"*Other cakes:* Take excellent African bread with sweet wine; remove the crust and soak it in milk. Make little balls of it and put them in the oven. Bake them only slightly, take them out, and sprinkle them with honey while still hot, having first pricked them in numerous places so that they will thoroughly absorb the honey. Pepper and serve.

"*Other cakes:* Take bread made of fine wheat flour; remove the crust and cut it in fairly large mouthfuls that you then soak in milk and fry in oil. Moisten with honey and serve.

---

[4] The Greek word *plax*, which serves to designate any flat surface, and by extension flat cakes, is the general term under which cakes, *plakous*, are subsumed.

"Bakeresses kneading bread to the sound of a flute." Terra-cotta, Greece. Musée du Louvre, Paris.

"Bakery, with mills for grinding grain, and an oven." Pompeii.

"*Cakes:* Grind pepper with *garum*, honey, undiluted wine, raisin wine, rue, and pine nuts; mix boiled spelt and crushed walnuts with these ingredients, and add toasted hazelnuts . . .

"*Other cakes:* Grind pepper and pine nuts with honey, rue, and raisin wine. Work the whole into noodle dough and milk, and form little balls of it that you then coat with beaten egg to brown them. Cook, moisten with honey, and serve.

"*Other cakes:* Take fine white flour; cook it in water, and make a very thick gruel of it. Spread this gruel on a pastry board, cut it into cubes, and cook it in the best oil, as though they were cakes. Take them from the frying pan, pour honey over them, sprinkle them with pepper, and serve. These cakes will be better if you use milk instead of water.

"*Tripatina:* Choose a rather large bowl for your milk and pour the milk into it; mix honey with the milk, as for desserts made with milk; add 5 raw eggs per *setier* of liquid, 3 eggs per *hemina*. Beat the whole well in order to obtain a smooth mixture; pour this mixture into a terrine from Cumae and cook over a slow fire. When your dish has thickened, pepper it and serve it.

"*Frothy eggs in milk:* Beat 4 eggs with a *hemina* of milk and an ounce of oil. Meanwhile, heat a little oil in an earthenware frying pan; pour your preparation into it. Turn it out onto a round dish before it is thoroughly done; moisten with honey, sprinkle with pepper, and serve."

This latter recipe might be called the birth of the omelette, which thus first enters history in the form of a sweet dessert. As Bertrand Guégan aptly remarks in a note to his translation of Apicius, the latter already recommends that an omelette be served "runny." Note that the dessert recipe immediately preceding that of the omelette, the *Tripatina* (so called because it contains three ingredients: milk, eggs, and honey), closely resembles today's molded custards, though these latter substitute sugar for the honey.

～C

We have already noted at several points the Greek penchant for aromatic herbs and spices. We shall find the same thing to be true in the vast domain of wines, which the ancient Greeks and Romans were fond of mixing with honey, that ingredient that is found everywhere in the recipes of antiquity; but it would be a mistake to conclude, as certain authors do too hastily, that only sweet wines were known in the Greek and Roman West.

What were the wines of antiquity like? What were European vineyards like in the beginning and how did they evolve between the dawn of Greek civilization and the fall of the Roman Empire? What were the most famous growths and in what circumstances were they drunk? How can we imagine the taste, the consistency, the flavor of the beverages that Agathon's guests get drunk on in Plato's *Symposium*, or the good bottles that Horace cautiously brings out from behind his pile of firewood to honor the visit of a friend passing by, or even to drink alone? These are the points that we shall now deal with, and our discussion will take us back to the birth of the modern Western vineyard, to the introduction of wine grapes into Gaul and even as far north as Germania, on the banks of the Rhine and the Moselle.

Wine existed in Babylon; it is mentioned in numerous passages in the Bible. Though great beer drinkers, the Egyptians also accorded wine a place of honor and their sculpture represents scenes of grape-harvesting and vinification. What is more, all fruits, all berries, all fermentable saps and juices have been used by man for the making of alcoholic beverages. Wild pears, apples, raspberries, blackberries, wild strawberries, grapes from wild vines have all been crushed and later drunk at the end of the period necessary for their fermentation. Apicius mentions wine made from dates, from figs, and from pomegranates.

Nothing that can serve as the basis for the transformation of sugar into alcohol has escaped the attention of *Homo sapiens*, beginning with honey (yet again!), since the oldest Greek beverage was hydromel, which is nothing other than honey that has fermented in around ten to twelve times its own volume of water. The sap of plants can also furnish strong drinks: Mexican *pulque* is sap of the maguey (a variety of large cactus) sucked up with a straw from the heart of the plant, where enough again collects to be gathered in about three days. It is then allowed to ferment; at the end of a first stage it results in what the Indians erroneously call hydromel (*agua-miel*), that is to say a light-colored, sweet, transparent drink with a very slight alcoholic content. After more lengthy fermentation, the liquid turns an opaque white resembling

milk and gives off a strong odor (which often puts Europeans and
North Americans off): this is *pulque*, properly speaking, with an
alcohol content of 8 to 9 percent. It is a viscous, slightly acid, very
thirst-quenching beverage that is impossible to store and ship, so
that it is best to drink it on the spot, in the country and not in a
city, where it risks being spoiled and where it is almost impossible
to find.

If every fruit juice can be "wine," why this exceptional destiny
of wine made from grapes? In the course of Prehistory and
Protohistory, grapes were no more than just another berry among
others. But from the moment that grapevines were first cultivated,
grapes demonstrated their superiority over all other fruits that
produced fermented drinks. This superiority stems essentially
from three properties of wine: its exceptional variation in taste,
depending on the vines, the soil, and the climate in which the vines
grow; its ability to age, to change, to be "improved," to lend itself
to all sorts of experiments as to the conditions under which it is
preserved; and, for certain wines at least, the possibility of being
transported elsewhere.

That is why wine has become the only alcoholic drink to have
spread to every corner of the globe and to be produced in very
different forms, for distilled alcohols are drunk all over the world
but each type is more or less uniform, and other fermented drinks
are at most popular refreshments, closely linked with local conditions. Despite the differences, which we will return to later—
differences that fans of beer maintain that they can detect in various versions of this drink—it must be admitted that its range of
flavors is rather limited. From Greek civilization onward, the
grapevine has ruled supreme.[5] This is all the more true in that it
has never ceased posing problems that challenge the perspicacity
of the grower and never ceased testing the memory of the connoisseur. Its many reactions, according to the place where it is
grown and the variety of wine, the infinite subtleties that result,
make wine-growing and wine-tasting a game of chess with endless
solutions that are never exhausted. Hence, since the beginning, it is
accepted that the lover of wines, once he has come under their

---

[5] On all the beverages prior to the royal reign of wine, see Maurizzio,
Geschichte der gegorenen Getränke (*History of Beverages That Have Disappeared*).

spell, is almost incapable of turning his mind toward anything else. Wine is associated with love and the lack of love; it accompanies both joy and sadness, success and failure; it presides over friendship; it has a profound effect on the life of the mind, on commerce, on war and peace, on the worker's leisure. In certain civilizations giving up drinking wine is more or less tantamount to renouncing all activity, any sort of exchange with one's fellows, even thinking; and the social, emotional, and moral implications of wine have resulted in the creation of a set of habits that go far beyond the need for alcohol, properly speaking. Certain wine-producing countries, such as contemporary Italy, are countries where obvious drunkenness (if not alcoholism, as an illness and a social plague) is almost never seen, and where the consumption of wine could nonetheless not be done away with without seriously affecting daily life.

The growing of grapes for wine in the Aegean region dates from the Minoan era. There were established practices for cultivation of the vines, which the Aegean islands would seem to have learned from the inhabitants of the Southeastern Mediterranean and doubtless from the Semites in the region of Syria. It was only gradually that Dionysus became the god of wine that he was essentially to be in Alexandrian and Roman poetry. Nothing is a better indication of the strong affective overtones of wine in Mediterranean civilizations than the Greek word *ganos*, used to designate, among others, new wine. *Ganos* refers to the sparkling quality of a clear, bright liquid; it was the word used to describe a spring flowing in the shadow of thickets in summer, and also to the flow of rivers, to honey, to a bunch of ripe grapes, to wine itself. More generally still, *ganos* meant "a smiling and joyous appearance." This was precisely the appearance attributed to Dionysus, he who, in the paean addressed to him by Euripides in his *Bacchae*,

> . . . in the joy of feasts bedecked in festive
> garlands of flowers, is
> the first of the blessed.
> It is he who has the honor of leading the processions
> with choruses of dances,
> of mingling bursts of laughter with the sound of flutes,
> of dissipating sorrows, when

the golden, joyous sparkle [*ganos*] of the grape
appears in solemn feasts, and when
at banquets one crowns oneself with ivy,
from the krater you drink in the all-enveloping vapor
of sleep . . .
. . . the god-son of Zeus
gives equally to rich man and poor
the peaceful enjoyment of wine.

For three thousand years Mediterranean Europe has been not so much a geographical area where grapevines are grown as a region dependent on its vineyards. Nonetheless wine in Greek and Roman territories was not as usual a drink at meals as it is today. The habit today is to drink wine at table and not drink any between meals, at least in any quantity, except in cases of patent dipsomania. In ancient Greece it was precisely the reverse. The habit was to drink only a little at table (except for that "shot" of straight wine at breakfast, not unlike the "little snort" in the morning taken by today's peasant), while on the other hand people gathered together especially to drink. This latter was the glorious Hellenic institution of the *symposion*, a term that in our day calls to mind high-minded conversations that in fact have little in common with its origin. For though Plato's *Symposium* is one of the great texts of Western philosophy, and though Xenophon's work by the same name also shows dialectical and ethical questions being embarked upon during the conversation at table, let us not lose sight of the fact that such exchanges always took the form of elegant badinage, without a trace of pedantry, even when, thanks to Socrates, this playful banter extended to the realm of metaphysics. What is more, it often had what today we would call cabaret numbers as an accompaniment and a background. In Xenophon's *Symposium*, the host, Callias, has engaged an impresario from Syracuse and his two "artists": a young man and a young girl, both handsome creatures, who perform dances, acrobatic tricks, and feats of skill, and as a finale offer a ballet-pantomime of the loves of Dionysus and Ariadne so realistic that, according to Xenophon, the guests completely lost their heads: "Those who were bachelors swore that they would take a wife as soon as possible and those who were already married rose from their couches in great haste to leap on their horses and gallop home to join their wives and possess them."[6]

At what time of day was the *symposion* held? (We leave the word in the Greek, since it is neither a French "drinking bout" nor an English "party"; as we shall see, for the Greeks it was a ceremony that followed very definite rules.) After the *akratismos* the Greeks ate a snack, the *ariston*, in the middle of the day. The principal meal of the day, the only one which saw friends gathered together, was dinner, *deipnon* (the reader will remember that the word occurs in the title of Athenaeus' work, the *Deipnosophistai*, or "dinner of savants"). This repast was served very late in the day, often after nightfall. This explains why the Greeks often had another snack in the late afternoon, the *hesperisma*. If the dinner was a holiday one or a special occasion among friends, it was followed by a *symposion*. This gathering was divided into two quite separate and distinct parts; during the first part the guests ate and during the second part they drank, though nothing prevented them from continuing to nibble on dried fruits, almonds, and fresh grapes. During the dinner, "tables were brought," for Greek servants did not set the food out on a table. Rather, they brought tables in with all the food already laid out on them and put them in front of the guests as they reclined on couches, after which they took them away and brought others when everything on them had been consumed. What we would call the first and second courses were referred to as the "first tables" and the "second tables." The Romans organized their dinners in similar fashion. In the course of a formal dinner (*coena recta*) or *comessatio* ("fancy repast," an "orgy"), the *ante coenam* (cf. Italian *antipasto*), consisting of fish, vegetables, and shellfish, was brought in first, followed by the *in coena*, consisting of game, boar, roe deer, and Picenian bread. This "second table" (*secunda mensa*) was followed by the "fruit table" (*mensa pomorum*), which also included jams and preserves (*bellaria*).

In classical Greece, once the last tables had been taken away,

---

6 Women were never present at these gatherings. Greek society was made entirely by and for men, and Socrates, seeing the dexterity of the young girl juggler brought by the Syracusan, states in the form of a paradox that when all is said and done, except for a lesser physical strength, a woman is not the inferior of a man.

the *symposion* officially began. The dinner that preceded it had a tendency in fact to be a rather hurried repast; even though it was a sumptuous meal it was "in silence" (according to Socrates) that Callias' guests partook of it in Xenophon's text. After the last tables had been removed, wine was brought in a krater along with wine-cups. The guests rose to their feet, the host made a libation, a rite that consisted of pouring out a little wine in honor of the divinity, and then everyone said the *"symposion* paean" or hymn in honor of Dionysus, thus formally opening the *symposion,* properly speaking. A *symposion* leader or symposiarch was then named, who determined the number of cups of wine that would be drunk, as the guests drank only in unison, at the bidding of the symposiarch. He also decreed the quantity of wine that these cups would contain and, even more important, the proportions of water and wine—hence the degree of intoxication of the mixture—which was then prepared by the slaves. This was an ancient practice, for as early as the *Iliad,* when Achilles receives Agamemnon's ambassadors, he turns to Patroclus and says to him: "Take the largest krater, o son of Menoetius, make a stronger mixture, and give wine-cups to all."

This text is proof that the krater was definitely not the recipient from which wine was drunk by the guests (the public's astonishment at the enormous size of kraters in museums is unjustified), but rather the recipient in which the water and the wine were mixed; individual cups of wine were then dipped out of it with the aid of a sort of long-handled cup or ladle, the *kyathos.* As each guest drank the same number of cups, the degree of inebriation could be judged by the number of kraters that had been emptied during the night. Each new krater brought in called for a new libation, and it was thus that the first krater, the second, and on to the twentieth was "blessed," so to speak. It was the symposiarch's privilege to order the slave to dilute the wine with more water as the night wore on, which he did if he was wise; but the custom was to "bludgeon" the participants in the beginning by having them swallow one after the other several cups brimful of almost straight wine so as to "create an atmosphere," as we would say. It is this, moreover, that Socrates in Xenophon's *Symposium* gracefully asks the company to avoid:

"Drink, my friends; I for my part am entirely disposed to do so

too. For it is quite true that by moistening souls, wine puts trou-
bles to sleep, as mandrake root puts people to sleep, while at the
same time it awakens joy, as oil stimulates a flame. But it seems to
me that the same thing happens with the human body as with
plants. When in fact the divinity waters them too copiously, they
cannot stand upright or allow themselves to be penetrated by the
breeze; but when they drink only as much as pleases them, they
grow quite straight and tall, flower, and produce fruit. It is the
same with us: if we have great brimming cups poured out for us
our body and our mind will soon vacillate and we will not be able
even to catch our breath, let alone proffer a few words. But if the
servants cause a fine and frequent rain to fall for us in small cups—
to express myself in the manner of Gorgias[7]—we will not be led to
drunkenness beneath the constraint of wine, but rather its gentle
persuasion will lead us to more gaiety."[8]

In our day there exists in English colleges a type of after-dinner
gathering that is altogether mindful of the *symposion* of antiquity.
After having dined at their table with the students in the main dining hall of the college, the dons retire to a small dining room
where they find a table laden with dried fruits and other delica-
cies. They seat themselves around it, as a "drinking master" (ordinarily the don of the college in charge of the cellar and the
purchase of wines) sends the bottle of Port and the bottle of
Madeira around, having first announced the year (an 1890 Port, a
1910 Madeira, etc.), and the bottles pass from hand to hand coun-
terclockwise. The dons converse, never touching on their particular areas of professional competence, however, for this is strictly
forbidden, and give themselves over to one of the great English
pastimes: wagers. A notebook for recording them makes the
rounds of the table as often as the bottles, and the bets of each of
those present as to the results of a coming election or a sports com-
petition are written down in it.

The Greeks were fond of another type of amusement, a sort of
fortune-telling game for lovers known as a *cottabos*, which along

---

[7] A celebrated rhetorician, who furnished the title of a no less celebrated dialogue by Plato.

[8] This translation is based on the French version by François Ollier (Les Belles
Lettres, Paris). (*Translator's note*)

with songs, dances, music, and conversation was one of the diversions of the assembled drinkers. The *cottabos* consisted of imitating a libation, that is to say of pouring out wine, but in this case it was aimed at a saucer placed some distance away and what was uttered was not the name of the god but that of the beloved. If the wine landed in the saucer it was an auspicious sign for the lover. This game, of Sicilian origin, was very popular at evening gatherings attended by young Athenians, and was more than a passing vogue, for Greek came to have a whole family of words having to do with this game: there was one for "playing *cottabos*," another for "cup for playing at *cottabos*" (*cottabis*), still another for "metal basin for playing at *cottabos*" (*cottabeion*), the metal in this case being expected to have a certain ring to it if the sign was a favorable one, and, finally, a word for "winner's prize at the game of *cottabos*" (*cottabion*).

Wine, the consumption of wine, the wine libation, the *cottabos*, the hymn that opened the *symposion*, the fact that the guests wore crowns of flowers and laurel all indicate at least a vague survival of a religious and magic context to which Euripides' *Bacchae* bears witness. Later on in Rome, though the libation is still practiced, drunkenness takes on secular overtones. More and more frequently wine is consumed not only in the course of fancy banquets, but also in private, among friends. The custom of giving banquets continues and even becomes more widespread under the Empire, but the distinction between a dinner and a *symposion* becomes blurred: the guests get drunk as they eat, as in Petronius' *Satyricon*, and with Horace one witnesses the creation of a new figure, the lover of good wine, who is pleased to enjoy a great vintage with a friend in his country house. Whereas in classical Greece the consumption of wine was collective and ceremonial, it now becomes personal and private, marked by individualism and a critical turn of mind. With Horace's *Odes* the aesthetic of the modern "tippler" enters the history of Western sensibility.

Though bacchic customs are fairly easy to reconstitute from the texts that have come down to us, it is less easy to draw any conclusions as to what the taste of different wines of antiquity might have been like. The great problem is to know whether there existed in the classical period the equivalent of what we call a dry wine today, that is to say, a wine that does not have the trace of a sweet taste. It seems probable that such a thing did exist, since both the Greeks and the Romans distinguished between sweet, dry, and "intermediate" wines. But does "dry" in this case (the adjective is the same in both languages: *æsteros* in Greek and *austerus* in Latin) mean "with a high alcohol content" or "the contrary of sweet"? The adjective can be interpreted in both senses. The so-called "intermediate" type of wine (which Athenaeus calls *mesos*) might have been either what we call a "demi-sec" wine or "a wine of average strength," since it was also called *autocratos*, or wine "mixed with itself," that is to say, one that does not need to be diluted with water to weaken it or to be strengthened by the addition of a wine with a higher alcohol content. (In Italian too, we might point out, *secco* means "high in alcohol"; the word for "nonsweet" is *asciutto*.) It is not unlikely that the still-imperfect processes of vinification of the time prevented the ancient Greeks and Romans from making completely dry wines, in the sense that we today call a Pouilly-Fuissé or a Muscadet dry. Certain varieties of vine in certain soils and in certain climates would appear however to have sometimes produced grapes that by themselves furnished light, dry white wines like ours: this would seem to be the case with Mareotic wine, an Egyptian wine from the region of Alexandria.

Another problem: Why was wine diluted? The custom of mixing water with wine before serving it would seem to be explained by the wish to keep guests at a *symposion* from becoming drunk too quickly, but it also seems to have stemmed from other necessities. The wines of antiquity were doubtless rather heavy and must have had an alcoholic content as high as 16 to 18 percent. Let us not forget that, on the whole, wine grapes were grown in regions much farther south than today. There were no vineyards north of the Mediterranean regions. The principal wine-growing region in Italy was situated around Naples. The earliest wine to become famous, according to Homer, was Maronean wine, from the Thracian coast. Homer tells us that Maronean wine, the wine that Ulysses gets Polyphemus drunk on in the *Odyssey*, must be mixed with twenty times its volume of water. Doubtless a certain amount of epic exaggeration enters the picture here, and what is meant is probably something like "a wine of prodigious strength." In point of fact, a wine of normal strength was considered to be one to

"Baking bread." Hebrew manuscript, end of the fifteenth century:
Recueil de prescriptions rituelles concernant les observations reli-

gieuses (Compilation of Ritual Prescriptions Concerning Religious Observations).

which one should add three parts of water to one of wine. Cratinus (an author cited by Athenaeus) provides a portrait of a wine-lover attentively watching over the aging of a Mendean wine (from Mendaios, in Macedonia): "Let him spy a little Mendean wine that is still very young, and he follows it, he accompanies it, and says: 'By my faith! How pretty and white it is! Will it take three-quarters water?'" meaning: "Will it become strong enough, take on enough body, to permit the normal mixture?" This mixture must have had an alcohol content of no more than 5 to 6 percent; hence the endurance of drinkers at *symposia*. But later, in Italy, as certain great vintages became distinguishable and took on a personality of their own, it became less and less a question of stretching them out with water. Not for anything in the world would Horace have allowed water to be mixed with his Falernian, and from the Empire onward, authors speak not only of wine but expressly use the word *merum*, meaning undiluted wine.[9]

In Book XIV of his *Natural History*, devoted to wine and viniculture, Pliny estimates the number of highly regarded growths of his time to be around eighty, and the number of varieties of wine at one hundred and twenty-five. Among Greek wines the most celebrated were those from the islands Lesbos, Thasos, Chios. The wine of Cos was diluted with sea water, a frequent practice in the Greek islands and one that apparently permitted wines to be shipped more easily. The best Greek wines were in fact exported in the direction of the Western Mediterranean. According to certain texts, diluting wine with sea water was considered to be a method of improving it, while according to others this practice was restricted to wines of inferior quality. In Italy there was no such thing as recognized growths before the end of the second century B.C. Julius Caesar caused a sensation in 45 B.C. when he had four different growths served at the banquet cele-

---

[9] *Dissolve frigus ligna super foco*
large reponens, atque benignius
deprome quadrimum Sabina,
O Taliarche, merum diota.

(Horace, *Odes*, I, 9)

(*Banish the cold by piling plenty of logs on the fire*
And, my dear Taliarchus, pour out with a more generous hand
This pure, four-year-old wine
From the Sabine amphora with two handles.)

brating his fourth consulate. Previously the only designation was that of the year, indicated by the name of the consul then in office. One of the most highly praised years was 121 B.C., under the consulate of Lucius Opimius. The expression "Opimian wine" became a synonym for "a very great year." "Such was the temperature [the grapes cooked, they say] beneath the effect of the sun [that] these wines, now more than two hundred years old, are still around, reduced to a sort of bitter honey," Pliny tells us.

Italian growths, still unknown to Plautus and Cato, began to come to the fore in the course of the first century B.C.: first Cecubo, from a vineyard planted in the middle of the Pontine Marshes, and then the wines of Campania: Falerno, mentioned for the first time by Catullus, from one precise vineyard, situated near Capua, in a place today called San Giovanni in Ponte Campano. Around Falerno properly speaking, a larger wine-growing region produced wine that went by the general appellation of Falernian. Among them was Massic wine, praised by Horace, who also thought highly of the wines of Alba. Sicily had a highly regarded growth, Mamertino, from the region of Messina. The classification of growth, according to Pliny, was, in decreasing order: Cecubo, Falerno, Alba, Mamertino. Numerous other growths could be cited—Tarentum, Ancona, etc.—but since there is no way of having any very definite idea of their qualities, such an enumeration would be pointless and boring.

It is nonetheless worth mentioning Spanish wine districts (Tarragona, Valencia), already great producers and exporters, and wine-growing in Gaul, to which we shall return, for its development in the very last years of classical antiquity and the beginning of the Middle Ages is a capital step in the progression of viticulture toward colder latitudes.

In the Gallo-Roman era, only two regions in Gaul were important: that around present-day Vienne, producing what we would today call *côtes du Rhône*, and the Narbonnaise, the region around Béziers, a large-scale producer ever since. One regrets having to mention the fact that the reputation of wine-growers in the South of France was no better at the beginning of our era than it is today. "The reputation of the wines of Béziers is confined to the Gauls," Pliny says. "Of the other wines of the Narbonnaise, there is nothing that can be said, for manufactories have been set up in which they are disguised with smoke, and thank heaven not with herbs and harmful ingredients as well, for wine merchants even use aloes to alter the taste and the color of it!" In defense of the wine-growers of Gaul, it should be said that they were not the only ones to engage in these regrettable practices. Columella describes processes for adulterating wine in Italy and Greece that were just as dishonest. The Gauls, alas, were held to be at once quite unscrupulous wine-growers, frightful drunkards ("a race gluttonous for wine," *vini avidum genus,* Ammianus Marcellinus calls them), and also cutthroat tradesmen, already specialized in barefaced overcharging. Speaking of the price of wines, Pliny the Elder declares: "Before now one has rarely seen, and then only out of [the buyer's] prodigality, a *testa*[10] bringing a thousand sesterces. The Viennois alone, it would seem, demand a higher price for their sticky wines, but only on the domestic market and out of national pride."

But let us not dwell on the subject of Gallic trickery and instead examine the question of the aging of wines. Given the shortcomings of vinification processes in antiquity and the fact that fermentation in vats was more or less unknown, one might expect the Greeks and Romans to have drunk their wines young, since these wines were necessarily fragile. But quite the contrary was the case, at least with regard to the famous growths. Authors speak only of wines to be drunk at the end of five, seven, fifteen, twenty-five years. Fifteen or twenty years are common figures; today only truly exceptional growths gain anything by reaching that age. According to R. Billiard, the author of the most careful study of the subject thus far, *La Vigne dans l'Antiquité* (*Wine-growing in Antiquity*),[11] Greek and Roman wines took on a syrupy consistency as they aged. "The bitterness of rancid wines is the result of various *casses,*[12] of aging, and of bacterial diseases peculiar to great growths," he states. As we have seen, Pliny speaks of Opimian wine as "bitter." The question is complicated by the fact

---

[10] An amphora of forty liters.

[11] Lyon, 1913. Let us also cite the remarkable commentaries of J. André in his edition of Pliny the Elder (Les Belles Lettres Collection); it is this text and translation that have been followed here.

[12] A disorder of certain wines, causing them to lose color and deposit sediment. (*Translator's note*)

that the authors of antiquity never specify whether they are speaking of a dry wine or a sweet wine, of a natural or an artificial sweet wine, of a liqueur or of a cooked wine. In this latter case, keeping it a long time was more understandable. White wine was more highly regarded than red, which does not make much sense without further description, and Apicius even gives a recipe for turning "black wine into white wine." Let us note in this regard that if Greek and Roman texts speak of red wine and black wine, we must not leap to the conclusion, as certain modern authors do, that there eixsted in this period a "black" wine that has since disappeared. We need think only of present-day Italian usage, whereby red wine is called either *vino rosso* or *vino nero*. A waiter in an Italian trattoria will ask you *"Bianco o nero?"* to find out whether you want white wine or red. Old wines were often used in antiquity to dilute young wines, which is as inconceivable today as though one were to pour a half liter of vintage Pommard into an ordinary 11-percent red wine to make the latter taste better!

But this is inconceivable only if we are thinking in terms of modern wines. The Greeks and Romans considered wine less as a product to be distinguished by growths that each had separate and distinct characteristics than as the basis, the point of departure, of all sorts of beverages that also contained water, either salt or fresh, honey, pitch, resin, and all sorts of perfumes. Aromatizing wines, with different flowers especially, was an important feature of the art of wine-making, and indeed there exists in Greek a special term to designate wine "with the scent of flowers," *anthosmias*. Apicius speaks of wine aromatized with roses and violets. Pliny speaks of "aromatic wine prepared almost like perfumes, those with myrrh first of all, and then also with Celtic spikenard, sweet rush, and tar, in little balls thrown into must or sweet wine." Among other scents, he mentions cinnamon, absinth, saffron, lavender, and gentian. The scent chosen was either introduced into the must itself during fermentation, or when it was put into jars, or when it was served. Certain herb wines seem to have been the equivalent of our present-day vermouths.[13] When honey was mixed with wine dur-

---

[13] We should also mention wine made from raisins, *passum*, which was greatly esteemed in the Hellenic and the Roman world—a sweet wine, since Martial calls

(continued on next page)

ing fermentation, it was not so much for the purpose of flavoring it as of sweetening it, as in the modern process of *"sucrage,"* adding sugar so as to increase its alcohol content. The Greeks and Romans often smoked their wines by keeping them for a time in the *apotheca,* a room on the second story through which the smoke from the chimney passed. Greek wine flavored with resin (which still exists today) is cited by Pliny as a characteristic aromatized wine, and although he wrote in the first century A.D. he speaks of it as though it were a traditional product and seems to indicate that the method for making it, consisting of mixing resin with fermenting must, had been known by Greek wine-growers since earliest antiquity. In short, wine in the classical world was almost always used as a sort of raw material, to be combined with various additives ranging from sea water to smoke.

This habit of aromatizing wines was to persist for a long time, until the end of the Middle Ages.[14] But as early as the Empire, new vineyards came into being that produced wines with both a lower alcohol content and particular characteristics (thus prefiguring our modern "growths"), so that the addition of extraneous ingredients became superfluous.

---

it "the honeyed wine of the poor." Women were permitted to drink it. In general, wine was forbidden women, and historians report cases of husbands in the second century B.C. who killed their wives because they had gone to tipple secretly in the wine cellar. The stricture would appear to have become less severe later, for Livia Augusta (the wife of the Emperor Augustus), who died in A.D. 29 at the age of eighty-six, "said she owed her eighty-six years to Pucinum wine, the only one she ever partook of" (Pliny). This was a vineyard on the Adriatic, either at Procecco or Duino. We have an equivalent today of *passum:* the *vin de paille* of the Jura.

[14] Today we find *kir* (white wine mixed with *cassis,* an alcoholic currant syrup) and, less often, red wine and *cassis* (called *cardinal* or *communard* or *rouge-gorge*), which are basically a survival of the old school of mixtures. Until World War One, *vin blanc gommé* could be found. The "gum" that was added was a sort of sweetish syrup that was used to mask the taste of inferior wines. The need to "fill the glass all the way up with gum" meant that the wine in question was more or less pure rotgut. And finally, as another product of the age-old tradition of blending flavors, which is the contrary of modern oenology, which aims at affirming the distinct personality of each type of wine, let us mention *argenteuil,* a mixture of red and white wine that as recently as 1966 we saw still being served in certain very popular cheap Parisian bars.

CHAPTER FOUR

AT LAST
TAILLEVENT
CAME ON THE
SCENE . . .

We have discussed the cuisine of antiquity in detail for several reasons: first, because it is the cuisine of eras the most remote in time that we find hardest to imagine; second, because the texts that give information as to what this cuisine was like are usually difficult to consult, unlike those about more recent periods (and nothing is as good as the actual reading of a precise, concrete recipe to give one a fair idea of a given gastronomical style); and finally, because the cuisine of antiquity in fact long outlasted the classical period itself.

There indeed exists an argument according to which, after the complicated and erudite cuisine of Apicius, there was a return to more barbarous and primitive food habits, with cuisine arriving only by imperceptible degrees at certain improvements. Then a gastronomical revolution took place, according to this argument, in Italy at the time of the Renaissance and spread to France in the middle of the sixteenth century at the time of the marriage of Catherine de Médicis and Henry II, thus giving rise to a first form of modern cuisine.

In the following chapter, devoted to the Renaissance, we shall see whether the facts support this second point.

As for the first point of this argument, we shall see that the differences between the cuisine of the Middle Ages and that of antiquity are much less substantial than the resemblances. The differences stem first of all from the fact that the Middle Ages, at least at the beginning, had fewer cooking methods. Until approximately the thirteenth century, ovens were more or less unknown. Fireplaces were the principal means of cooking, with spits turning in front of them for cooking meat and hooks for pots inside them to boil vegetables. Thus baking, whose importance in antiquity we have seen, was precluded, as were stews and meat sauces, for fireplaces provided no source of moderate heat. Nevertheless, we note that meats were prepared in the same way as in antiquity: in the Middle Ages as well, fowl, game, and roasts from the butcher's were generally boiled in water before putting them on the spit. We must point out, however, that the andirons (called *landiers*) of these huge fireplaces had not only complex branching arrangements at either end for supporting the entire edifice of spits, but also hollow receptacles that coals could be put in, over which small saucepans could be placed.

It was not until the end of the thirteenth century, however, that medieval cuisine reached the level of that of antiquity, by rediscovering the art of stews, sauces, and cooking in an oven, usually a bakery oven. Medieval cuisine also bore another resemblance to that of antiquity: a persistent abuse of spices, and a fondness for disguising foodstuffs—the habit, for example, of serving "dressed pheasant" or "dressed swan," that is, birds cooked and then redecorated with all their feathers, and the fondness for novelties, tricks, and jokes, which, as we shall see, lingered on until the very end of the sixteenth century. Moreover, compared to antiquity, the Middle Ages had a slightly inferior sense of what ingredients should be mixed together: cooks were generally content to juxtapose them. It was an age that took great visual pleasure in serving enormous accumulations of meat. Its idea of a feast was to bring in gigantic roasts of veal, roe deer, red deer, and boar, served whole on enormous silver platters, surrounded by geese, partridge, and grouse. Very often perfumes were burned in the banquet hall. This habit persisted until the beginning of the eighteenth century.

The diet of the wealthy class, one realizes, thus contained a great deal of meat. Mixing meat and fish together was the normal practice. We are told, for instance, of an ass's foal served in Dagobert's reign stuffed with little birds, eels, and aromatic herbs. For even the simplest meals, two vast vessels were placed on the table, one of them containing all sorts of animal products, both fish and meat, the other, the "herbs," or boiled green vegetables. The mixture of salt and sweet, the use (beginning in the fourteenth century) of sugar in sauces, replacing the honey of antiquity, the association of fresh fruits and meat in stews, were also general practices, which lingered on until the middle of the sixteenth century and even the seventeenth century and beyond. There was also the medieval habit of consuming fresh fruit at the beginning of meals, a habit that historians generally take to be characteristic only of the Renaissance. This is inaccurate, for as early as the seventh century we find, for example, a text in which the Latin poet and bishop Venantius Fortunatus writes to the abbess of Poitiers: "I ate so many good things that I have a stomach swollen like a balloon. Dishes filled to the brim with exquisite foods rose above the table like hills; I was first presented with sweet fruits that common folk call peaches, etc. . . ." With this image of hills, we again note the persistent obsession with sheer quantity, which will continue to manifest itself even at the very heart of modern cuisine, though in the latter its only usual forms are "mountains of fruit" and fancy pastry creations.

We find fruit at the beginning of a meal in the reign of Saint Louis. Here is the menu of a meatless dinner offered by the king in the refectory of a convent at Sens, a dinner described by an Italian monk: "We had cherries first, then very white bread, after which we were served quantities [*quand et quand*] of excellent wine in great abundance, as was fitting for royal magnificence, and according to the custom of the French,[1] several persons hastened to invite and urge those who did not care to drink to do so. After this we were given new broad beans cooked in milk, fish and crayfish, eel pâté, rice pudding with almonds, sprinkled with cinnamon, roasted eels, accompanied by a very good sauce, meat pie and *caillebotte*, and finally a quantity of fruits."[2] *Caillebotte* is milk that has been curdled and drained of the whey. As for the wines mentioned, they might have been either wines from the Paris region, which at this time was entirely covered with vineyards, or wines from Greece, Palestine, Malvoisie from Cyprus, highly regarded as a luxury wine, or perfumed wines, consumed in great quantities in the Middle Ages: wines aromatized with absinth, aloes, hyssop, myrtle, anise, rosemary, cloves, nutmeg, ginger, cinnamon, sage, etc. Burgundy wines were, nonetheless, considered to be the best, and in 1395 an ordinance by Philip the Bold was promulgated intended to prevent its adulteration.

We find that eel was widely eaten in medieval times (in the *Roman de Renart*, the fox is always trying to catch an eel in the river), and herring too was an important food. River fish and crayfish were generally abundant and easy to catch, since not many people fished for them and the population was extremely sparse. In this regard, moreover, one is struck by the fact that there was not as much difference between the diet of the people

---

[1] That is to say, the inhabitants of what today is called the Île de France.

[2] The serving of sweet dishes between two meat or fish dishes was the general rule.

"Tapestry of Queen Mathilde," c. 1080. Musée de l'Évêché, Bayeux.

and that of the ruling classes in the Middle Ages as there was to be later on, at the end of the seventeenth and eighteenth centuries. Let us also point out that when it is said that the peasants of the seventeenth century lived on "roots," what was meant by the term at the time was such vegetables as carrots, turnips, celery root, and so on . . . Even as late as the beginning of the nineteenth century, the word "root" is still used in cookbooks to designate anything that grows underground. The festive dish of the people in the Middle Ages was *galimafrée*, half a soup and half a stew, into which went chopped meat, chicken, bacon, wine, spices, verjuice, and *cameline*.

These latter two terms merit comment. Verjuice played an important role in cuisine in this period. It was put in everything, and

we find it everywhere. As late as 1660 the Hôtel-Dieu, the great hospital in Paris, consumed forty *muids* (a *muid* was 268 liters) of it a year, which proves that medieval cuisine, like scholastic philosophy, lingered on even at the height of the classic century. Verjuice is an acid stock prepared in advance in various manners, either from an acid herb, such as sorrel, or lemon, or, when lemons were too costly, from the juice of green grapes. As for *cameline*, this was a sauce with cinnamon, ginger, cloves, pepper, and sour wine or verjuice.

For the greater part of the Middle Ages we unfortunately have no written source, no treatise on gastronomy properly speaking, and are reduced to relying on an inadequate source of information —accounts of banquets for special occasions. Beginning in the

"*Butchering a pig.*" *Miniature from a thirteenth-century Provençal Codex,* Le Bréviaire d'Amour (The Breviary of Love), *by Ermengol de Béziers. Biblioteca Royal del Escorial.*

fourteenth century, things change, for the first cookbooks since Apicius make their appearance. In 1306 there appeared a *Traité où l'on enseigne à faire et à appareiller et assaisonner toutes viandes selon divers usages de divers pays* (*Treatise teaching how to prepare and combine and season every sort of viand according to different customs of different countries*). In it we read, for example, a recipe typical of the era, for eel *sarraginée*, in which we find, in addition to eel that has been fried beforehand, bread, sugar, wine, and verjuice, all boiled together, along with a great many spices, cinnamon, lavender, cloves, etc. . . . . It should be noted that sugar was considered a spice. Discovered in the territory of Tripoli by the Crusaders, the "honeyed reeds," or sugarcane, of the Middle East furnished the only sugar available to Western Europe at the time. Beginning in the thirteenth century, sugar replaced honey as a sweetener, as we have said, and sugarcane was subsequently successfully acclimated in Crete, Sicily, Madeira, and Andalusia.

Around 1350 there appeared another book, the *Grand Cuisinier de toute cuisine* (*The Great Cook of Every Variety of Cuisine*), an anonymous work which circulated only in manuscript form and was printed for the first time in the middle of the sixteenth century by a chef of the time, Pierre Pidoulx. But like the *Traité* of 1306, the *Grand Cuisinier* of 1350 was familiar to cooks in the fourteenth and fifteenth centuries, for one finds recipes copied word for word from these two works in later manuals. Two other capital works were to appear during the second half of the fourteenth century: the *Ménagier de Paris* (*The Paris Household Manager*), composed in the last decade of the century, a work that is largely a treatise on domestic economy; and standing out from all these books, Taillevent's *Viandier* (*Cookbook*), the great document synthesizing medieval cuisine which appeared in 1490.

Guillaume Tirel, known as Taillevent, born around 1310, was the first Christian "star" of gastronomy. He foreshadowed the long series of chefs who, from Carême to Escoffier, successfully allied theory and practice, made their mark on the cuisine of their time, and became semilegendary figures and unquestioned authorities. In his *Grand Testament*, the poet François Villon, looking for the way to make a fricassee, consults his Taillevent:

"Royal banquet." French miniature, fourteenth century, from Livy's Histoire romaine (Roman History). *Bibliothèque publique et universitaire, Genève.*

"Honey." Italian miniature, end of the fourteenth century, from the Tacuinum sanitatis in Medicina (Manual of Health Remedies in Medicine). *Bibliothèque nationale, Paris.*

Mel.

G. naturc. c.a.f.i.z. meli creo q̃ est ĩ fiuo. .... miamentri
mõdificat larit ꝛ ꝓbula coꝛuptionẽ carnium. ꝛ aliorũ
bunectat. noẽtri. sirũ effiat exꝗntur. ....
ꝗ pꝛimis murtis.

*Si allé veoir en Taillevent
ou chappitre de fricassure.*

*(So I went to see in Taillevent
the chapter on fricasseeing . . .)*

The complete title of Taillevent's collection of recipes, not at all a long work, is *Ci apres sensuyt le viandier pour appareiller toutes manieres de viandes que Taillevent queulx du roi nostre sire fist tant pour abiller et appareiller boully, rosty, poissons de mer et d'eaue doulce, saulces, espices et aultres choses à ce convenables et necessaires comme cy apres sera dit . . . (There follows the cook-book for preparing all manner of viands that Taillevent, the cook of the king our sire composed, both for dressing and mixing boiled foods, roast foods, salt-water and fresh-water fish, sauces, spices, and other things suitable and necessary for this purpose as will be set forth hereinafter . . .)* The king mentioned is Charles VI; and let us also recall here the fact that *viande* at the time meant not only meat in general but also all foodstuffs, *habiller* means to prepare a fowl or game or any animal served whole, and *appareiller* refers to the art of combining several ingredients.

What was Taillevent's contribution, his special innovation? Tradition has it that it was essentially the importance he attributed to sauces. Outside of *cameline*, which we have already mentioned, whose smooth consistency he perfected by putting its ingredients through a sieve (which would seem to prefigure the great Antonin Carême), he is the inventor of three *dodines:* white *dodine*, verjuice *dodine*, and red *dodine*.[3] The first is a sauce made of milk, egg yolks (called *moyeux d'oeufs* in the vocabulary of the time), sugar, salt, and parsley. The second is made of verjuice, yolks of hard-boiled eggs, poultry livers, bouillon, herbs, and a little sugar. Red *dodine* is made of toasted bread (referred to as "browned" bread) soaked in red wine, onions fried in bacon, cinnamon, nutmeg, cloves, sugar and salt, and duck fat. These three sauces were prepared *underneath* the roast as it turns on the spit, which means that drops of meat juice fell into them. In this period, *roux*, thickeners made of flour and butter, had not yet been invented,

---

[3] Correctly used, this word does not refer at all to a variation of the *terrine*. A *dodine de canard* is a duck *in dodine sauce.*

and it was the "browned" bread that served to give body to these various sauces accompanying meat dishes.

Taillevent's inventions were not limited to the introduction of new recipes. They also included improvements and refinements of old ones: the popular *garbures*, different sorts of thick soups with vegetables and bread and, a name still borne by an admirable soup from the Béarn: *le chaudumer*, the ancestor of our *materlote d'an-guilles* (eel stew with red wine and onions), and ragouts, which now make their appearance or reappearance. The *Viandier* also includes several recipes for very simple clear soups, for example, one with ginger, garlic, and verjuice, rather like Provençal garlic soup or Périgord *tourin*. It was also one of Taillevent's habitual practices to *"verdir,"* that is, to add at the last minute the juice of green vegetables to a dish that has just been prepared.

It is difficult to appreciate fully the originality of the *Viandier* as compared to the *Grand Cuisinier de toute cuisine* that had appeared earlier. These two works are representative of precisely the same moment in the history of gastronomy and should be studied together, for they form a whole. But what is striking about these two books is how close in many respects both of them remain to antiquity. The list of spices in use in the fourteenth and fifteenth centuries is virtually the same as the one placed at the head of Apicius' extracts ten or twelve centuries earlier. Moreover, when we take a look at the various cuisines of Europe in the same era, we note that cuisine in those days was very international. There is evidence, naturally, of local particularities: in Italy, macaroni and vermicelli made a first timid appearance (at this point they were used only as an ingredient in stews). But one can find in Taillevent a recipe for tuna with pears, seasoned with oregano and lemon, that formed part of the Tuscan cuisine of the Quattrocento. There is also an English recipe for eggs with tripe and saffron (saffron had been introduced into Spain by the Moors and was highly esteemed throughout the Middle Ages), a recipe that was invented in 1390 by one of Richard II's cooks.

Taillevent himself provides a recipe for a German broth with bouillon, wine, bacon, onion, almonds, cinnamon, ginger, cloves, "seeds of paradise" (cardamom?), saffron, and verjuice. All these spices define a certain style of cuisine that is a direct carry-over from antiquity. That the tradition is a continuous one can be seen

Le liure de tail=leuent grant cuy=sinier du Roy de France

"*A kitchen boy.*" Detail of a fifteenth-century miniature by Évrard d'Espingues, from the Livre de la Propriété des choses (Property Owners' Handbook), *by Barthélemy l'Anglais. Bibliothèque nationale, Paris.*

"*Guillaume Tirel, known as Taillevent.*" Title page of Le Livre de Taillevent, grand cuisinier du Roi de France (The Book of Taillevent, Master Cook of the King of France), *Paris, c. 1520. Bibliothèque nationale, Paris.*

from a recipe such as "Charlemagne's deer," which consisted of a marinade for red deer or roe deer. This marinade contained raspberries, lemon, and honey, along with the ingredients that still figure in all modern marinades: onions, carrots, celery, and parsley. In order to account for this cuisine based on spices, we must of course not forget the influence of the Middle East (and of the Arabs in particular), of Muslim Spain, and also of Sicily: we have a recipe for *gratin* of chicken with pistachio nuts and almonds, the creation of Ibnath-Thumma, emir of Catania, and another for meat croquettes with cumin, from the caliph of Palermo. These dishes are no longer praised as highly as they deserve to be, but they did, understandably, circulate all through the West, especially at various courts.

In later years, from the seventeenth and in particular the eighteenth century on, the use of spices declined considerably. In his *Grand Dictionnaire de cuisine*, Alexandre Dumas *père* speaks of saffron with the greatest scorn. What we are confronted with here is, in fact, two prototypes of cuisine: one in which individual spices are used very liberally, initially, and later all mixed together with no thought as to the spices' compatibility. The other cuisine consists of reducing the use of very pronounced flavors to a minimum or, rather, using them only to reinforce, to heighten the natural flavor of a given food. In accordance with this latter school of thought, spices are used only in such small doses that they are almost homeopathic, and barbarous marriages in which many different flavors risk neutralizing and destroying the essential flavor of the basic foodstuff to which they are added are carefully avoided. The adepts of this second school are eloquently defended by the great chef Curnonsky when he writes: "Cuisine is when things taste like what they are."

According to the modern conception, it is not only spices that will serve to flavor other foods, but also other natural foods themselves. The idea of using a decoction of shrimp to flavor a filet of sole, or a purée of morilles to scent a chicken wing obviously eliminates the need to resort to an excess of nutmeg or cloves to season a tasteless dish. Our contemporaries are at present returning to spices. They can be found in great quantities, both fresh and dried, in supermarkets as well as in fancy grocery stores, and once

"Absinth." Italian miniature, end of the fourteenth century, from the Tacuinum sanitatis in Medicina *(Manual of Health Remedies in Medicine).* Bibliothèque nationale, Paris.

Absintum

Nature. c. q. f. j. 2. melius creo. habes foleas albae
reddit apetitum a custodit panos atneis l'euse.
sucus ei nocet stomaco. remocio noci. si sumat bz
ba et nõ sucus.

again hot pepper, saffron, great amounts of thyme, dill, paprika, rosemary, savory, sage (the use of which never disappeared in Italy) are used with a lavish hand both by amateur cooks and in commercially prepared food. This is a happy development in one sense, for it is a proof of imagination, but it is not one when an abuse of spices masks the weakness and the primitive nature of the basic preparation. Herbs and all extrinsic flavorings are often an overly facile solution, and their excessive use may well mark a certain regression of culinary art in our day. The practitioners of the "New French Cuisine" born since 1970 are quite aware of this and have reacted by once again striving for subtle natural flavors.

With regard to the art of combining aromas by using them only in ideal proportions and never to excess, one cannot help comparing Western cuisine to another which the West was to discover much later: that of China.

Let us note first that cuisine, which in China was already 3,500 years old at the end of our Middle Ages, has always been considered an art by the Chinese. A thousand years before Christ, they were experimenting, inventing new dishes, trying out foods that had never been eaten before, writing their recipes out on silk and bamboo. In 1115 B.C. the imperial court hired a dietician who was also a master chef. There exists in China a vast gastronomical literature. For four thousand years, writers and poets in this civilization were gourmets. Although a man of letters in the West, and particularly in France, is not looked down upon if he manifests an interest in gastronomy, it would nonetheless not be considered a serious endeavor were he to write treatises on cuisine. Alexandre Dumas's *Grand Dictionnaire de cuisine* is an exception, but Dumas *père* is not exactly considered to be a representative of literature at its highest and purest. China, on the contrary, is perhaps the only country in the world in which scholars, philosophers, moralists, political thinkers, and poets have personally written treatises on food and put together collections of recipes.

This perhaps explains why Chinese cuisine is based on aesthetic experience, both as regards the combination of aromas and flavors and as regards that of colors. The Chinese, moreover, add a supplementary element to these harmonies—the contrast in consis-

"Cheese-making." Italian miniature, end of the fourteenth century, from the Tacuinum sanitatis in Medicina *(Manual of Health Remedies in Medicine).* Bibliothèque nationale, Paris.

Caſcus recens.

Al. nature. f. ꝛ. b. melꝰ ergo. teperaũ lacte aīalıꝰ ſanı
Aıuamenti. molıficat corpꝰ ꝰ ꝺ pıgnat. noeumentũ. op̄ılat
ıemono nocı. ꝺı nuabꝰ amıgꝺale et melꝰ.

tencies and textures: many dishes juxtapose and oppose crisp vegetables and soft ones, harsh sauces and smooth condiments. But the care taken by the Chinese never to go beyond a sort of chamber music of cuisine sometimes results in dishes that to unsophisticated palates may appear to be entirely lacking in aroma and flavor. The fact is that each dish has its own proper proportions, its own dominant element, and as the Chinese have been the first to demonstrate with their eight thousand codified recipes, cuisine depends as much—and perhaps even more so—on the education of the tastes of *consumers* as on the talent of master chefs.

The Chinese certainly did not lack gastronomical imagination, since long before the West, and often far more adventurously, they explored all the resources of the earth and the sea, even going so far as to include flower petals in their cuisine. Nonetheless, the evolution of their gastronomical art tended toward *an increasing complexity as to conception and an increasing simplicity as to the result.* It is a fascinating cuisine that offers as many possibilities of refinement to the poor as to the rich, to the family cook as to imperial chefs. This is obviously not true of every recipe, but it is true of a great many of them. And the mark of great art in cuisine is precisely that: making use of a certain number of *principles* that are applicable both to simple and cheap dishes and to costly ones, and applicable both in times of famine and in periods of prosperity.[4]

Let us also not forget that the methods of cooking in Chinese cuisine were essentially determined by a particular scarcity: that of fuel. This led Chinese cooks to perfect methods that allowed a dish to be cooked in ten or twenty minutes over coals or a fire on the stove. More time was thus spent planning the mixture of ingredients before cooking than to the cooking itself. No corrections could be made, and the art of proportions was thus a capital one.

What is striking about medieval cuisine, in contrast to the Chinese cuisine that we have just briefly described, and in contrast to the Western cuisine of a later period, is that proportions are only

---

[4] Dr. Édouard de Pomiane's work, *Bien manger quand même (Eating Well Regardless)*, published during World War Two, is a good example of the application of considered gastronomical principles to raw materials that at the time were monotonous or scarce due to difficulties in procuring food supplies.

very sketchily indicated or are not even mentioned at all. When we think of the precise measurements that sometimes became a mania with a Carême or an Ali Bab in the nineteenth or twentieth century—12 grams of salt, 8½ grams of Hungarian pepper, and so on—which sometimes seem to border on a sort of mathematical abstraction, we are surprised at the scant importance that Taillevent or Pidoulx appear to attach to such instructions.

Ought we to conclude that medieval cuisine was not an art? Later commentators on gastronomy, from the eighteenth century on, have always refused to so honor it. There is no discipline with as great and as naïve a belief in progress—and in decadence—as cuisine. Carême professes sovereign disdain for almost all of those who preceded him. But on the other hand, one also finds, again from the eighteenth century on, recriminations against the "new cuisine" from which great modern cuisine evolved. The Maréchal de Richelieu declared: "It is principally after the death of Louis XV that real gastronomical knowledge and, as a consequence, the science of the cook have gone to pieces." For us, however, it is officially from this moment on that modern cuisine began to take shape. When it was suggested to the Maréchal de Richelieu that he should marry the widow of Monsieur de Brunoy, he replied: "We would quarrel continually over salads with cream and spun-sugar sultanas that stick to the teeth; she is infatuated with this new cuisine that is bitterly stupid and everything to eat at her house has so many frills that one has no idea what one is partaking of. She's a woman who adores hodgepodges, and may the devil take her!"

There are two reasons why speaking of decadence or of progress in cuisine is difficult. The first is that every good quality offered by a new style risks causing the disappearance of certain very positive old qualities that were possible within another style. It is conceivable that the medieval cuisine that breathed its last during the Regency brought out certain natural flavors, in green vegetables in particular, that were sacrificed in the more sophisticated style known as "the cuisine of the Financiers." As for artificial flavors, certain ragouts, the recipes for which appear crude to us, perhaps had a charm, an original personality that certain food-lovers were sorry to see disappear. Moreover, innovators are always inclined to say nothing of the most refined aspects of their predecessors' accomplishments. This is as true in cuisine as in philosophy. Hence the widespread belief that all really subtle dishes are a modern invention. In point of fact, nothing could be further from the truth. One sees from sixteenth-century *dispensaires*[5] that carp tongues and livers of anglerfish braised in Spanish wine were served at the table of Francis I. Our *potage à la Reine*, made of puréed white meat of chicken and filberts, a variety of hazelnut, was served every Thursday at the Valois court and was a particular favorite of Queen Marguerite, whence its name. Such facts are proof that subtlety was not totally lacking in the old-style cuisine.

The second reason why it is difficult to pass judgment on the question is that a written recipe is far removed from the finished product. Between the two there lies the indefinable domain of tricks and knacks and basic tastes that are always implicit, never explained in so many words, because the books are addressed to people who speak the same language. Any recipe read in a house-wife's handbook on sale today in bookstores calls to the reader's mind a register of very precise tastes. When we are told to add this or that rare condiment to *moules marinières*, we see immediately what the result will be because the expression *moules marinières* immediately summons to mind a very particular flavor. When, on the contrary, carp tongues and livers of anglerfish braised in Spanish wine are mentioned, we cannot be sure of the gastronomical reality implied by this expression, for, in the first place, we do not know if this wine was sweet or dry, and we have no idea how long the cooking time was.

Another characteristic, in fact, that distinguishes the old-style cookbooks from the new ones is that in the former the cooking times are no more precisely indicated than the proportions, but this perhaps stemmed from their supposedly being common knowledge.

Attempts have been made in modern times to offer meals cooked according to old recipes. In 1888, Pierre Loti experimented at doing so at his "Rochefort" in Aunis, and in 1926, Prosper Montagné tried his hand at it. But we are not told whether the celebrated amateur chef satisfied his guests, nor are we informed of what reception the novelist's meal received. It is to be feared

---

[5] Manuscript cookbooks containing old recipes. (*Translator's note*)

that this culinary "gothic revival" was far removed from the original recipes, despite following them to the letter.

These archaeological banquets lead us to examine the question of the composition of meals and menus, a subject with which we will deal in conjunction with Renaissance menus and banquets.

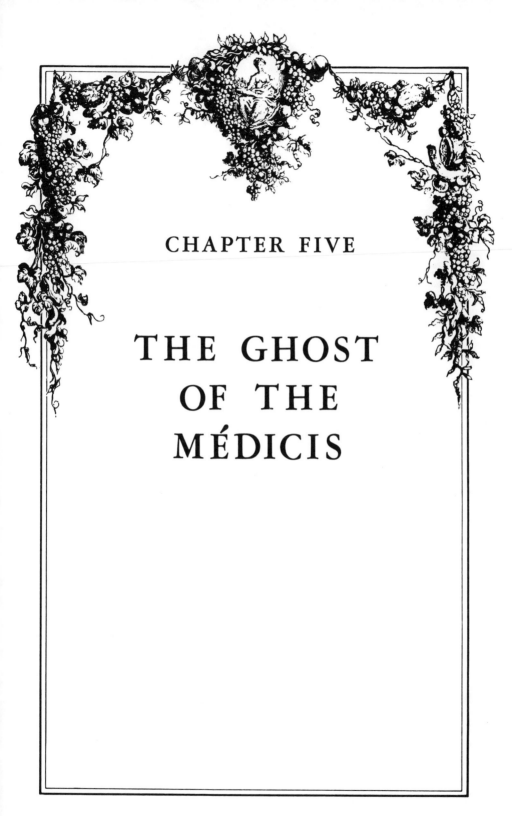

CHAPTER FIVE

THE GHOST
OF THE
MÉDICIS

One can say without posthumous flattery that, in the eyes of official history, sixteenth-century culinary art is almost wholly dominated by the family of the Médicis. From the pontificate of Giovanni de' Medici, who took the name of Pope Leo X, and who imbued civilization on the banks of the Tiber with a spirit of witty and theatrical epicureanism at the beginning of the century, to the marriage of Marie de Médicis to Henry IV of France in 1600, and noting between times the marriage of Catherine de Médicis to the future Henry II of France in 1533, the Médicis family greatly influenced court life in Europe and consequently greatly influenced the art of the table in the West. These facts have led historians of gastronomy, especially those of French gastronomy, to suppose that the sixteenth century saw a gastronomic revolution due to the sudden advent of Italian cuisine in the rest of Europe. Though ordinarily xenophobic, the French in this particular case—one instance does not constitute a tradition—date the beginnings of modern culinary art and the origins of "grand" cuisine from the arrival of Catherine de Médicis in France with her Florentine chefs. I have heard the great contemporary chef Raymond Oliver himself cite this as dogma. What are we to think of this view?

If we consult works of the period devoted to the art of the table, we do in fact note that the most influential work in the sixteenth century, both in Italy and in France, was a book by Platina of Cremona, the pseudonym of Bartolommeo de' Sacchi, a member of an illustrious Italian family that held important offices at the court of Rome. This work, which appeared at the end of the fifteenth century (in 1474 to be precise), was originally written in Latin. Its title in that language is: *De honesta voluptate et valetudine* (*On Decent Enjoyment and Good Health*). The first French translation appeared in 1505 at Lyon under the title *Le Livre de l'honneste volupté*. Numerous re-editions followed one upon the other throughout the sixteenth century, and it can be said that "Platinus" served, alongside Castiglione's famous *Il Cortegiano* (*The Courtier*), as a manual of etiquette and the art of living for humanist Europe.

It is, in fact, to a humanist that we owe this book, a man who acknowledges his debt to Epicurus, who has studied the ancient authors, Varro, Columella, Pliny the Elder, Apicius, and the Greek physicians. His aim, as the title of the book indicates, is at once to permit his reader to enjoy the pleasures of the table without violating certain moral and aesthetic rules (this is the double meaning of "*honesta*") and to advise him on what is good for his health. This latter aspect, moreover, is a constant in amateur manuals of gastronomy down to almost the nineteenth century. Since ancient medicine consisted in large part of rules for diet with a strong admixture of magic, the author of any treatise on cuisine felt obliged to point out the real or supposed properties, both physiological and psychic, of various foods and of various methods of preparing them. All Greek cookbooks laid claim to being books on medicine as well. In the Middle Ages the medical school called the School of Salerno also became a school of nutrition; in the twelfth century Giovanni di Milano, a celebrated physician, composed, under this same name of the School of Salerno, aphorisms in Latin verse addressed to the King of England. They were medicogastronomic precepts, repeating numerous ancient beliefs as to the properties of various meats, wines, and starches. It is worthy of note that as late as the beginning of the nineteenth century in his *Physiologie du goût*, Brillat-Savarin, being still under the sway of a long-standing tradition, does not quite manage to separate the medical aspect (although he was definitely not a physician himself) from the purely hedonistic aspect of culinary art. He gives recipes for various "magisterial restoratives," that is, beverages supposed to have a tonic effect, and he attributes erotic properties to truffles.[1] Before Pasteur's day, it is true, the absence of proper hygiene brought on so many sudden and apparently inexplicable illnesses that it is understandable that people endlessly racked their brains to discover intrinsic properties conducive to good health in different foods.

The other aspect of Platina of Cremona's book has to do with good manners, the art of living and of setting a table, and of behaving at the table. It was with regard to these questions of etiquette and decoration, of proper manners, and of refinement that

----

[1] If Brillat-Savarin's theory is correct, one trembles to think of the debauchery we risk witnessing since the development by agronomists of a cultivable truffle which can henceforth be produced in unlimited quantities (1978).

THE GHOST OF THE MÉDICIS

his book constituted a sovereign authority, and it is to these questions that his treatise is largely devoted. *Le Livre de l'honneste volupté* is a cookbook only to a very limited extent. Exactly as was the case later with Brillat-Savarin's *Physiologie du goût,* which we have just mentioned, those who viewed it as a gastronomical work were wrong to do so. Both were, rather, books owed to cultivated men who were more painters or teachers of the manners and morals of the worldly class of their time than they were technicians peering into the bottom of pots and pans for a new or an old truth. The recipes, properly speaking, that one finds in Platina are few and far between and absolutely medieval. Sometimes they are simple literary diversions borrowed from the writers of antiquity. Hence it is not in the *Livre de l'honneste volupté* that we should seek the principles of the "gastronomic revolution" that supposedly took place in the sixteenth century.

But should we perhaps look for the source of this revolution in historical facts rather than in a book? It is the cooks and the pastry-makers brought to France by Catherine de Médicis who are said to have completely revolutionized the art of gastronomy and to have had as disciples several generations of French chefs who thus supposedly learned the secrets of the new cuisine directly from them, mastering them to such a point that Italians were amazed at the culinary exploits of their French *confrères* and—ironically—even went so far as to deplore the influence of French cuisine on Italian cuisine, as they did, for example, at the court of the grand duke of Tuscany in the seventeenth century.

This historical schema is generally accepted even by the most critical scholars and thus has all the earmarks of the sort of vicious circle whereby something is taken to be proved that is not, after which the evolution of French cuisine from the middle of the sixteenth century on (which is in itself problematical) is linked solely to this imaginary fact.

This classic interpretation is open to very strong objections that might be summed up as follows:

1) French cuisine does not begin to evolve beginning in the middle of the sixteenth century but only from the middle of the seventeenth century, that is to say, a century later, and even then only hesitantly.

2) As we have no concrete proof, no trace in documents of the famous "revolution of 1533,"[2] is not the best way to measure its importance and above all to appreciate what it involved, to go back to its supposed *cause*, since we have no information whatsoever as to its effects—that is, to examine the state of Italian cuisine during the first third of the sixteenth century?

That is what we shall now proceed to do. In this chapter we shall deal with the second point since the first is pertinent to the chapter that follows.

As for the date of the supposed mutation, let us limit ourselves for the moment to pointing out a historical fact whose enormous importance is quite evident, namely, that between Taillevent's *Viandier*, which appeared in 1490, and Pierre La Varenne's *Le Cuisinier français* (*The French Chef*), which appeared in 1651, no cookbook that is really a cookbook, properly speaking, was published in Europe. All the books dealing with the subject of food that were composed during this period are really either books on diet or on good manners and the art of receiving guests, or on all these things at once, and all of them presuppose as their point of departure a certain type of cuisine that is more or less generally accepted. But the surest sign of a gastronomic revolution is the appearance of a great many cookbooks, as we shall see was the case during the second half of the seventeenth century and in the nineteenth century. Even more important, the fact that the first printed edition of Pierre Pidoulx's *Grand Cuisinier de toute cuisine* saw the light of day in 1540 and that this text was *continually reprinted* down to 1620 is ample proof of the persistence of medieval cuisine at the very height of the Renaissance. Let us recall that the first manuscript of the *Grand Cuisinier* dates from 1350 and that the conception of cuisine put forth in it is more or less identical to that of Taillevent. It is striking that without being promoted as "fashionably old-fashioned" this book could be put before the public two centuries later, in the second half of the sixteenth century, as a practical and up-to-date manual!

To return to the principal point of this debate, the best means,

_____

2 The date of the arrival of Catherine de Médicis in France.

_____

"*Title page of* Il Trinciante (The Master Carver), *by Vincenzo Cervio, gentleman carver to Cardinal Farnese.*" *Venice, 1610. Bibliothèque nationale, Paris.*

IL
TRINCIANTE
DI
M. VINCENZO
CERVIO,

Ampliato, e ridotto à perfettione dal Caualier
Reale Fusorito da Narni,

TRINCIANTE DELL'ILLVSTRISS.
& Reuerendiss.Sig.Cardinal Farnese.
CON PRIVILEGIO.

IN VENETIA,   M. DC. X.

Appresso Alessandro de' Vecchi.

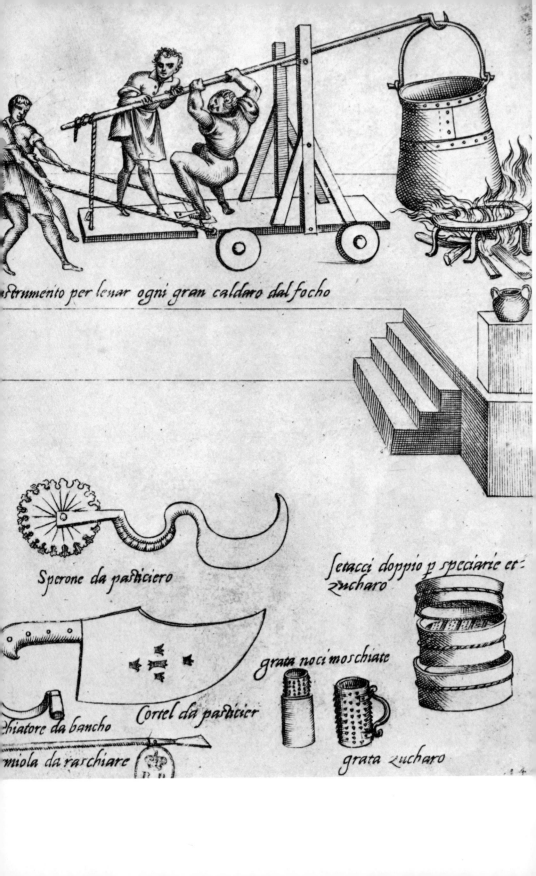

strumento per leuar ogni gran caldaro dal focho

Sperone da pasticiero

setacci doppio p speciarie et zucharo

grata noci moschiate

Cortel da pasticier

chiatore da bancho

grata zucharo

miola da raschiare

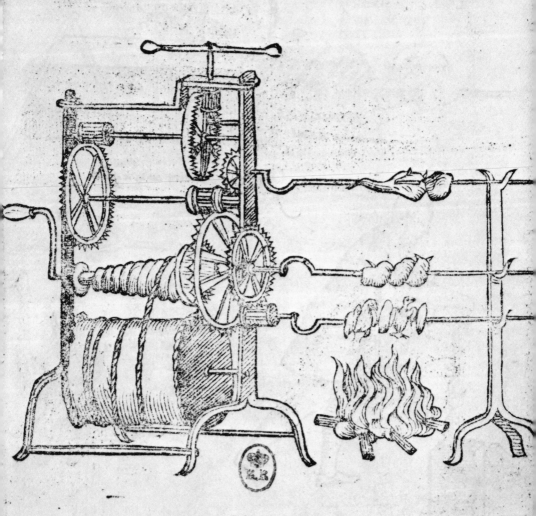

Molinello con tre fpedi, che fi volta da fe, per
forza di ruota, col tempo, a foggia di Orologio,
come nella prefente figura fi moftra.

"Method for lifting a large cooking pot. Various utensils for pastry-
making." "Spit." Two plates from the Opere (Works) of Bartolomeo
Scappi, Venice, 1570. Bibliothèque nationale, Paris.

PRECEDING PAGES:
"The Marriage at Cana," *detail. Painted in 1562–63 by Paolo Veronese (1528–1588). Musée du Louvre, Paris.*

as I was saying, of lighting our lamp of knowledge is thus to consult the history of Italian cuisine.

Let us take as an example the description of the banquet offered the Medici on September 13, 1513, by the city of Rome, a banquet that was among the festivities organized in honor of Giuliano de' Medici, who had just been named a Patrician of Rome. This banquet took place on the square of the Capitol and had as its privileged guests some twenty persons, all seated at the same table. The table itself was placed on a sort of platform, all around which tiers of seats were set up for common folk who wished to witness the feast.

According to the accounts of various chroniclers of the time, the festivities consisted of the following. First of all, each guest found in front of him a napkin of very fine linen in which little live birds were imprisoned. After water had been brought the guests for them to wash their hands, they unfolded their napkins and freed the birds, which began hopping about on the table and pecking. The hors-d'oeuvre had been set out beforehand on a credenza to one side, arranged on saucers which the servants brought to the table forthwith; they consisted of cakes made of pine nuts and marzipan, biscuits with Malmsey wine, sweet cup custards, figs, and muscatel wine. The first service saw the appearance of enormous platters laden with roasted warblers, quail, and turtledoves, meat pies, partridges seasoned Catalán-style, roosters cooked and put back in their skin and feathers, hens similarly put back in their skin and feathers and stood up on their feet, boiled capons in white sauce, *fouaces* of marzipan, quail pasties, and a ram with four horns, poached in water and put back in its skin, standing in a golden basin looking as though it were alive.

The enumeration of the following services, which all strangely resembled the first, would be interminable: pheasants, roe-deer pasties, more pheasants, also in their skin and feathers, boiled veal served with mustard, "sufficient for all the table" (as might be expected), sugared capons covered in fine gold, goat in green sauce, *blanc-manger* in a dish, a garden of jasmine set out on a table with an eagle inside it grasping a rabbit in its talons, casks from which flocks of birds escaped when they were opened, etc. . . . There followed twelve or thirteen other services, all more or less the same, that is, consisting of boiled and roasted meats, meat pies, and a great quantity of decorative dishes and surprise effects. Toward the end of the feast a great vessel giving off fragrant smoke was brought. As dessert there were preserves of all sorts and candied fruits, and at the very end perfumed toothpicks were presented to the guests. Wines from all over were as abundant as the food served. Overwhelmed by this lavish extravaganza and, as one chronicler puts it, "not only full but uncomfortable," the guests began to distribute what was being served to them to the spectators seated all around the square, and soon they too were stuffed full of food and began to throw portions of it at each other. Roe deer, rabbits, suckling pigs, pheasants, and partridges went flying through the air and soon the pavement of the illustrious square of the Capitol was strewn with them from one end to the other.

It is evident that such a banquet was markedly medieval in character and, indeed, shares, if I may say so, all the most disturbing features of that period. We note the accumulation of various sorts of meat, the mixture of sweet and salt,[3] the fondness for surprises, this latter a trait handed down from the nouveaux-riches of the last years of antiquity that became even more exaggerated in the Middle Ages. Moreover, there is no evidence here of any sort of revolutionary recipe at all. The menu and the cuisine, the spirit and the organization of this banquet are no different from that of other medieval festivities north of the Alps, of which we shall now offer several examples from the previous century.

At the "pheasant feast" given in Lille in 1433, there appeared, for instance, a pie containing twenty-eight live persons playing different instruments. Various roasted meats were brought in on blue and gold carts, presented in forty-eight different ways—though, alas, not prepared in as many different ways! At the marriage of Charles the Bold and Margaret of York in 1468, an entire whale was hauled into the banquet hall. It was not meant to be

---

[3] The fact that this feast *begins* with sweets is nonetheless purely Italian; it is the only novelty, and we shall see the reason for this below.

"The presentation of the pheasant." Flemish miniature (1450-80), from the Livre des Nobles Emprises du Roy Alixandre (Book of the Noble Enterprises of King Alexander), by Jean Wauquelin. Musée du Petit Palais, Paris.

orta di Guardia

Bottigliaria

Credenza

Ordine che si tiene in Sedia Vacante à seruire
gl'Emi et Rmi Cardinali al Conclaue, si di
robbe di Cucina, come di Credenza, et
di bottigliaria

Ruota del Conclaue

Mazziero

Rinceditori

...cina

Tauola, doue li Scalchi
presentano le uiuande delli
R.mi, Alli reueditori

Scala di ritorno

PRECEDING PAGES:
"Order observed for the presentation of dishes at the conclave of cardinals." Engraving from the Opere *(Works) of Bartolomeo Scappi, Venice, 1570. Bibliothèque nationale, Paris.*

eaten, of course, but rather was filled with various eye-catchers and circled the table to the sound of bugles and trumpets. Never, however, was the transformation of a meal into a spectacle as complete, perhaps, as in the case of the fêtes held at Bruges and Lille in the time of the dukes of Burgundy. When we read the description of them in the chronicle of Olivier de la Marche or in Barante's classic work on the dukes of Burgundy, we are not even able to guess what foods could have been concealed beneath all the complicated apparatus. Let us therefore go back to simpler meals, though not without first pointing out that this mixture of gastronomy and spectacle was a distinctive medieval trait that was merely perpetuated during the Italian Renaissance.

Here, for example, is the menu of the banquet served by Taillevent himself to King Charles VI: *"For the first service:* capons with cinnamon-flavored gruel, hens with herbs, new cabbages, and then venison. *Second service:* the best roast, peacocks or *seberereau,*[4] capon pasties, young hares with rosé-wine vinegar, and capons with Jehan must. *Third service:* partridge with trimolette,[5] braised pigeons, venison pies, jelly, and *leschées.*[6] *Fourth service:* as desserts, pear pastries, almonds, sugared tarts."

It will be noted that this menu is in many respects somewhat better balanced than the one offered in Rome in 1513. This is also true of a menu prepared in the fourteenth century at Weissenfels in Germany in honor of the bishop of Zeiz. Let us cite a part of it: *"First service:* egg soup with saffron, pepper, and honey; millet soup; mutton with onions; a chicken roasted with prunes. *Second service:* codfish in oil with raisins; plaice fried in oil, boiled eel with pepper; *bucklinge* [lightly salted herring], roasts with mustard. *Third service:* fish boiled and roasted; little birds fried in

---

[4] An edible fowl; modern equivalent unknown.

[5] An unknown condiment, perhaps a regional aromatic herb.

[6] Doubtless slices of bread and jam, according to Montagné.

La seconde partie conte-nant la façon & maniere de faire toutes confitures liquides, tant en suc-cre, miel, qu'en vin cuit.

Enfemble deux façons pour faire le fyrop rofat laxatif. Et pour faire le fuccre candi, penites & tourrons d'Hefpaigne.

Et premierement pour côfire l'efcor-ce, ou la chair du citron auec le fuccre.

CHAP. I.

O V S prendres le citron tout en-tier, & felon la groffeur qu'il fe-ra en feres fix ou fept parts tout du long, que pour le moins chacun car tier ait le large de deux doigts : & quand toutes les pieces feront coppees, vous aures la auprés vne

I 3

"*Method for making preserves.*" *Extract from the* Excellent opuscule à tous nécessaire qui désirent avoir connaissance de plusieurs exquises recettes (Excellent small work necessary for all those desiring to have knowledge of a number of exquisite recipes), *by Michel Nostradamus, Lyon, 1555. Bibliothèque nationale, Paris.*

lard, with radishes; ham with cucumbers." This German menu is really quite refined, balancing as it does fish and meat and refreshing vegetable dishes.

In the menu served in the square of the Capitol, we note the presence of a *blanc-manger*, which is one of Taillevent's most celebrated recipes, though it was perhaps not invented but merely standardized by him. *Blanc-manger* is nothing other than the *potage à la Reine* for which we gave the recipe in the preceding chapter. Here is how Taillevant prepared it: he first cooked a capon in boiling water, then removed the white meat, ground a great quantity of almonds with it, mixed in bouillon, and put the whole through a sieve. Then he reboiled this mixture to thicken it, after which he fried a half dozen peeled almonds, poured the soup in a plate, put the fried almonds in it, garnished it with pomegranate seeds, and added sugar.

One last remark: it must be stressed that the habit of setting out aromatic fumigations in the banquet hall was in answer to a very precise need stemming from the presence of so many cooked animals that had been stuffed back into their skin and feathers, for in view of the time necessary to thus prepare them these animals naturally had a tendency to decompose somewhat. Though they may have been a delight to the eye, they delighted the guests' sense of smell far less, and the latter had to be dulled with the aid of scents that would mask the animal odor. Such excessive use was made of these aromatic burners set about in the room and sometimes under the table that cases are cited in which several guests nearly died of asphyxiation from the fumes.

Documents of Tuscan cuisine dating from a slightly later period nonetheless show an increased tendency toward lightness and the use of raw vegetables. These documents mention hors-d'oeuvre that are no longer composed of pastries but of lettuce, carrots, radishes, and so on . . . Cured meats are also mentioned: sausages, mortadella, hard sausage, cows' udders, and so on . . . We see the basic elements of future Italian cuisine taking hold in this period: meat pies, polenta, gnocchi, macaroni, lasagna, ravioli, tortellini, etc. . . . The sauces are more or less the same as those of the Middle Ages, green sauce, *cameline*, garlic sauce. Sugar, pepper, saffron, rosemary, sage, and onion continue to be used as condiments. There is nothing very new in all of this save for a definite

reaction against the heavy cuisine of banquets and a certain tendency to return to simplicity. Aretino, for instance, praises a radish
salad (the "radish" in question was doubtless the *radicchio rosso di
Treviso*, a salad vegetable that is not a radish but a variety of very
tasty reddish dandelion) in these words: "I believe that the inventor of such a thing could only have been a Florentine." Aretino
thereupon goes on to say that the Florentines are past masters in
the art of arranging a table, of decorating it with roses, of washing
the glasses, of preparing little poultry livers, brains, and blood sausage, and he attributes to them an innovation which in fact was
destined for a great future, even though, properly speaking, it is
not gastronomical: the custom of serving fruits at the *end* of meals
(rather than at the beginning, an idea erroneously attributed to the
Italians).

We could continue indefinitely this review of menus of banquets down to the end of the sixteenth century, both in Italy and
in France and Germany, without finding anything really different
from what we have already seen being served in the fifteenth and
the beginning of the sixteenth century, save for certain differences
stemming from the variety of local natural foods available. Yet
there are two points on which the Italians were the educators of
Europe: the refinement of manners and the invention of pastry
and sweetmeats. This latter aspect is obviously the most important
one as far as the art of preparing food is concerned.

The good manners introduced by Italy consisted first of all in
greater cleanliness, in particular the habit of washing one's hands
before eating (as we have seen), next, in the use of forks, and
finally in a greater elegance, a greater discrimination with respect
to food habits in general. And second, the Italians would appear to
have trained excellent maîtres d'hôtel capable of conceiving a succession of *mets*[7] and thinking through the composition of a meal,
even though this was as yet scarcely apparent from the results.

Here is what Montaigne has to say on the subject: "I have said
this with regard to an Italian with whom I have just had converse,
one who served the late Cardinal Caraffa as maître d'hôtel until his
death. I had him give me an account of his duties; he pronounced a

---

[7] This word, which in modern French means "dish," designated an entire
course or "service" in the Middle Ages; it is the word used, for instance, in the
menu of Taillevent that we have cited.

PRECEDING PAGES:
"Distillation." Detail of an engraving by Jean Stradan (1523–1605). Bibliothèque nationale, Paris.

discourse on this science of stuffing one's face, with gravity and a magisterial seriousness, as though he were speaking to me of some capital theological point: he distinguished for me a number of different appetites; the one that one has when one's stomach is empty, the one that one has after the second and third services, the means of sometimes pleasing it very simply, of sometimes awakening and piquing it; the order of sauces, first in general, and then describing more specifically the qualities of ingredients and their effects; the differences in salads according to the season; the one that ought to be heated, the one that ought to be served cold; the way to decorate and embellish them to make them still more pleasing to the eye. After that he took up the order of service, full of fine and important considerations:

> *Nec minimo sane discrimine refert,*
> *Quo gesto lepores, et quo gallina secetur.*

> *(And with equally careful discrimination,*
> *He describes how to carve hens and hares.)*

And all of this in the most high-flown style, with rich and magnificent words, the very ones that are used to treat of the government of an empire."[8]

The same precepts concerning etiquette continue to be set forth in more or less identical terms down to the end of the seventeenth century. A treatise on good manners attributed to a certain Nolfi and addressed to ladies of the nobility, published during the second half of the seventeenth century, recommends once again, for instance, among other things, washing one's hands in the basin of water presented at the beginning of the meal, though not without first having made a token gesture of refusal, waiting until the head of the house has shown one one's place before sitting down at table, beginning the meal by contenting oneself with what one finds in front of one, using one's spoon to eat everything that is

---

[8] *Essays*, I, 51.

presented in liquid form and one's fork for taking pieces of roast meat from the platter, after which the fork should be placed on one's plate and the meat eaten with one's fingers. This detail reminds us that the use of forks (which Nolfi describes, moreover, as being on the point of being abandoned) was long limited to fishing out bits and pieces of food from a dish. Among other advice, we read that one ought not to blow noisily on hot meats, that one should pass the best morsels to others when they ask to be served, and, finally, that one should not carry away in one's handkerchief or one's muff sweets that are served as dessert. And one last bit of advice: to eat with one's head held high rather than with one's face buried in one's plate.

However primitive these precepts may appear to be, they are proof of how long it took for what we consider today to be everyday manners to take hold.

We also learn that the order in which various foods were served and the places at table were not nearly as rigidly set as in modern times. The courses (referred to as *mets* or *services*) were really rather like successive buffets; all the dishes were put on the table simultaneously, and it is evident that no one was necessarily supposed to partake of *everything* laid out for the guests. In the first place, everyone's consumption was limited by the place at which he found himself at table and by how far away the various dishes were or how many of them his neighbors were willing to pass him, and also by the limits of his appetite. Service "by the head," whereby each guest eats exactly the same thing as the others at table and the list of dishes on the menu for the repast is what is really consumed by all of those present, with each guest being presented individually with each successive dish, does not appear until the eighteenth century. Let us also observe, to conclude this discussion of a subject that lies beyond the bounds of gastronomy, properly speaking, that the refinement of manners and the advice appertaining to it are found in many other countries besides Italy, from the very earliest days. Precepts in verse that circulated in England during the Middle Ages[9] recommended, for instance, that one not bite directly into one's chunk of bread, not speak with one's mouth full, chew slowly and silently, not wipe one's knife

[9] Cited by Dorothy Hartley, *Food in England*, London, 1954.

on the tablecloth, not eat with one's knife, not drink with one's mouth full, not ask for dishes that have already been removed from the table, blow one's nose discreetly, and so on . . . This is advice that could well be given to many people even today, and, what is more, the art of good table manners would appear to have been much more firmly implanted, and at a much earlier date, in England than in the Latin countries.

To return to cuisine, as we have already hinted, it is in the domain of sweets, preserves, fruit pastes, and constructions in sugar that the Italians were radical innovators. In this realm Europe owes them everything. Their experience in this area must have gone back a long way, for in Boccaccio one constantly sees gentlemen and gentlewomen consuming preserves and sweets, the majority of the repasts in the *Decameron* seemingly consisting only of these two things; this indicates that sweets were considered to be elegant foods, whereas sausages or a *galimafrée* would have taken away the poetry of a collation.

In 1541 there appeared at Lyon a book entitled *Bastiment de recettes* (*The Edifice of Recipes*), a translation of an Italian book published a few months before in Venice. The *Bastiment de recettes* was to be reprinted regularly down to the eighteenth century. It introduced into France the art of making jams, preserved fruits, and candied orange peel, an art that previously had been totally unknown. During the second half of the sixteenth century several French works on the art of making sweets appeared. One of the most remarkable of them is owed to the celebrated prophet Nostradamus. It appeared in Lyon in 1555, under the title *Excellent et moult utile opuscule à tous nécessaire qui désirent avoir connaissance de plusieurs exquises recettes* (*Excellent and very useful little book necessary for all those who desire to become acquainted with a number of exquisite recipes*). As is also true of the *Bastiment*, one finds in it, all jumbled together, medical advice, recipes for perfume and cosmetics, and, finally, recipes for sweets. Nostradamus explains in it "the manner and fashion of making preserves of several sorts, in honey as well as in sugar and cooked wine." He shows how to go about "preserving whole little limes and oranges, quinces in quarters with sugar, making *cotignac*,[10]

---

[10] A fruit paste.

pignolat,[11] sugar candy, syrups, pear preserves, Spanish nougat, and marzipan tart." Also given is "a way of making a jelly of *guignes* that is very delicate but expensive and for noblemen." (*Guignes* are a variety of cherry. This fruit is still used today to prepare *guignolet*, a cherry liqueur; it is a specialty of the city of Angers.)

Thus the art of preserves and sweetmeats of all sorts is really the only truly new contribution to gastronomy made during the Renaissance. Outside of this, all the works that follow one upon the other in the second half of the sixteenth century and the first half of the seventeenth belong to the medicoculinary category previously mentioned. Among them we might cite the *Sommaire traité des melons contenant la nature et l'usage d'iceux, avec les commodités et incommodités qui en reviennent* (*Brief treatise on melons, dealing with their nature and use, with the advantages and disadvantages appertaining thereunto*), by Jacques Pons, which appeared in 1583, or *Le Trésor de santé* (*The Treasure of Health*), or *Mesnage de la vie humaine* (*The Husbandry of Human Life*), an anonymous work that appeared in 1607. This latter book gives in passing, however, a few recipes such as one for baked carp stuffed with roe, egg yolks, ground almonds, butter, and good herbs. Its author seems less prodigal with spices than predecessors of his who wrote cookbooks, an interesting sign. But it is a very faint sign, for during the first decade of the seventeenth century, under Henry IV, we still find, in another book, *Le Portrait de la santé* (*The Portrait of Health*) (1606), recipes for bacon pasties and herb pasties in which ground almonds, bacon, stewed leeks, and egg yolks are mixed with sugar and an excessive quantity of cinnamon, in a spirit that is immutably medieval.

In any event, the recipes in question are still put before the reader for dietetic purposes. To correct what I said earlier about this habitual mixture of medical advice and advice for food-lovers in old-style cookbooks, I must add that such a mixture is never the work of professional chefs. Taillevent did not claim that his book was a medical one, and the same is true of La Varenne's later volume, *Le Cuisinier français*.

The sixteenth century has buried us in manuals of etiquette, in dietetic precepts that were necessarily absurd and arbitrary, in an

---

[11] Pine-nut nougat.

avalanche of fruit pastes and an ocean of preserves: it was not the century of any real gastronomic revolution. By giving it the benefit of the doubt, one might credit it with demonstrating, at most, a greater sagacity and a moderation in the use of aromatic spices and condiments than the Middle Ages.

On the other hand, the sixteenth century saw the list of vegetables used in cuisine grow considerably longer. These were vegetables of European origin, first of all, that had seldom been grown in gardens up until then or rarely eaten: artichokes, which Pliny says came from Sicily and which did not begin to be grown in France until around 1560–70, asparagus, already cultivated in the preceding century, but viewed with mistrust in the Middle Ages, and spinach and peas, of which the same was true. And finally and most importantly, we must mention the edible vegetables imported into Europe as a result of the discovery of the New World: corn, tomatoes, hot peppers, beans,[12] all of which were to play a considerable role in the whole of Western cuisine, not to mention the potato, which was discovered at this time but was not yet eaten. During the Renaissance, gardening and tree-growing were the objects of particular care, as can be seen from paintings and engravings of the period, and from this time on, progress was made in growing that most civilized of all fruits: the pear, esteemed to be the "queen of orchards" in the Renaissance. And finally, the Renaissance saw the appearance of brandy, or, rather, of brandy for ordinary consumption.[13] Since early processes of distillation were primitive, brandy still had a bad taste and it became the habit to mask this bad taste with various aromatic products and syrups, thus resulting in the first liqueurs, flavored with rose petals, orange flowers, musk, anise extract, angelica, or rosemary. *Ratafias,* or fruit liqueurs, were also made; the best known of these is maraschino, which originated in Dalmatia. Along with pastry and preserves, these sweet liqueurs were introduced into France in the middle of the sixteenth century.

As we have often had occasion to mention, the gastronomical documents that have come down to us are often deceptive, either

---

[12] Mutton stew with beans (*aux haricots*) gave rise to a constant confusion with mouton *halicoté,* a medieval term meaning "cut into pieces."

[13] It had previously been used as a preservative, and as a restorative for the sick.

"The pastry cook." Anonymous wood engraving, sixteenth century. Bibliothèque nationale, Paris.

because they describe exceptional festivities, or because they are evidence of a cuisine intended for a single social class (even a royal, imperial, or pontifical court), or because they are educational works aimed at creating a vogue, at proposing an ideal rather than describing a current state of affairs. That is why it is only in rare instances that we are able to cite a document reflecting daily habits, the impressions of the man on the street, or ordinary cuisine. By chance, however, we possess such a document for the Paris of the sixteenth century, owed (as was often the case) to an ambassador, the Venetian Girolamo Lippomano, and dating from 1577. We shall cite his account *in extenso*, as it is quite difficult to find:

"The French eat little bread and fruit, but a great deal of meat; the table is loaded with it at their banquets. Moreover, it is usually well roasted and well seasoned. People in France are even fonder of pastries, that is to say, meats cooked in a frying pan, than people elsewhere; in the cities and even in the villages, one finds roast cooks and pastry cooks who purvey all sorts of already-prepared dishes, or at least ones put together in such a way that all they require is to be cooked. There is something that long seemed incredible to me, the fact that a capon, a partridge, a hare already prepared, larded, and roasted, cost less than buying them alive at the market or on the outskirts of Paris. This is due to the fact that roast cooks buy them wholesale at a low price and can thus resell them at a similarly low price; they are content to earn eight or ten deniers, provided that their money circulates and gives them some profit each day. Pork is the usual food of poor people, but of those who are really poor. Every workman, every merchant, however badly off he may be, wants to eat, on meat days, mutton, roe deer, and partridge as the rich do; and on meatless days, salmon, cod, and salted herrings that are brought in from the Lowlands and from the northern islands in very great abundance. The shops of Paris are full of them. Fresh butter and milk products are also eaten. There are also vegetables in abundance, especially white and green peas: these latter are more tender and easier to cook. As for other sorts of vegetables, not much use is made of them; in some places a small quantity of lentils is eaten, but never broad beans.

"Paris provides an abundance of everything that can be desired. Goods flow in from every region: provisions are brought by way of the Seine from Picardy, the Auvergne, Burgundy, Champagne, and Normandy. Hence although the population is enormous it lacks for nothing: everything seems to fall from heaven. Yet the price of food is not at all high, really; for the French spend money for nothing as willingly as they do to buy food and for what they call living well. That is why butchers, meat dealers, roast cooks, retailers, pastry cooks, the owners of public houses, tavern keepers are found there in such great numbers that there is real confusion; there is no street, however unremarkable, that does not have its share of them. Do you wish to buy animals at the market, or

meat? You can do so at any hour, anywhere. Do you wish your
food, either cooked or raw, all prepared beforehand? In less than
an hour roast cooks and pastry cooks arrange a dinner, a supper
for ten, for twenty, for a hundred persons; the roast cook provides
your meat, the pastry cook the pâtés, the meat pies, the entrées,
the desserts; the cook provides your jellies, sauces, and stews. This
art is so advanced in Paris that there are owners of public houses
who give you a meal at their establishment at all sorts of prices,
for a *teston*, for an *écu*, for four, for ten, for even twenty per person if you so desire. But for twenty *écus* you will be given, I hope,
manna in soup, or roast phoenix; in short, everything in the world
that is most precious. Princes of the blood and the king himself
sometimes go there."

(Let us note in passing the expression "pastries, that is to say,
meat cooked in a frying pan," which seems to refer to a little-
known use of the word *pâtisserie*, or perhaps it bears a relationship
to the Italian word *pasticcio*, which means pâté, a mixture, and
also *gratin* [bread crumbs and grated cheese]; or it may refer to a
sort of *fritto misto . . . alla francese*, a French-style assortment of
fried meats.)

To conclude, two lessons can be learned from this text: the first
is that popular cuisine is less poor in quantity and quality, we
repeat, than historians ordinarily lead us to believe; the second is
that there is little difference between good eating at the end of the
sixteenth century and good eating at the end of the fifteenth century. The spectacle of the shop-lined street such as Villon paints
in his *Grand Testament* is not very far removed from the description of one provided about a century later by our Venetian ambassador.

But as you leaf through the books of the time, and when you
enter a kitchen, the smells are, nonetheless, not the same as in the
fifteenth and sixteenth centuries: when you raise the potlids of the
Middle Ages, there rises to your nostrils a harsh meaty steam with
the odor of cloves, saffron, pepper, ginger, and cinnamon mingled
with the acidity of verjuice; as you lean over the cooking vessels
of the Renaissance you breathe in a sweet, fruity cloud that smells
of cooked sugar and pear or currant juice, all silently boiling together. The Middle Ages was the era of seasoned stews, the
Renaissance the age of tasty sweetmeats.

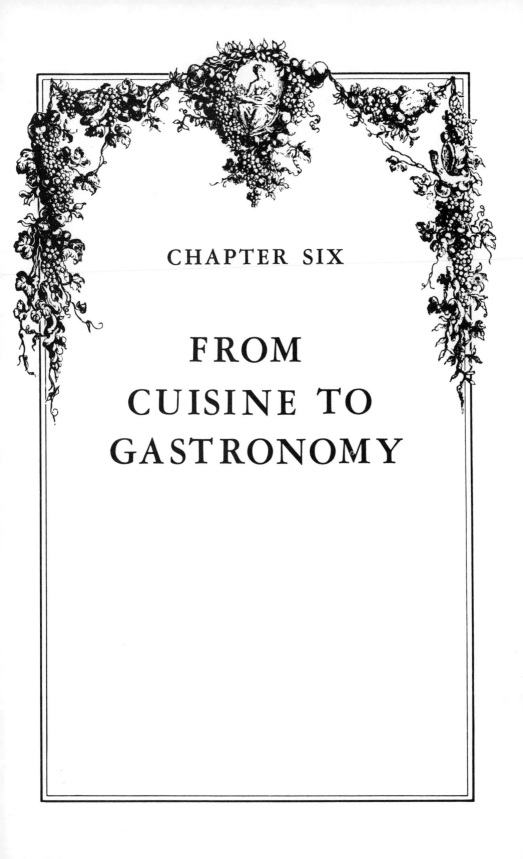

CHAPTER SIX

FROM
CUISINE TO
GASTRONOMY

The word *gastronome*, a learned word taken from the Greek, does not make its appearance until the beginning of the nineteenth century, but the corresponding figure is born in the seventeenth century. Tallemant des Réaux writes of Madame de Sablé: "Since she has become devoutly religious, she is fonder of good food than anyone else in the world; she maintains that there is no one who has such discriminating taste as herself . . . She is always inventing some clever new trick. She has been seen to rail against the book entitled *Le Cuisinier français*, composed by Monsieur d'Uxelles' chef. 'He makes nothing that is worth anything,' she said; 'he ought to be punished for taking people in.'" What he has shown us is the modern gastronomical spirit in action.

The gastronome is neither emprisoned by tradition nor impressed by novelty. With gastronomy cuisine ceases to be collective. Everyone prides himself on exercising his own original opinion and perhaps contributing his own personal creation. I do not know if Monsieur de Béchameil, the king's secretary, a financier and lover of paintings, furniture, and gardens, was really the author of *sauce béchamel;* I do not know if it is really to him that the invention of this celebrated (and currently unfashionable) sauce based on a white *roux* must be attributed, if it was really he who first had the idea of putting flour, butter, parsley, shallots, and milk together in a pan, but it is not without interest that this sauce bears his name.

A word was needed to designate this new attitude, and although the very ugly word *gastronome* came on the scene later, it was during the second half of the seventeenth century that we see the first signs of the phenomenon that in cuisine, as in politics, heralds the modern era, namely, the reign of opinion.

The gastronome is at once curious and suspicious, venturesome and timid; he explores, but he does so faintheartedly. He seeks new sensations and at the same time fears them. He spends half his time recalling past satisfactions and the other half making skeptical conjectures as to possibilities to come. The Maréchal de Richelieu, whom we have already mentioned, declared: "I have never rejected happy innovations; but with the exception of bisques made from a purée of small crabs, timbales with quail eggs and glazes of whole-wheat bread alternating with glazes of fresh butter, I can assure you that nothing satisfying or distinguished has been invented in the seventy-five years that I have been eating and inviting others to eat with me." And when the Duc de Nivernais learned of some novelty that seemed acceptable to him, "he had the patience and the conscientiousness to have it served to him and partake of it for eight days in a row, so as to bring and cause the thing to reach the acme of perfection."

It must not, of course, be thought that all the dishes, all the sauces, all the garnishes labeled "Richelieu," "Conti," "à la Maintenon," or "à la Colbert" were actually created by the very own hands of the great figures whose names they bear. But the fact that they were created for them, perhaps at their instigation, that they were placed under their aegis is proof of the gradual formation of a gastronomical patronage capable of subsidizing the spirit of discovery. There is gastronomy when there is a permanent quarrel of the Ancients and Moderns and when there is a public both competent enough and rich enough to arbitrate this quarrel.

But though the seventeenth century, and more particularly Paris, gave birth to such aspirations, it was far from having satisfied them, fulfilled them, and realized them fully in a new cuisine. We are, in fact, struck by the contradiction that exists, in the treatises on cuisine that we are about to speak of, between the fairly clear expression of a new ideal in the general introductory section of the text and the lack of application of this ideal in the chapters devoted to details of execution and kitchen practice. Thus in the book entitled *Les Délices de la campagne* (*The Delights of Country Life*) (1654), for instance, the author, Nicolas de Bonnefons, exclaims: "Let a healthful soup be a good bourgeois soup, full of good meats that are well chosen, and reduced to a small quantity of bouillon, without forcemeats, mushrooms, spices, or other ingredients, but rather let it be simple, since it bears the name of health; let a cabbage soup smell and taste entirely of cabbage; a leek soup of leeks; a turnip soup of turnips, and so on with others, leaving compositions for bisques, forcemeats, breading, and other disguises, which one should merely taste rather than gorging himself on them. And you will see that your masters will be in better health, will always have a good appetite, and that you and the cooks will receive praise for it. What I say of soups I mean to be taken as a universal rule, as a law for everything that is eaten." In this same general introduction, Nicolas de Bonnefons also complains that the majority of cooks fry all the meats from which they make their soups and stews in bacon fat, which ends up giving all dishes the same aftertaste, a capital defect of bad cuisine. He thus has a thousand pieces of good advice to offer, but unfortunately when the reader comes to his personal recipes he perceives that they do not conform at all the program of authenticity and lightness that Bonnefons preaches to others with so much conviction.

This is likewise the case of the author (as yet unidentified, who goes by the initials L.S.R.) of a book entitled *L'Art de bien traiter* (*The Art of Good Catering*) (1674). When we read his preface, at once edifying and polemical, we note that he condemns the abundance of stews and *galimafrées* (a term that thus takes on the pejorative connotations of the word *rata* in French today), stigmatizes "the extraordinary combination of meats . . . that confused accumulation of various spices, those multiple changes of flying plates and courses served in a bizarre way, wherein it seems that artifice and nature are about to be entirely exhausted, etc. . . ." This mysterious L.S.R., who served in the most illustrious households and organized repasts in the most marvelous châteaux, he tells us, calls for discrimination in the seasoning of food, for an exquisite choice of meats rather than simply great quantities of them, and advises against barbarous combinations. Unfortunately, he too provides recipes that are extremely monotonous: his meats are always simmered in bouillon and are always seasoned with the same spices: a "packet" composed of a scallion, thyme, chervil, parsley, and two cloves, the whole rolled and tied up in a slice of bacon. This is the ancestor of our *bouquet garni*, with bacon added. For L.S.R., the living antithesis of Bonnefons, bacon is "the soul of almost all the best stews." He puts it in everything. He cooks vegetables and fish in water, but proposes a pike, half of which is fried and the other half cooked in sauce, an innovation with merit. The method of preparing fish at the time was to half-cook them in water and finish cooking them in sauce. L.S.R. is also credited with being the creator of pigs' feet à la Sainte-Menehould. But on the whole it is only his general ideas that distinguish him and that depart from the old cuisine.

Nicolas de Bonnefons preaches, as we have seen, a culinary art essentially intended to bring out the *natural* flavor of each food. Even though he does not apply it, he nonetheless thus expresses the basic principle of every real renewal in the realm of gastronomy. There is a gastronomical impasse whenever complication and sheer accumulation end up confusing flavors, masking natural properties. Instead of aiding and complementing nature, cuisine effaces it, although it cannot replace it. The remedy obviously then lies in a return to simplicity and quality. Yet very often this return to simplicity either remains entirely theoretical or is followed by no new gastronomical invention. This is most frequently the case. But it must also be noted, in all fairness, that what has come to be known since 1970 as the New French Cuisine is so difficult to carry into practice, that this balance between naturalness and complexity requires so much skill, professional conscientiousness, and financial probity that it is not surprising that we usually find, on the level of commercial food purveying, only its mediocre apparition, in which imposture rivals rapacity. In the face of this danger, which rears its head not only in false Grand Cuisine but also in its young rival, "New" Cuisine, it is understandable why certain countries, certain provinces, have instead clung tenaciously to the simplicity of their forebears.

This is the case with Italian cuisine and in particular Tuscan cuisine, and, in France, with the cuisine of Provence or the Aveyron. Though the Tuscans are not responsible, as we have demonstrated, for the birth of modern cuisine, they nonetheless have the merit of having made of their province a marvelous conservatory of age-old recipes, based directly on the natural resources of the region. There exists, for example, a recipe—or, rather, I should say, a technique, though by that word I do not mean to imply that it requires the skill of a professional chef—for preparing little birds on a spit: larks, thrushes, warblers, alternating with poultry livers wrapped in bay leaves and little bits of filet of pork pricked with sage, interlarded with crusts of bread and slices of bacon, the whole of which is roasted over a wood fire —a recipe that can be found in fifteenth-century texts and that can still be eaten today,[1] absolutely unchanged, in Tuscany. The es-

---

[1] This "today" is now a yesterday: truly wild game, with its pronounced flavors and aromas, has disappeared from Italy as it has from France.

sential thing, when all is said and done, is to retain a clear notion
of what one wants to accomplish and to remain faithful to a certain style of cuisine without attempting to introduce into it
disparate elements that this style cannot organically incorporate.
"A light cuisine," Prezzolini writes in his *Life of Niccolò Machia-
velli*, "with little fat, savory, full of wit and perfume, made for a
people who have lively minds and do not want to acquire the pot-
belly of those who live a sedentary life; a cuisine that never
dreamed of risotto, that did not invent macaroni, that successfully
kept fat at a distance, that remained faithful to roasting on a spit
and grilling, with the purifying flame of wood and charcoal, that
insisted that fried and roasted meats be accompanied by no sauce."
There are of course many other regional schools in Italy, often superior to the Tuscan school, but this latter remains a very clear-
cut historical example of a "return" to simplicity that did not immediately backtrack in the direction of complication.

As this cuisine was becoming fixed in its habits, that adventurer,
gastronomy, for its part was timidly exploring the unknown paths
of nature and endeavoring to write new roles for it. We have already mentioned *Les Délices de la campagne* (1654) and *L'Art
de bien traiter* (1674). To these there must be added *Le Cuisinier* (*The Chef*) by Pierre de Lune (1656), *Le Nouveau et
Parfait Maître d'hôtel royal* (*The New and Perfect Royal Maître
d'Hôtel*) (1662), by the same author, followed, interestingly
enough, by a *Cuisinier à l'espagnole* (*The Spanish-style Chef*) as
an appendix. In 1662 there appeared an *École parfaite des officiers
de bouche* (*The Perfect School for Maîtres d'Hôtel*), by Jean
Ribou, and in 1691 *Le Cuisinier royal et bourgeois* (*The Royal
and Bourgeois Chef*) by Massialot. But of all the cookbooks which
—a revealing phenomenon—succeeded each other at a rapid pace,
at least compared to the void of the two preceding centuries, and
commented on each other, the most important historically, the one
that had the greatest success and dominated the market up until
the Regency, was *Le Cuisinier français* (*The French Chef*), by a
certain Sieur de La Varenne, the kitchen equerry of the Marquis
d'Uxelles, a nobleman who gave his name to quail à la Duxelles
(Duxelles sauce always had chopped mushrooms with onions,
shallots, butter, and oil as its base). The *Cuisinier français*, published in 1651, was received so enthusiastically that the title, as is

frequent when a book sells well, served as a prototype for others down to the death of Louis XIV: a *French Gardener*, a *French Pastry Chef* (1653), and so on soon saw the light of day.

We have merely cited a few of the books that appeared, the authors of which tried to make a personal contribution to the debate. The revolutionary value of these books is very uneven. *L'École parfaite des officiers de bouche* is a pure and simple fraud (perpetrated by the widow of Pierre de Lune's publisher to sabotage the sales of de Lune's book when the latter decided to publish it himself, thus depriving her of the profits) in which the author limits himself to hashing over medieval recipes copied directly from Taillevent and the *Grand Cuisinier de toute cuisine*, without even taking the trouble to adapt them to the tastes of the day. It was a dreadful book but, thanks to its pretentiousness, it went through fifteen editions,[2] whereas poor Pierre de Lune's book saw only two. Nicolas Bonnefons's *Les Délices de la campagne*, which we have already commented upon, went through ten editions, and La Varenne's *Le Cuisinier français* thirty.

The two authors responsible for the greatest number of innovations, Pierre de Lune and Massialot, did not enjoy great success among the general public, but, on the other hand, they were held in high esteem by the professional chefs of the eighteenth century. They were to exert an influence on the long-term evolution of cuisine, not so much because they were read directly by consumers as because they were reflected upon by their *confrères*, the chefs. As for La Varenne, a moderate revolutionary, his book, though written with less talent, represented what the *Cuisine de Tante Marie* (*Aunt Marie's Cookbook*) or *La Cuisine pour tous* (*Cooking for Everyone*) by Ginette Mathiot were to represent in our time for the French bourgeoisie.

La Varenne, Pierre de Lune, the mysterious L.S.R. were all chefs in noble households. As we have said, La Varenne served the Marquis d'Uxelles, who died at the siege of Gravelines in 1658, and his book was dedicated to his master. Pierre de Lune was kitchen equerry in the household of Duc Hercule de Rohan (who "considered his chef a man capable of giving his table a soul"—an

---

[2] And was translated into English!

expression that is unthinkable outside of what we have called the gastronomical spirit), and then entered the service of the Marquis de Mauregart, the chief magistrate of the Cour des Aides. Pierre de Lune writes that it was in seasoning the meats destined for the table of this latter that he found the secret of satisfying a man with finicky tastes. We thus see here the beginnings of that dialogue between the food-lover and the creator that allows the former to find an interpreter capable of realizing his ambitions and the latter to give free rein to his imagination, knowing that its labors will be understood.

As for L.S.R., the author of *L'Art de bien traiter*, we are not certain what household employed him, for we do not know exactly who he was, but he himself tells us that he is familiar with the châteaux of Fontainebleau, Saint-Cloud, Rueil, Vaux-le-Vicomte, and Liancourt. He is a marvelous teacher of the art of setting out collations in gardens, of organizing *ambigus*, repasts at which meat and dessert were set out at the same time, and he gives most tasteful and discriminating advice on how to set tables, to decorate them with flowers, to make crystal glasses filled with wine sparkle in the light of torches. In this he is the heir of the talents for stage-setting of the maîtres d'hôtel of the Renaissance, though possessed of more refinement and subtlety.

Massialot, for his part, was the guiding light of the tables of the dukes of Chartres, Orléans, Aumont, and the great Louvois himself, to cite only a few of his patrons. His practice was soon imitated at court.

Periods of gastronomical changes are inevitably also periods of gastronomical *polemics*. When there are no polemics, there is no experimentation, since controversy does not arise if there is no tension between tradition and invention, or between on the contrary invention and academicism. The polemic, for instance, of L.S.R. against La Varenne, who was relatively conservative and addressed himself to a cautious bourgeoisie, can be considered to be an avant-garde polemic against a certain static *status quo*, whereas, on the contrary, the attack of Jean Ribou, the author of *L'École parfaite*, against Pierre de Lune represents routine practice up in arms against modernity.

The first of these two polemics is naturally the most interesting

PRECEDING PAGES:
"A seventeenth-century kitchen." Painting by Diego Velázquez (1599–1660). Château de Villandry.

since it is proof of at least a theoretical effort to do away with medieval cuisine once and for all. "I believe," L.S.R. writes, "that in these pages the reader will not see the absurdities and the disgusting lessons that the Sieur de La Varenne dares to put forth and argue in favor of, with which he has for so long deceived and hoodwinked the stupid and ignorant populace by passing off his productions as so many infallible truths and the most widely approved doctrine in the world as regards cuisine . . . Do you not shudder at the description of a teal soup with hippocras, of larks in sweet sauce? Can you look without horror on his soup of leg of beef with lemon slices, cooked in a vulgar stewpot? Does not the one made of fried calf's head make you laugh, or, rather, weep with compassion? Read on, and consider the soups made of stewed shoulder, of pumpkin and herbs without butter, of frogs with saffron, of bran, of hops, of parsnips, of raspberries and, of various other nastinesses of this sort . . . ."

In the midst of these anathemas, the historian must be careful not to take sides. If we view the question from the persepective of the *terminus ad quem*, there is reason to consider the cuisine of the end of the eighteenth century as the ideal toward which the evolution of gastronomy was tending, just as the old-school historians of Italian painting considered works painted between the twelfth and the fifteenth century to be merely a series of approximations leading to Raphael or Titian. Hence, as I have pointed out in the preceding chapter, a goodly number of people doubtless deplored the partial disappearance of the old-style cuisine and expressed themselves in much the same terms as Noël du Fail in a text that antedates the period we are discussing, entitled *Le Sire d'Eutrapel* (*The Master of Eutrapel*): "In the time of the great king Francis [I], the pot was still brought to the table, on which there was laid out nothing more than a huge platter with beef, mutton, veal, and bacon and the great armful of herbs that were cooked and mixed together to make a *brouet*, a true restorative and the elixir of life.

"Light repast prepared in a garden." Engraving by Charles N. Cochin (1688–1754). Bibliothèque nationale, Paris.

From this mixture [*sic*] of food thus laid out, each one took what struck his fancy, and according to his appetite; everything about this arrangement was straightforward." It is evident that the country gentleman who is the author of these lines considers the complicated serving of food in little side dishes which gradually became the fashion to be a barbarous and inconvenient innovation. He for his part would like to see the mountains of roasts that Nicolas Boileau was later to poke fun at in his *Le Repas ridicule* (*The Ridiculous Repast*).

From *our* point of view, it is quite difficult to see any very great difference between the recipes of the various authors of the seventeenth century that we have just mentioned. Massialot and L.S.R. were considered, as we have said, to be more discriminating than the prolific La Varenne, who is not only the author of *Le Cuisinier français* but also certainly the anonymous author of *Le Pâtissier français* (*The French Pastry Chef*). But if we leaf through the recipes of these various kitchen equerries, we note, for example, that they all used perfumes to excess, in cuisine as in pastry: rose water, musk, and, above all, ambergris, which was held to be an aphrodisiac. Moreover, by virtue of a curious reversal due to historical perspective, certain recipes that struck those who were in the vanguard of cuisine at the time as being dreadfully unsophisticated appear to us today to be the most interesting when viewed in the context of our own gastronomical academicism. I shall cite in this regard the raspberry soup owed to Pierre de Lune, and his melon soup with pullets. The first of these is really a dessert, for a *potage*, which today has only the meaning of *soup*, meant in that period anything cooked in a "pot." Certain stews, as well as certain syrupy sweets, were also desserts. But the second *potage*, the one made with melon and pullets, is not unlike certain present-day experiments aimed at using meat and fruit in the same dish. Pierre de Lune's *potage* consisted of a chicken bouillon, seasoned with *fines herbes* and salt, to which was added a purée of cooked melon that had been put through a sieve with the juice of a filet of veal. The whole was then garnished with slices of fried melon and served with mutton juice and lemon juice. We also owe

"Dinner for Louis XIV at the Hôtel de Ville de Paris, January 30, 1687." Fêtes pour le rétablissement de la santé du Roi (Festivities in Honor of the Recovery of the King's Health). *Anonymous engraving. Bibliothèque nationale, Paris.*

LE DINE DV ROY A L'HOTEL DE VILLE DE PARIS

CALENDRIER POUR L'ANNEE BISSEXTILE MDCLXXVIII.

Par vn excez de friandise
Icy lon donne du ragoust;

Chascun y trauaille à son tour,
Châcun met la main à la va

Pour de l'argent on donne à tous   Cette boutique à des delices,
Des maccarrons, des darioles,   Qui charment en mille façons

PRECEDING PAGES:
"Pastry cook's shop, seventeenth century." Engraving by Abraham Bosse (*1602–1676*). Bibliothèque nationale, Paris.

to Pierre de Lune the first recipe for *boeuf à la mode,* and to *L'École parfaite* the first recipe for fattened pullet *à la provençale,* with capers, anchovies, and pitted olives, but without tomatoes, while Massialot gives us a very modern-sounding recipe, for truffled pullet with olives, lemon, and foie gras. Should duck with oysters (yet another creation of Massialot's) be considered a hold-over from the Middle Ages or as a forebear of a modern dish? There is no satisfactory answer. We feel the same perplexity in the face of Pierre de Lune's *pâté à la portugaise,* into which went the white meat of turkey with beef marrow, lemon rind, dates, pistachio nuts, prunes, Corinth raisins, bacon, sugar, orange flower extract, and pomegranate seeds. Is this the cuisine of the thirteenth century or that of the twenty-first century? La Varenne's fricassee of artichokes with white wine would honor any weekend meal cooked today by a good amateur gourmet cook, while the violet marmalade for which Massialot gives the recipe in his *Instruction pour les confitures (Handbook of Preserves)* (1692) would today be considered at the very least an interesting curiosity, if not something more.

As we might surmise, the realm of pastry in this revolution-minded period was no less turbulent than that of cuisine. In the seventeenth century the *tourte* still reigned supreme, and it was to do so for more than a century afterward.

A *tourte* was an all-purpose pastry that lent itself both to salty entrées and to sweet desserts, or, as was very popular in this era, a mixture of the two. It was a hollow pastry shell with a top crust made of pastry dough as well, of approximately the consistency of today's pizza, filled with forcemeats or sweets—or with fish, cheese, or green vegetables—and then baked either beneath coals or in an oven. The *tourte* is the ancestor of our *vol-au-vent* and *pâtés en croûte.* One of the most frequent *tourte* fillings consisted of *godiveaux,* a sort of forcemeat ball, and *béatilles,* which are giblets, rooster crests, poultry kidneys, lamb sweetbreads, etc. . . .

(*Béatilles* are still served in Tuscan cuisine; cooked in a frying pan with sage and served separately, they are known as *rigaglie alla salvia*.) At the beginning of the nineteenth century, the "divine" Carême in his treatise on *Entrées chaudes de pâtisseries* (*Hot Pastry Entrées*) was to write that the *tourte* "is not luxurious enough to have a place on our opulent tables, for the reason that its appearance is too vulgar; even the bourgeois class disdains it and no longer eats anything but hot *pâtés en croûte* and *vol-au-vent*, whereas great merchants of the past feasted *en famille* on the modest *tourte d'entrée*."

And, indeed, when we read the menu of the great banquet that Louvois gave for Monseigneur, Monsieur, Madame, and a whole retinue from the royal court at his château in Meudon on August 25, 1690—a repast prepared by Massialot at which only the king was missing—we note that pigeon *tourtes*, *tourtes* of crisp pastry filled with apricot marmalade, and other pastries with meat or sweet fillings were served. In this period, a cook who prepared any food, whether sweet or salt, meat or milk product, in a baked crust was known as a *pâtissier* or pastry cook. Even today, one can still find at the *pâtissier's* not only pies and cakes for dessert but also *vol-au-vent* with mushrooms or anchovy turnovers. The cakes of this period were known as *casse-museaux* (jawbreakers), so named because they were so hard, *darioles, talemouses*, and so on . . . Sweetmeat cooks, known as *confituriers*, were responsible for the preparation not only of jams and jellies but also of cordials and liqueurs. One of the most fashionable liqueurs was *rossoli*, of Piedmontese origin, with a base of rose petals, orange flowers, and jasmine, plus cinnamon and cloves, one of the variations of which was *populo*, to which anise, musk, and amber were added. In this period old-fashioned hippocras, an aromatized, sugared wine, was also widely drunk.

But the great revolution at the end of the seventeenth century, so far as desserts were concerned, was, first of all, the increasingly widespread consumption of ices and sherbets, which had originated in Spain and Sicily, and, second, the accompaniment of dessert with tea from China, coffee from Arabia, and chocolate from America. There would be no point in recalling the countless debates regarding the properties of coffee and chocolate, ranging from the question as to whether chocolate (which at the time was prepared with water) was to be considered as breaking the rules for fasting imposed by the Church, and whether coffee was good or bad for the health, whether its comsumption would be a lasting habit or a passing fancy ("Racine will pass [out of fashion], as will coffee," Madame de Sévigné wrote) to the question of the virtues of the three new beverages as a cure for venereal disease. A slim volume published in Paris in 1687, entitled *Le Bon Usage du thé, du café, et du chocolat* (*The Proper Use of Tea, Coffee, and Chocolate*), recommends these new products "to all those who have the misfortune of finding themselves afflicted with the most universal of maladies occasioned by love." These celebrated alkaloids were, alas, no enemies of syphilis.

Ices, coffee, tea, and chocolate were not the only new foodstuffs or the only new dishes invented in this period. It was in the seventeenth century that turkey began to be more widely consumed, after having been imported from America in the preceding century. Green peas, too, began to figure more importantly on menus and, indeed, were the object of a veritable craze which we learn of, once again, from one of Madame de Sévigné's famous letters to her daughter: "The chapter on peas is still going on, the impatience to eat them, the pleasure of having eaten them, and the joy of eating them again are the three points that our princes have dwelt upon these last four days," she writes. Asparagus, as well, came to be a more and more common dish: Pierre du Lune provides a recipe for an asparagus omelette, which is cooked according to principles that are the precise opposite of those leading to today's creamy, runny omelette, since it is cooked in a *tourte* pan over a slow fire until it is completely solidified. And finally, cauliflower, which had originated in the Middle East and had been known in Italy since the sixteenth century, became more and more highly esteemed, as did broccoli, another member of the cabbage family. To conclude these remarks on vegetables in the seventeenth century, let us note the timid appearance of eggplant, from the Indies, which in this period was given only a lukewarm reception.

But another great revolution, this time affecting the realm of wine, took place during the last years of the seventeenth century. It was due to a man of the cloth whose name can still be found today on certain bottles and has taken on the dimensions of a commercial myth and a basic value judgment: Dom Pérignon. *Sparkling* champagne[3] dates, in fact, from 1668. In that year, the cellar-master of the abbey of Hautvillers, Dom Pérignon, noticed that the wine of Champagne sometimes was subject to a secondary fermentation that made it bubbly, a phenomenon that was considered to be a disease. Dom Pérignon decided, on the contrary, to encourage this fermentation. He adopted the use of corks to close the bottles[4] and also developed a rudimentary process for champagnizing the wine of the region. In point of fact, the process consisting of tossing a piece of sugar into a bottle of wine or cider had been known in Normandy since the thirteenth century. Dom Pérignon's contribution was to transform this curiosity into a definite technique, and to mix various growths of champagne, as is still done today.

On the whole, the cuisine of the seventeenth century, daughter of the Middle Ages, unquestionably smells a little too much of bacon, cinnamon, and verjuice, but the change of mental attitude toward cuisine was already a foretaste of what was about to take place in the cooking pot.

---

[3] Still champagne, the wine of the region in its natural state, dates from much earlier.

[4] Instead of closing the bottles with the aid of a layer of oil on the top, as is still done in Italy today.

CHAPTER SEVEN

THE OLD
AND
THE NEW

We now enter a period in the history of gastronomy in which an amateur's knowledge of cuisine is no longer sufficient, not only to follow but, I venture to say, even to understand the new culinary techniques. When we read various cookbooks in the course of this history, the same thing happens, more or less, as when we read a history of science or mathematics: the lay reader follows the historian's account without difficulty up to the critical period in which the science in question becomes a real science. To read a recipe in Apicius or Pierre de Lune is to experience the delightful, relaxed pleasure that comes from browsing in the anecdotal sector of prescientific cuisine; to read a recipe in Carême, de Gouffé, or de Nignon is to be constrained to pay close attention *merely to reading it* (not to mention actually making the dish!) and, even so, one's effort is not always rewarded with perfect understanding. For just as it is almost impossible for the man in the street to understand the detailed account of a surgical operation, just as a person who has merely a literary knowledge of clinical medicine cannot hope to comprehend the results of the biological analyses of modern laboratories, so a truly refined recipe, from about 1800 onward, is really accessible only to professional chefs. The eighteenth century leads to a sharp break in the language of cuisine, and there is as much difference between Pierre de Lune and Carême as between the scientific observations of Rabelais and Newton's physics, between Paracelsus' alchemy and Lavoisier's laws of chemistry, between the music of the madrigalists and an opera by Mozart.

The eighteenth century saw the application of ideas formulated in the seventeenth century but never actually put into practice. It tended to return to ideals of simplicity and at the same time found elegant and ingenious solutions to difficult problems. Lying halfway between the old-style cuisine of superimposition and mixture, and the new cuisine of permeation and essences, the gastronomy of the eighteenth century was still within the reach of the zealous amateur, even though its guiding lights were professionals with a reflective cast of mind. This was the era when King Louis XV himself fixed omelettes, eggs *en chemise à la fanatique*, lark pâtés, and chicken with basil. The Duchesse de Berry, the daughter of the Regent, invented or was responsible for her chef's inventing filet of young rabbit *à la Berry* and Madame de Pompadour filets of poultry *à la Bellevue* (from the name of her château). Several dishes that are still called *à la Bellevue* or *en Bellevue* today originated with Madame de Pompadour, who also created a recipe for timbales, doubtless to rival *timbales Agnès Sorel* (which Agnès Sorel, the fifteenth-century favorite of Charles VII, probably never tasted, since they contain *purée Soubise,* which was invented in the eighteenth century).

In this century the French nobility attached its names to sauces or combinations of food, just as in the following century it would lend them to horse races, thereby giving the thoroughbred more importance than a sauce. It was the eighteenth century that saw the birth of *Soubise,* a purée of onions prepared with rice, and of *mirepoix,* a mixture that became a classic, consisting of diced carrots, onions, celery, and so on (a fatless variation of which, called *brunoise,* was to have the honor of going into the making of crayfish *à la bordelaise*).

This century also saw the appearance on the Western European scene of *baba au rhum* (imported from Poland by Stanislas Leczinski) and of the first of the great basic sauces—the first radically new sauce since Taillevent's *dodines* and the green sauces of the Italian Renaissance—mayonnaise, an invention attributed to the Duc de Richelieu. Having captured Port-Mahon on June 28, 1756, he supposedly gave to a sauce made with his own hand the name *mahonnaise.* Others claim that the original name of the sauce was *bayonnaise.* Carême, on the other hand, gives it as *magnionnaise,* which, according to him, comes from the verb *manier,* to work one ingredient into another; this is the name it goes by in chefs' kitchens, he maintains.

A century later, no sauce, no dish could legitimately bear the name of a mere amateur cook if it was to meet the standards of nineteenth-century *haute cuisine;* new dishes invariably bore the names of professional chefs such as Véron, Foyot, and so on . . . The mere reading of the formulas for a *sauce Richelieu,* a *sauce Soubise,* a *sauce Mornay,* or of a *sauce Villeroi* is enough to prove that though the original idea behind them might possibly have crossed the mind of an amateur, the perfecting of them lay beyond the simple good will of the individual gourmet cook, even a highly cultivated one.

In *La Physiologie du goût*, Brillat-Savarin writes that no one can know what the life of a true gourmet is like unless he lived through the last years of the Ancien Régime. I believe that this statement is something more than the classic nostalgia for the days of one's youth, for Brillat-Savarin, who was born in 1755 and died in 1826, lived in perhaps the most interesting period in the entire history of gastronomy and was on hand to appreciate all the developments, the rare flowers that first bloomed at the beginning of the nineteenth century. It is indeed true that the period corresponding to his youth offered a unique synthesis between amateur and professional cuisine, traditional and new-style cuisine, country cuisine and laboratory cuisine, peasant cuisine and bourgeois cuisine, provincial cuisine and international cuisine. It was financiers, the nouveaux-riches of the eighteenth century, whom the Duc de Richelieu, as we have seen, blames for what he calls the absurdities of modern cuisine, as it was they who subsidized the most costly experiments and entertained the sort of guests capable of appreciating the importance of them. Brillat-Savarian calls them "the heroes of good eating," and, he adds, "it was a real battle." What battle does he mean? It suffices to read these protests by certain aristocrats and certain bourgeois against the new-style chefs to appreciate that food is undoubtedly the domain in which man clings the most stubbornly to his habits. The case is cited of a soldier from Franche-Comté whose regiment found itself in Paris and who died after two weeks because he could not come by the cabbage soup and smoked bacon that he was accustomed to eating daily back in the region where he was born. But we should also quote Voltaire, who wrote to the Comte d'Autray: "I confess that my stomach cannot get used to the new cuisine," following which he cites various recipes belonging to the old-style cuisine, among them a forcemeat of turkey, hare, and rabbit with an excess of pepper and nutmeg.

In his *Confessions*, Rousseau deplores the over-elaborate cuisine of his patrons. What would I not have given, he exclaims, for a simple chervil omelette! He was perfectly right to wish for one, for Grand Cuisine was to "improve" the omelette considerably. And Diderot, for his part, writes long letters to Sophie Volland describing the meals he has eaten in the country house of the very rich Baron d'Holbach. After lunch, he writes, one takes a stroll

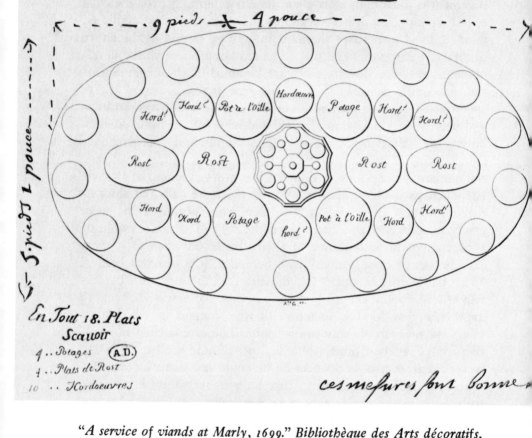

"A service of viands at Marly, 1699." Bibliothèque des Arts décoratifs, Paris.

"Menu of a supper for Louis XV and Madame de Pompadour at the Château de Choisy, November 4, 1757 (Friday fast-day menu)." ("Oille": a pot-au-feu, with or without meat, thicker than a soup.) Bibliothèque des Arts décoratifs, Paris.

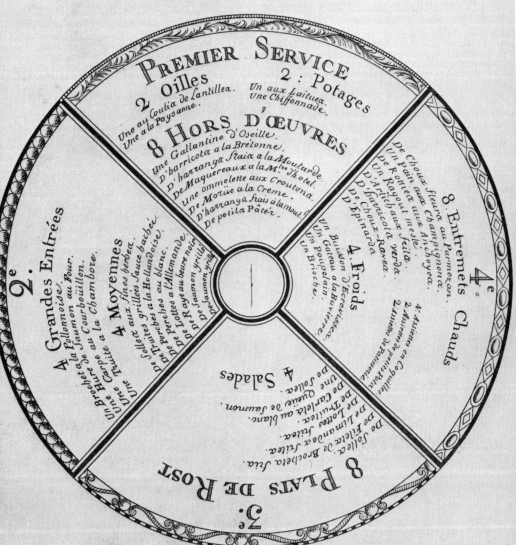

and digests, "if one is able to." The financiers and men of letters were allied in the gastronomic revolution by common interests that were to bring them together again as partners in political revolution. Under the reign of Louis XIV, Brillat-Savarin tells us, "men of letters were drunkards; they followed the fashion, and the Memoirs of the time are most edifying in this regard. Nowadays they are gourmands, which is an improvement."

In the year 1780 a group of friends decided to play a trick on a certain Chevalier de Langeac, a professional gourmet. They decided to invite him to supper in order to hold him up to ridicule in the following way: an agreeable, tasty, very copious meal, but one with no particular refinement, would first be served. The chevalier would be certain to do it full justice. The other guests, all of whom were in on the plot, would give various excuses—a cold, a headache—for having merely nibbled at this good, hearty meal. The moment everything had been eaten and the table cleared, a second supper would be brought in, a much more sophisticated one and even more copious than the first, which the company, suddenly cured, would do full honors to with a vengeance, while the poor chevalier, stuffed to the gullet by all the food previously served would be incapable of eating a single bite.

Why retell this story? Because it is interesting to compare the two menus, since the first one, according to its planners themselves, is excellent but not at all adventuresome, whereas the second expresses the most secret aspirations of the gourmet of 1780. We see here a living antithesis between the ancient and the modern, set side by side by representatives of the very generation in the best position to pass judgment on the difference between them.

Here is the first menu:

First service: an enormous sirloin of beef in its own juice; a well-garnished chicken fricassee, a slice of veal, a very fine stuffed carp. *Second service:* a turkey, a pike served rare, the whole flanked by six side dishes of vegetables and (an exotic though simple little note) macaroni with Parmesan cheese. Numerous salads and cheeses, followed by a glass of Malaga, for the chevalier never ate sweets.

After making fun of those who were not hungry as he ate and drank, the Chevalier de Langeac noted to his great surprise that instead of clearing the table the servants put the tablecloth back on

again and served the second menu, which consisted of the following: *First service:* veal sweetbreads in crayfish broth, roe with
truffles, larded and stuffed pike, *bartavelle* wings with mushroom
purée (*bartavelle* is a variety of red partridge that is also known as
"Greek partridge"). Nothing is said about the second service, but
the third consisted of the following: several dozen snipe, "white
with fat, lying on *rôties officielles*," that is, slices of toasted bread
spread with stuffing and melted cheese; a pheasant, a fresh tuna,
and "the most elegant side dishes possible in the form of *petits
four*."

Several things call for comment here, the fact first and foremost
that the second menu is distinguished by *scents*, by purées whose
aroma comes not from extrinsic condiments but from natural
foods—crayfish broth, truffles, purée of mushrooms—that are ab-
sorbed into the dish and permeate it. And then we should note the
appearance of the *rôties*, followed by that of the side dishes in the
form of *petits fours*, not the little sweet cakes that are the only
thing referred to by this name today but dishes with baked crusts,
which are the product of the pastry chef's art (the pastry chef
being the one who makes pâtés). These, then, replaced the good
old side dishes of boiled vegetables and salads with many ingredients. In this new cuisine, aroma plays an important role in linking
everything in the meal together, and Brillat-Savarin, who recounts
this story, says that the scent of the entrées of the second menu
"rose to the heavens." The gastronomic revolution of the time, or,
rather, its most revealing sign, was the conquest of the air.

We also note, on the other hand, that this menu, like the "ancient" one, alternated fish and meat or even allowed them to be
served together, a possibility that gastronomical rules later eliminated in favor of the simple sequence of fish and meat.

The feeling of something new at hand was so constantly present
in the eighteenth century, in this domain as in others, that people
of the period could not help but be amazed by the continuous
renewal of their cuisine. Just as there was talk in the realm of ethics and science and philosophy of the progress of enlightenment,
so people constantly congratulated themselves on belonging to the
century of modern cuisine. *Le Cuisinier moderne* (*The Modern
Chef*) is indeed the eloquent title of one of the most important
cookbooks of the time. The preface is an astonishing reflection of

the spirit of the age, with its mixture of confidence in the eternal norms of human reason and the certainty that to follow the changes brought about by the course of history is to further the Good: "Arts have universal rules," the author of the *Cuisinier moderne*, Vincent La Chapelle, writes. "Nonetheless, these rules do not suffice, and perfection demands that one work untiringly to improve on a constant practice, which is subject, however, like every other thing, to the vicissitudes of the times." And La Chapelle adds: "The table of a great noble set out at present in the same manner as twenty years ago would not satisfy the guests." A mere twenty years! No culinary revolution has doubtless ever been swifter. In 1786 Sébastien Mercier writes in his *Tableau de Paris* (*Portrait of Paris*): "In the last century considerable quantities of meat were served, and served in pyramids. Little dishes, which cost ten times more than a big one, were not yet known. The habit of eating in a refined way is only a half century old . . . Who could count all the dishes of the new cuisine? It is an absolutely new language."

In truth, the terminology of meals had not changed all that much. Most of the time, the terms "first service" and "second service" (not first course or second course) were still employed, an indication that for each service (which itself contained a variety of dishes), everything was still placed on the table at the same time, according to the old custom. There was still talk of entrées, of dishes served after the soup, and of main dishes, although we still are unable to determine exactly what the difference was between them. La Chapelle writes of a certain sirloin of beef that if it is presented on an oval platter it will serve as the course after soup and if it is served on a round plate it will be the entrée . . . This more or less resembles the case today when an hors-d'oeuvre can also serve as the main dish. Side dishes were of all sorts, sweet or salt, meat or fish, vegetables or little pâtés, *vol-au-vent* or timbales. Hors-d'oeuvre, like side dishes, were served at any time during the meal, preferably at the end, and doubtless served to occupy the guests between more substantial dishes.

All these designations continued to be used for a very long time in the terminology of menus. Even today one finds the word *entrées* on what are called "complete bills of fare." These are not at all dishes intended to *begin* the meal, as logic might suggest, but

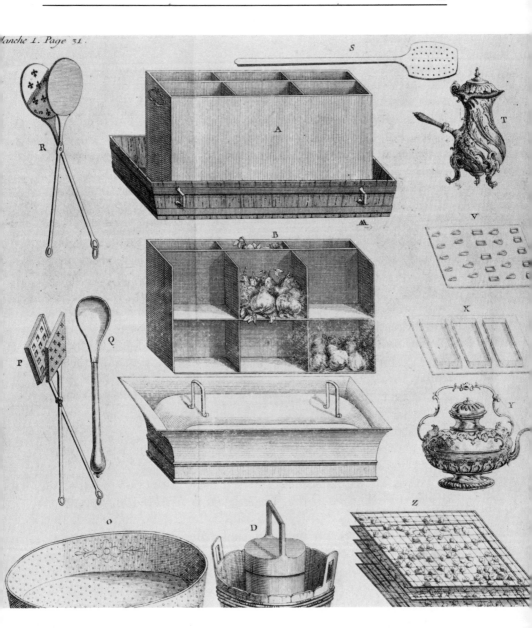

"Cooler for storing fruit (center)." Plate *from* Le Cannaméliste français (The French Confectioner), *by le Sieur Gilliers, Nancy, 1751.* Bibliothèque nationale, Paris.

are, rather, a survival of the old entrées brought in at each "service."

Changes in cuisine came about, as we have said, both because of the birth of gastronomical snobbism and because of the experiments undertaken by professional practitioners of the art of cuisine. In his *La Vie privée d'autrefois* (*The Private Life of Yesteryear*), Franklin writes: "For the Regent's little suppers, food was prepared in places that were purposely all on one floor, and all the utensils in them were made of silver; the *roués* often put their hand in along with the cooks." The *roués*, as is well known, were the epicureans in the Regent's entourage. The world of finance was no more able to get along without chefs than the aristocracy. Doubtless Madame de Lauzun shone at making scrambled eggs, doubtless Hénault, the chief magistrate of the Paris Parlement, knew how to make broth of game better than anyone else, doubtless the Comte de Laplace was the first to conceive of serving strawberries in orange juice, but the professional chef, nonetheless, was becoming more and more indispensable. "Sixty years ago," Duclos writes in 1765, "there were chefs only in first-class households. More than half the magistrates employed only female cooks."

But everything was changed now; everyone was eager to have his own chef, a chef who could think. Naturally such a chef, Sébastien Mercier tells us in his *Tableau de Paris*, "is made much of, humored, pacified when he is angry; and all the other servants of the household are ordinarily sacrificed to him."

This is the first time that we see a clear distinction being made between the cuisine of the female cook, transmitted by a tradition of manual skills and instruction within the family, and the cuisine of the chef, based on invention and reflection. This antifeminist distinction should not, of course, prevent us from noting that often chefs are women and vice versa. In any event, there are regrettably more false great chefs than true good women cooks.

What is a chef? For this new class of financiers or aristocrats who resided in cities and were given over entirely to life in worldly circles, a chef is a man capable of inventing what has not yet been eaten in the houses of others.

This inventive gift, a daily requirement, supposedly gave birth to a rather mysterious dish called "epigram of lamb." The episode

"Table layout for desserts." Engraving from Le Confiturier royal (The Royal Confectioner), *1791. Bibliothèque des Arts décoratifs, Paris.*

that purportedly gave rise to this dish happened around the middle of the eighteenth century (the recipe,[1] in any case, appears in texts a bit later). Hearing one of her guests at table one day say that those present had enjoyed excellent epigrams at the Comte de Vaudreuil's the evening before, a woman of the world believed, in all good faith, that what was meant was a new dish. Once her dinner party was over, she called in her chef, a certain Michelet, and said to him, according to the oral tradition that reached print much later: "You must prepare me a dish of epigrams for tomorrow."

---

[1] As it was made at the time (and ought to be made more frequently today), it consisted of two pieces of lamb, a slice of breast and a cutlet, breaded *à l'anglaise* and either grilled or sautéed and served without a sauce. The mixture for breading *à l'anglaise* is prepared from bread crumbs and egg yolks. If Parmesan cheese is added it becomes breading *à la milanese.*

The chef spent the night mulling over the problem, questioned his colleagues at dawn, consulted old formularies,[2] but found nothing. Obliged to have the "epigrams" ready for dinner (that is to say, by noon, since in the eighteenth century one "dined" at noon or eleven in the morning and "supped" at six or seven in the evening), he invented a new dish, which, incidentally, is very different from the one that goes by that name today and is much more subtle. The agreeably surprised guests asked what this unknown masterpiece was, and the maître d'hôtel dryly replied: "Epigrams of lamb *à la Michelet.*" The guests, who were the same ones who had been present at the lady's dinner the night before, burst out laughing and the young woman, thinking that it was Vaudreuil they were laughing at, flushed with pleasure.

La Chapelle's *Le Cuisinier moderne,* which I have mentioned, appeared in 1733. Carême, who had nothing but scorn for old-style cuisine (even that of the Age of Enlightenment!) nonetheless writes of La Chapelle's book: "*Le Cuisinier moderne* is the only book among the dispensaries antedating the Empire that is worthy of attention." La Chapelle was the inventor of *sauce espagnole,* which, along with mayonnaise, is one of the great basic sauces of cuisine. In all truth, preparing this sauce presupposes the mastery of the basic stocks of "Grand Cuisine," to which we shall return later. In a word, these stocks include all the *roux, mirepoix,* veal stocks, and *blond de veau,* which was invented in the eighteenth century (it is used for what are called "little mixed brown sauces"). More precisely, sauces are made by combining *roux* and stock. Hence *sauce espagnole* (which, despite its name, is totally absent from Spanish cuisine) has *as its point of departure* three preparations *that have been cooked beforehand:* a *roux* for thickening, a brown stock made from beef, veal, vegetables, pork rinds, and so on, and *mirepoix,* which we have described. To this is added lean bacon, onions, carrots, thyme, and bay leaf. This brown preparation, which requires six hours to be skimmed, deacidified, passed through a sieve and reduced to a *gelée,* serves in turn as the base for a great many common sauces, such as *bigarade,*

---

[2] Manuscript formularies or *dispensaires* containing old recipes customarily circulated in kitchens. That is why the *Grand Cuisinier,* for instance, which did not reach print until 1540, had nonetheless served as a manual for the two preceding centuries.

bordelaise, bourguignonne, chasseur, etc. . . . When it has reached its point of absolute perfection, *sauce espagnole* is called *demi-glace,* a sauce obtained by adding to it clear brown stock and Madeira. As for meat glazes, they are stocks simmered down to a consistency that is almost that of honey or resin.

Later, the refined and civilized Nignon, the owner of the Restaurant Larue in the days when Proust was a customer, boasted of having rid cuisine of "abominable *sauce espagnole.*" And, indeed, this method based on stocks, *roux,* glazes and demi-glazes, created with the best intentions in the world (namely, to make it possible to separate essences in order to reincorporate them into various dishes), this cuisine of the very first order—a cuisine within a cuisine—clearly presupposes, one realizes, the greatest expense and the greatest probity. In unscrupulous hands, the technique of stocks can lead to dreadful messes. This is what often happens, and the vulgar "all-purpose sauce" that comes straight from the sewers of a "Grand Cuisine" fallen into decadence, of a cuisine that is dishonest and lazy, is often, unfortunately, the lamentable final metamorphosis of the discoveries of the great chefs of the past.

With the triumph of *roux* and of *sauce béchamel,* it began to be the practice, or rather the practice became firmly established, of coating with flour meats that are to be fried or stewed.

In 1738, Lebas's *Le Festin joyeux (The Joyous Feast)* or *La Cuisine en musique (Cuisine Set to Music)* appears. It is a cookbook in verse, with the familiar tunes to which the verses are to be sung indicated. The author's purpose is to permit ladies "to teach to some of their servants how to make stews and sauces by singing." Here is the recipe for crayfish broth, to be sung to the melody of *Petits moutons qui dans la plaine:*

> *"Les écrevisses bien pilées,*
> *mitonnez-les dans du bouillon;*
> *joignez-y du pain qui soit bon,*
> *et que toutes soient bien passées."*

> (*"Take your well-ground crayfish,*
> *In bouillon simmer them;*
> *To them add good bread,*
> *And strain well."*)

Outside of his talents as a versifier, and an eminently fallible one at that, Lebas's name comes down to posterity only because he advised eating oysters raw instead of cooked (a piece of superfluous advice, since they were already being eaten that way before he came upon the scene), and because he was the inventor of solidified and soluble bouillon, which he called "consommé in lozenges," that one could carry while traveling—a debatable reason for fame, if one can judge by the latter-day bouillon cubes of which Lebas's lozenges were the forebear.

The book by François Marin, Madame de Gesvres's chef, entitled *Les Dons de Comus ou les délices de la table* (*The Gifts of Comus or the Delights of the Table*), printed in Paris in 1739, is much more important in the gastronomical bibliography of the time. This work, which Carême unjustly neglected because Marin did not have the inventive genius of La Chapelle, is, nonetheless, the most faithful inventory of the state of cuisine in the era in which new acquisitions are truly consolidated. It has another merit: whereas La Chapelle addresses himself solely to professionals, and like Taillevent or Pierre de Lune puts forth his ideas higgledy-piggledy, presupposing that his reader is familiar with the basic techniques and not taking the trouble to classify his recipes in any logical order or present them according to the degree of difficulty, *Les Dons de Comus*, on the contrary, stands out as the first really modern cookbook, in the sense that it is a *methodical* and exhaustive book in which Marin reviews all methods of preparing, of cooking, of executing recipes.

Like La Chapelle, he advises increasing discretion in the use of salt, pepper, and spices, the amounts of which become, with his light hand, infinitesimal. He uses champagne in certain dishes and presents a recipe for a first-rate pâté of trout with truffles, foreshadowing the future "New Cuisine" of the end of our own century, that one would like to see prepared more often today.

But François Marin's work attracts our attention thanks to another novelty, which admittedly is not attributable to him: the preface. It is a novelty not because it is a preface in the form of a manifesto, the case, as we have seen, with the *Délices de la campagne* and *L'Art de bien traiter*, but because it sets forth strikingly profound ideas and, above all, because it is the work of two Jesuits, the Reverend Fathers Brunoy and Bougeant. Naturally, neither of the two signed his name, but critics are certain that this anonymous preface is actually the work of Brunoy and Bougeant, which does them honor. Jesuits thus proved more enlightened in matters touching upon cuisine than Voltaire! Let us dwell for a few moments on this key text.

"Old-style cuisine," the authors state, "is the one that the French set the fashion for all over Europe, and the one that was almost universally followed only thirty short years ago. Modern cuisine, established on the bases of the old, with less pomp and circumstance, although with as great variety, is simpler and can be even more erudite. The old style of cooking was very complicated and infinitely detailed; the modern style is a sort of chemistry. The science of the chef consists of decomposing, of making meats digestible and of reducing them to their quintessence; of extracting juices that are nourishing yet light, of mixing and blending them together, so that no ingredient dominates the others and the taste of all of them comes through; and, finally, of giving them that unity that painters give to colors and of rendering them so homogeneous that all that remains of their diverse flavors is a fine and appetizing taste and, if I dare say so, an overall harmony of all the tastes thus brought together. That is the entire art of the profession, and the masterwork in cuisine."

This text is as important in the history of cuisine as Parmenides' poem in the history of philosophy. In it, cuisine is made the object of thought and no longer simply that of sensation—and here I am of course speaking of its execution and not of its consumption. Here we put our finger on the difference between a cuisine flavored with the aid of added spices and condiments, a cuisine within the scope of any amateur who has taken the trouble to learn a few things, and modern cuisine, which creates new entities not only by mixing diverse ingredients together, but by combining and fusing natural foods so as thus to constitute new gustatory unities.

This new cuisine could definitely be executed only by professionals. Hence we witness the appearance, alongside erudite cookbooks, of a branch of gastronomical literature that is still indispensable today, a branch devoted to simplified Grand Cuisine, brought within the reach of everyone, and consisting of works intended for the mother (or the father) of a family, for the empirical "cordon bleu"[3] and the megalomaniacal self-taught chef. Easy cookbooks thus "double," as one says of musical instruments, the series of books that in order to be put to use require what in music is called "transcendent virtuosity." The first of these practical works, a manual by Menon whose very title, *La Cuisinière bourgeoise* (*The Bourgeoise Family Cook*), is significant, appeared in 1745 and was destined to be reprinted many times down to the end of the nineteenth century. Massialot's book of the preceding century bore the title of *Le Cuisinier royal et bourgeois*, but it admittedly was more royal than bourgeois. During the Revolution *La Cuisinière républicaine* (*The Republican Family Cook*) by Madame Mérigot and an anonymous book, *Le Petit Cuisinier économe* (*The Economic Little Cook*), appeared. These two books were the first, in France at least, to give a prominent role to the potato; this tuber had already been widely eaten for several decades in Germany and the British Isles.

To the three classic books already cited—*Le Cuisinier moderne, Les Dons de Comus,* and *La Cuisinière bourgoise*—a fourth must be added: *Le Cuisinier gascon* (*The Gascon Chef*), published in 1740 and reprinted in 1857.

Le Cuisinier gascon is in reality the first cookbook written by a great aristocrat, a noble amateur chef, the Prince de Dombes. But using a literary device that was to become a classic one, the Prince pretends to be merely the patron to whom the manual, supposedly written by his chef, has been dedicated. The dedication in question is completely transparent however: "I will cry out on the rooftops," this pretended author-chef writes, "that you, Monsei-

---

[3] The emblem of the knights of the Order of the Holy Ghost was a blue ribbon, and a man decorated with this ribbon was referred to as a "cordon bleu." I do not know why or by what steps the shifting of the term from members of this Ordre du Saint-Esprit to wielders of pots and pans took place. The Littré dictionary merely cites these meanings that I have given, and adds: "familiarly and jokingly, *cordon bleu:* a very skillful cook."

gneur, are one of the best cooks in France. I have seen your hand at work a hundred times. If I have acquired a certain reputation in my profession, I owe it more to the emulation that you have inspired in me than to the desire that I have always felt to tickle your palate. And, finally, the work that I here take the liberty of presenting to you is none other than the fruit of my reflections on your practice."

This is as clear as it could possibly be, and is mindful of the words of Menon, who writes in his *Nouveau Traité de la cuisine* (*New Treatise on Cuisine*) (1742) that "refinement at table has been recently increased by the exquisite taste of several noble gentlemen who have contributed to the perfecting of their chef's art."

The Prince de Dombes, moreover, has the virtues and the defects of the amateur practitioner—he gives proof of more imagination than the professional when it comes to inventing dishes but is less precise about the practical directions for making them. He puts forward a wealth of ideas but presents far fewer techniques, and the intermediate steps that go into the making of a dish have a tendency to be skipped over. Whimsy often replaces real invention; his "stuffed calf's eyes au gratin," for instance, in which the pupil is replaced by a whole truffle, appear to us to be a very debatable use of truffles. The recipes for his sauces, though numerous and sophisticated, lack precision. On the other hand, his *poulet en musette à la financière* is nothing other than a chicken cooked in a bladder, an excellent method. It is accompanied by a *salpicon*, a garnish of diced meat and vegetables. *Le Cuisinier gascon* is also the only cookbook of the eighteenth century to give us a correct method for the preparation of noodles and macaroni. While the majority of the other manuals advise us to boil such *pasta* for an hour (!), Dombes recommends cooking them quickly, in the Italian style, *al dente*. Hence, although his text is very often addressed more to the imagination than to the hand, he is resolutely modern in his defense of the subtle chemical cuisine that had just come into being.

This cuisine, it should be pointed out, was made easier by a new piece of kitchen equipment. Until the reign of Louis XIV, kitchen equipment had remained almost the same as it had been in the Middle Ages, as I have described it in Chapter Four. Under Louis

XIV, various small-sized utensils in tin and wrought iron were added to it, but the only source of heat was still the vast fireplace, plus little portable braziers that permitted more delicate cooking. In the eighteenth century a new piece of equipment was developed that had a great deal to do with the gastronomic revolution: the large stove called a "soup stove" (*potager*), with twelve to twenty burners. It is evident that this new instrument permitted fires of different intensities to be used, thanks to which slow cooking, rapid cooking, simmering, grilling, and keeping preparations warm over a low fire gave rise to registers as varied as those of an organ. It also permitted the simultaneous preparation of various "first steps," beneath the very eyes of the practitioner—all those broths, purées, *salpicons*, *mirepoix*, and so on that were then to go into the final dish. Each of them could now be brought to the point of perfection in accordance with its own requisites, just as the skillful coachman can drive a team of six or eight horses.

From this time on, the writing of recipes is "tailored," so to speak, along different lines. Since this stove permitted the cook to occupy himself with new preparations while a first stage of the dish being prepared was beginning to cook, recipes were now written in several sequences. Even a dish that was simmered was no longer a sort of receptacle for a single cooking to which things were added more or less progressively; it might even be prepared in several small separate pans. Thus the cook could turn his attention to forcemeats, grind with the pestle, continue to slice and crush while the fire did its work in other sectors that could be watched out of the corner of his eye. But all these points of departure eventually led to a single point of arrival. Hence we can understand the importance of a term that was to be one of the keys of cuisine after 1750, the word *liaison* (thickening). Thickening or binding a sauce was often the final operation whereby hours of preparation ended either in glorious success or dismal failure. But at the same time the techniques for thickening were to be precisely one of the features whereby the new cuisine risked becoming heavy. The excessive use of flour, cream, and butter was to be the principal defect of certain sauces that no longer served to set off culinary science and stand as its supreme exemplar, but, rather, masked a chef's lack of it.

From this time on, the three great branches of the profession were firmly established. In former days, a distinction had been made between the *officier de cuisine,* who was the chef, and the *officier de bouche,* who was the maître d'hôtel. Sometimes the word *officier* was replaced by the word *écuyer.* Let us point out in this regard that the famous Vatel, whose name we purposely omitted in the preceding chapter and whose suicide made him immortal, was never a chef: he was the *officier de bouche* of the Prince de Condé and, as such, was charged with organizing meals and obtaining supplies for them (in particular, for the fatal evening when Condé entertained the king, an unexpected occasion for Vatel to display his talents, or, if not, to disappear forever from the scene). As Madame de Sévigné recounted in a celebrated letter, Vatel killed himself because provisions on which he was counting did not arrive in time. He had sent to Boulogne for fresh fish, relying on a successful catch that was not made that day. It was thus his capacities as an administrator that were inferior to his office and not his talents as an artist. In the normal course of things, if he had not committed suicide, he would have been put to death by either the *officier de cuisine* or the master of the household.

From the eighteenth century on, three separate and distinct branches of the art of cooking are recognized, the practitioners of which are the chef (*cuisinier*) and, under him, the pastry chef (*pâtissier*) and the meat chef (*rôtisseur*). For as Grimod de La Reynière so nicely put it, "no man can be at once great at the oven, great at the stove, and great at the spit." The *pâtissier* rules over the oven, and not only for pastries in the modern sense. The chef, the supreme artist who rules over the stoves has, to help him with the entrées, an aide who will become the modern specialist in charge of hors-d'oeuvre and cold dishes. It is the chef at the stove, in any event, who is in command of the others, and it is for this reason that at this moment in the history of gastronomy he begins to be referred to as the *chef de cuisine,* the head of the kitchen, a term which soon was to be shortened to *chef.*

The difference that existed, up to the end of the seventeenth century, between ordinary, everyday bourgeois cooking and aristocratic cooking was a difference in quantity and in elaborateness of presentation. Beginning in about 1750, the cuisine of ordinary days and that of special occasions were separated by a difference in kind, quality, and method. Ordinary cuisine naturally remained

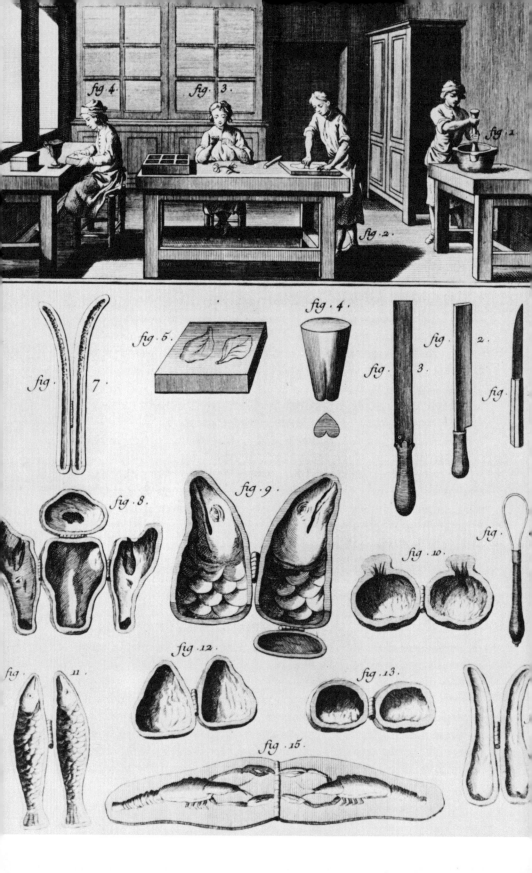

fig. 4.
fig. 3.
fig. 1.
fig. 2.

fig. 7.
fig. 5.
fig. 4.
fig. 3.
fig. 2.
fig.
fig. 8.
fig. 9.
fig. 10.
fig.
fig. 11.
fig. 12.
fig. 13.
fig. 15.

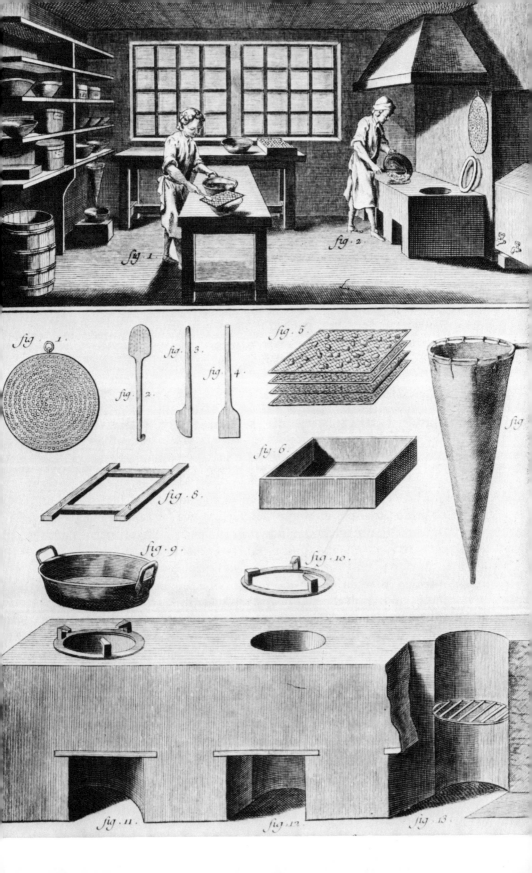

fig. 1
fig. 2

fig. 1
fig. 2
fig. 3
fig. 4
fig. 5
fig. 6
fig. 8
fig. 7
fig. 9
fig. 10
fig. 11
fig. 12
fig. 13

PRECEDING PAGES:
"1. Decorative sugarwork and molds for ices. 2. Making preserves."
Plates from Diderot's Encyclopédie. *Bibliothèque des Arts décoratifs,*
Paris.

closer to the old-style cuisine, for reasons of cost and convenience.
According to Brillat-Savarin, who had gathered his information
from the inhabitants of several *départements*, a dinner for ten persons around the year 1740 was composed of the following:

> *First service* . . . boiled meat;
>   an entrée of veal cooked in its own juice;
>   an hors-d'oeuvre.
> *Second service* . . . a turkey;
>   a vegetable dish;
>   a salad;
>   a cream (sometimes).
> *Dessert* . . . cheese;
>   fruit;
>   a pot of jam.

This order, with the succession of the boiled and the roasted as
its principal distinguishing characteristic, was to remain practically
the same in private homes down to the end of the nineteenth century. In Zola, it is the typical bourgeois menu.

As for Grand Cuisine, we shall now review some of the stages
marking its gestation by quoting in full a few sample recipes, ranging in time from the end of the seventeenth century to the middle
of the eighteenth. We shall comment upon them briefly as we go
along, so as to show what they still retain from the past and what
they incorporate from the new style of cuisine. The difference between past and present, I repeat, was so noticeable that mention of
it occurred again and again, like an obsession. Menon, for one,
writes quite naturally in 1742: "The *officier* who works in the new
[style] is preferred to the one who follows the old method."

"Cook, pastry cook, caterer, roast cook." Plate from Diderot's Encyclopédie. *Bibliothèque des Arts décoratifs, Paris.*

"*Duck with oysters:* Your duck being braised, put 2 or 3 mush-rooms through a sieve and 2 or 3 truffles with a little melted bacon fat and moisten them with duck juice. Once cooked, thicken them with a good *coulis* of veal and ham. A moment before serving take oysters; once they are opened put them in a dish and leave them in their water; put them on a stove and stir around 2 or 3 times. Take them off immediately and clean them one after the other; toss them into your stew and put the stew on the fire a little while. Ar-range your duck on the dish and put your stew over it and serve hot. It is to be observed that an oyster should not be boiled be-cause it shrivels up." (Massialot, *Le Cuisinier royal et bourgeois,* 1691)

The most interesting thing in this recipe is the sauce thickened with veal and ham *coulis,* a sort of purée. The use of cooked oys-ters, which was frequent in this period, is more debatable. They were usually delivered already shucked, in large baskets.

Here is one of Massialot's most notable inventions:

"*Royal sausage:* It is necessary to take some raw partridge meat, young pullet or capon meat, also raw, a bit of raw ham, a little veal thigh and some raw bacon, parsley, and scallions; the whole thoroughly chopped, with mushrooms and truffles, and seasoned with fine spices, a clove of garlic, salt and pepper, 2 whole eggs, and 3 or 4 yolks, and a dash of cream. Roll this forcemeat into large pieces according to the quantity of it that you have; and to cook them in such a way that the forcemeat does not fall apart, cut very thin slices from a round of veal and flatten them on the table; roll your forcemeat in that, making the rolls of the thickness of an arm at least, and of a reasonable length. Having thus prepared them, it is necessary to have an oval pan with many bardes of bacon in the bottom; arrange the sausages in the pan, fitting them in tightly, cover them with slices of beef and bardes of bacon, and cook them by braising them, taking care that the fire be not too hot; they must cook about 8 to 10 hours. Being cooked, push them to the back of the fire, allowing them to cool in the same pan; and when it is time to serve them, remove all the fat with your hand and take out your sausages, being careful not to break them. Re-move all the meat that is around them and let no fat remain. Then cut them in slices with your knife or a bacon-slicer that cuts well,

and arrange them nicely in a dish or on a plate and serve cold."
(Massialot, *Le Cuisinier royal et bourgeois*, 1691)

The subtlety of the forcemeat and the slow braising make this dish worthy of our attention.

"*Sturgeon à l'espagnole:* Take slices of sturgeon, in a quantity that you judge proper for a dish; put them in a pan, season with salt, pepper, 2 or 3 cloves of chopped garlic, a half glass of oil, a half bottle of champagne for 2 slices, a couple of glasses of water. Cook your sturgeon with coals above and below; once cooked, pour off all the bouillon from it into a pan and skim all the fat from it. Put in some good *coulis* to thicken it, or else *sauce à l'espagnole*. Bring your sauce to a boil; when it is as it should be, pour it over your sturgeon and keep it hot. When it is time to serve, put your slices of sturgeon in a dish and serve hot. Salmon, trout, pike, sea perch, and whatever other fish you like may be prepared in the same way. When you wish to have it without meat, you need only to use meatless *coulis* and juice and make it in the same way." (Vincent La Chapelle, *Le Cuisinier moderne*, 1735)

What is of principal interest in this recipe is the appearance of *sauce à l'espagnole* and of champagne (in considerable quantity, moreover, in this particular instance) in cuisine.

"*Mackerel with fennel and currants in season:* Your mackerel being washed and gutted, slit them down the back, put them in a dish with salt, pepper, and melted butter, and turn them so that they acquire a taste; put fennel on the grill and then your mackerel; once they are grilled on one side, put fennel on top and grill them on the other side; put a good-sized piece of butter in a pan along with a pinch of minced fennel and season it with salt, pepper, and nutmeg, a pinch of flour to thicken the sauce, and a dash of vinegar and a little water; put your sauce on the fire and thicken it; your sauce being thickened, put white currants in it, and your mackerel being cooked, arrange them on their dish; let your sauce have a good taste and put it on top and serve hot as an entrée." (Vincent La Chapelle, *Le Cuisinier moderne*, 1735)

What is meant here by "white currants" is gooseberries, which are difficult to come by in markets today. The use of branches of fennel during cooking is suitable for a fish with fat such as mackerel.

"*Filet of braised sirloin à la royale:* Carve [from a side of beef] a filet of sirloin from which you remove all the fat; lard it with bits of seasoned fat. Tie it carefully to give it the form you find most suitable, for it is a good idea to calculate whether you will need to serve it as a *relevé* on a large oval platter, or as an entrée on an average-size round platter. In any case, place in the bottom of a braising pan bardes of bacon and slices of veal, 5 to 6 onions, 2 cloves of garlic, with a *bouquet garni.* Then place the filet in the braising pan, cover it with bacon and add only a small quantity of salt; begin by boiling it on a very hot stove, and then simmer it for 6 hours. At the end of this time, take the stew stock and reduce and clarify it; skim off the fat carefully and make of this stock a very clear *demi-glace* that you serve on the filet of beef, after having given it a good color. If you wish the filet of beef to have a still finer appearance, allow it to cool so as to prepare it for the table more tastefully; heat it in a part of the liquid in which it cooked. You will also be able to serve it jellied if you have taken care to add a calf's foot and an ounce of deer horn to the braising pan." (Vincent La Chapelle, *Le Cuisinier moderne,* 1735)

To be noted here is the cooking in two stages so as to obtain a *demi-glace,* thus already foreshadowing Carême.

"*Chervil sauce:* Put in a pan 4 glasses of consommé, a glass of champagne, 2 cloves of garlic, a *bouquet* [*garni*], 2 mushrooms, two spoonfuls of oil. Simmer the whole for a half hour and put it through a silk strainer so that the oil does not pass through. Blanch crushed chervil and put it in a pan with a pat of butter and flour. Mix in some of the above bouillon. Stir over the fire and add the juice of a lemon at the very end." (Marin, *Les Dons de Comus,* 1739)

This is an extremely subtle and aromatic sauce, in which we again note the use of champagne (the one feature that makes it resemble modern cuisine), and the thickening with flour. An easy recipe.

"*Oyster and truffle sauce:* Peel fine truffles and slice. Mince half of one with parsley, scallions, shallots, salt, and pepper. Rub all these minced things into 2 pats of butter. Grease a pan with a little of this butter. Arrange slices of truffles on it. Then put in a little more butter, and then your oysters, green or otherwise, after having blanched them in their own liquid and removed the beards and the hard parts. Put in still more butter and some truffles. Cover your pan well, make it sweat on warm ashes for a quarter of an hour. Then remove the truffles and the oysters. Pour half a glass of champagne and a little quintessence of veal stock over what remains. Bring to a boil and skim off the fat. At the very end, add the juice of a lemon. You can serve this sauce on anything you think suitable. You can even serve it alone as a side dish with croutons." (Marin, *Les Dons de Comus*, 1739)

A typical sauce of the "new cuisine": after having gone into the making of it, the truffles and the oysters disappear during the final step, leaving behind only their scent, mingled with that of veal stock.

"*Garbure:* Put in a cooking pot a certain quantity (*un combien*) of ham rinsed thoroughly in hot water and scraped, some beef round, 2 goose thighs; make them sweat and stick to the pan over a good fire until the meat is browned; moisten with some good bouillon. Then put in a *mignonnette*, 3 or 4 onions, carrots, parsnips, a stalk of celery, a green cabbage blanched in boiling water and tied with string, and a piece of blanched bacon. Simmer on a slow fire until the meat is cooked; allow the soup to simmer with this bouillon, some whole-wheat bread cut in slices, and the cabbage; allow it to simmer until a brown crust forms in the bottom. Place on top the *combien* of ham, the goose thighs, and the bacon; moisten with bouillon, though not so much as to make the soup too clear." (Menon, *Les Soupers de la Cour* [*Suppers at Court*], 1755)

Garbure is a very old "soup" and it is interesting to see it still presented in a book as radically modernist as this. *Mignonnette* is a little bag filled with pepper and cloves. Among the old-style recipes that still exist in this period is chicken with verjuice.

"*Crayfish à la Choisy:* Take fine crayfish; cook them in water with a little salt, then peel the tails and the bodies and leave only the big legs, cutting off the ends of them. Remove all of the insides also without taking off the tail; put in their place a bit of carp roe in each crayfish. It is necessary that this roe be well blanched and diced and marinated with a little good butter, parsley, scallions, and shallots, the whole chopped very fine with salt, pepper, nutmeg, and a little basil. On your crayfish, covering the whole up to the big legs, put a fish forcemeat made of carp or some other fish that is very velvety. Brown them in butter, in which you will have put an egg yolk; bread with very fine white bread crumbs and make them take on color without drying out. For the sauce, take little crayfish tails that you will cut into small cubes; put them in a pan with a little restorative or some other good bouillon, or some reduction, along with a piece as large as your thumb of good butter rubbed into little minced herbs of ravigote sauce and a little flour; stir over the fire; add lemon juice at the very end. Place on the dish that you are to serve with the crayfish on top. One can also make them with meat stuffing and put foies gras or something else in place of the roe, as convenient." (Marin, *Les Dons de Comus*, 1739)

To be noted here: the cooking in two stages, with the main ingredient (in this case crayfish) being accompanied by a sauce based on the same ingredient. Crayfish furnished the scent most sought after in cuisine after 1700, which caused, through overfishing, their disappearance from the streams of France. Pigeon with crayfish was also a highly esteemed dish in the eighteenth century.

"*Epigrams of lamb cutlets:* Take a front quarter of lamb; carve off the shoulder and cook it on a spit; when it is cold, chop it very fine. Put in a pan a slice of ham, a little butter, 2 shallots, parsley, scallions, half a bay leaf, a little basil, and 2 cloves of garlic. Put all of this over the fire together, sprinkle liberally with flour, moisten with consommé, season with salt and pepper; allow it to boil until there is no more liquid left; then moisten with half a *setier* of thick cream; allow it to boil gently until the sauce is thickened. Put it through a sieve, put in the chopped lamb, and heat without boiling. As for the cutlets, lard them with thin slices of truffles and marinate them in melted bacon fat or the remainder of their marinade. Make a border for the dish that you are to serve with fillets of soft white bread that you hold together with slightly heated egg white. Serve the chopped lamb in the middle of cutlets placed around the edges . . ." (Menon, *Les Soupers de la Cour*, 1755)

"The Tavern Keeper." *Anonymous engraving, seventeenth century. Bibliothèque nationale, Paris.*

Le trone de baca

Cedy est mors

Reste mon reste

Les enfans san Soucis

Le Cabaretier

Le temps passe n'est plus, à la Prouidance,
Beuuez, mes chers Amis, car le uin n'est plus cher :
Et puisque nous trouuons aussi dequoy mâcher,
Profitons du bonheur de l'aimable Abondance

A Paris Chez la veue le Camu rue St Jacques a la teste d'Or   Auec Priuil. du R oy

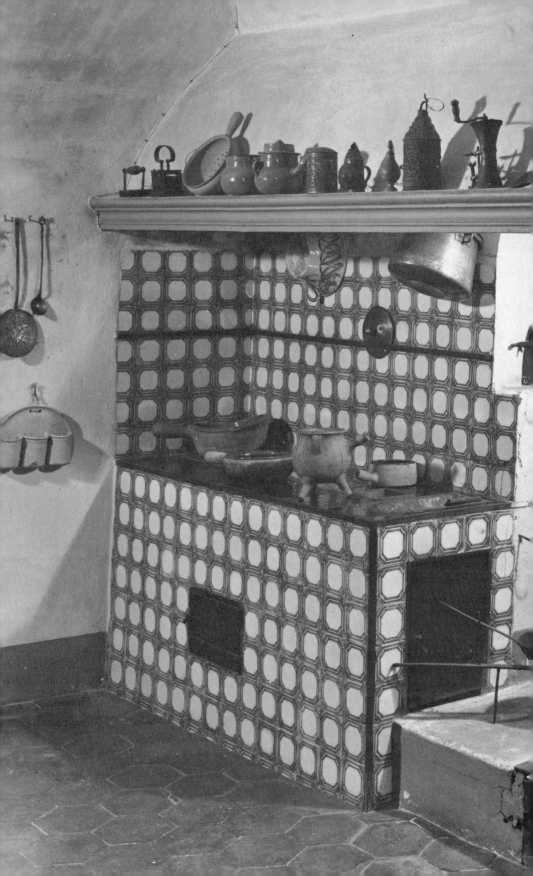

We do not know whether this is the recipe of Michelet, the chef whom we have mentioned previously, but in any event it is much more subtle than the dish, already described, that goes by the name of "epigram of lamb" today.

৵

Among the factors that were at once the cause and effect of a new gastronomical culture, mention should be made of the appearance not only of meringue, camembert, cognac, and foie gras in the eighteenth century, but also of restaurants as well.

From the end of the eighteenth century on, there was no lack anywhere of taverns, inns, caterers, pork butchers, pastry cooks, and *cafetiers* (in the literal sense of "coffee roasters," rather than the modern sense of "owners of cafés"). Their professions, moreover, were strictly regulated, according to the guild rules of old Europe. Thus a *rôtisseur* did not have the right to prepare stews or baked goods. Inns, especially those of rural areas just outside the great cities, at once the goal of excursions into the country and the theater of amusing and more or less moral repasts, had always existed. There is mention in the eighteenth century of a young woman, named du Ryer or Duriez, who had an eating house at Saint-Cloud. In his *Historiettes* (*Vignettes*), Tallemant des Réaux recounted the life of this astonishing hostess, who would appear to have been the directress (she made her husband work in the kitchens) of the first snobbish "little bistro" in Paris, at least the first one that a writer who pens his memoirs tells us of in such a way as to give us something other than a legendary account of the place. It was frequented by the brother of Louis XIII, Gaston d'Orléans, and his faithful drinking companions Bassompierre and Puylaurens. In good weather, meals were served outdoors under the grape arbor. The author of the *Roman bourgeois* (*The Bourgeois Novel*), Furetière, confesses in a letter: "If I were curious, I should like to find out how many turkeys were eaten Tuesday at Du Ryer's place, how many dishes of fresh peas or strawberries."

Many other eating houses subsequently struck the fancy of snobs at one time or another: the Épée Royale in Passy, the Petit Maure (or Petit More) in Vaugirard, not to mention other more urban places. But the reasons for their success stemmed more from the possibilities they offered as meeting places than from the outstanding nature of the cuisine to be found there. Very often, moreover, a great part of the food served in them came from caterers and pork butchers. It was wines more than the food that distinguished one eating house from another, since in those days each owner bought his wine in different regions, so that one went to Boucingo's to drink Alicante and to La Guerbois to drink Sillery.

With commercialization and the blending of table wines, our era has witnessed the more or less total disappearance of one of the principal charms of traveling, the pleasure of finding a different wine at each stop, one that can still be enjoyed in certain regions not frequented by tourists, in Italy, Greece, and Spain, but almost never in France. In France, all table wines have become incredibly undrinkable, and, what is more, they are the same everywhere. The good wines or great growths offered by decent restaurants are likewise the same everywhere, necessarily, since they are from classic wine-growing regions. All attempts to react against this double uniformity and encourage "little local wines" have merely led in turn to other abuses and to new absences of variety. Almost nowhere in restaurants today does there exist a "house wine" that is neither an industrial product nor a great growth.

In his recollections of Jean-Jacques Rousseau, Bernardin de Saint-Pierre tells of an excursion to the country, somewhere just outside Paris, with the author of the *Confessions*. When Rousseau, who was very partial to good food and something of a tippler, entered the inn for the midday meal, the first thing he did was to order the wine of the house to be brought to him to taste. Having drunk a sip, he immediately decreed: "It is a little young." The innkeeper dutifully pointed out that his rival, just a few steps away, had better, whereupon Rousseau asked whether it would not be possible to have wine brought from this other inn and served to him and his friend with their meal. In an aside to his friend, Rousseau commented ecstatically on the honesty of this innkeeper who had not hesitated to point out that the wine served by his competitor was better than his. But this honesty was apparently not sufficient reason to persuade him to eat a meal accompanied by a wine that was too young, for when the innkeeper replied that unfortunately the rules of the confraternity prevented him from going to fetch wine for his customers from his rival's inn, Rousseau, expressing to the innkeeper his infinite regret that this was so, dragged Bernardin de Saint-Pierre off to the establishment across the street.

Until approximately 1760, the word *restaurant* meant "fortifying" and nothing else. It was applied to certain bouillons and eggnogs consumed to restore one's strength after an illness or great physical exertion. In 1765 a certain Boulanger posted on his sign the notice: "Boulanger serves divine *restaurants*." This indicates that his establishment was really a popular refreshment room and bar called a *bouillon*. It was not until around 1955 that the last *bouillons* in Paris disappeared. The very last one was probably the Bouillon Buci, in the rue de Buci. Servings of bouillon, chicken boiled with coarse salt, and eggs were sold there.

The aforementioned Boulanger, having added sheep's feet with *poulette* sauce to his menu, was attacked by the guild of caterers, which claimed that this was a ragout, and that a *bouillon* did not have the right to sell a ragout. *Poulette* sauce is made with egg yolks, a white stock, mushrooms reduced to an essence, lemon juice, and parsley. This sauce was simply poured over the sheep's feet, rather than the feet being cooked *in* it. The Paris law court, having had the case brought before it, nonetheless entered into lengthy deliberations before rendering a verdict as to whether sheep's feet *à la sauce poulette* did or did not constitute a stew. In the end, and rightly, the case was dismissed, but this much-talked-of lawsuit resulted in a vogue for the dish that eventually brought it to the royal tables.

We see the word *restaurant* appear for the first time, or one of the first times, in a decree dated June 8, 1786, authorizing caterers and *restaurateurs* to receive people in their public rooms and to serve meals in them. It was at this time, in fact, that the custom of the *table d'hôte* took hold. The expression has had several meanings since being coined, but in the beginning it meant quite literally that the caterer allowed the client to sit *at the table where he took his own meals* and eat, if he so desired, certain already-prepared dishes *instead of taking them out.* We still find a similar case today with oyster-sellers, who also let customers "taste" oysters on the spot rather than taking them home.

Until the end of the eighteenth century this new custom attracted no particular notice, though caterers seemed bound to enter into violent conflict with innkeepers sooner or later. But in the end this did not happen, since the National Assembly, once the Revolution was under way, did away with privileges and guilds, thus allowing the owners of such establishments to add roasts and stews, soups, pâtés, entrées, and side dishes to their menus. Freed at last of gastronomy governed by guild rules and thus able to practice "liberal" gastronomy, they were now in a position to give the whole of what they served their personal stamp, when they had one, whereas in former days innkeepers had brought this from the caterer's and that from the pork butcher's and the other from the *pâtissier* or the *rôtisseur.*

Other features created a radical distinction between the restaurant and its ancestors the public house, the tavern, or the inn: on the one hand, the cleanliness and even the luxury of the décor, and, on the other, and even more importantly, the fact that they put Grand Cuisine within reach of the public. We read in an almanac dating from the end of the eighteenth century: "These new establishments, which have sprung up and taken the name of restaurants or health houses,[4] owe their implantation in this capital to Sieurs Roze and Pontaillé, in the year 1787."

It was not that inns had been really squalid, though the testimony of travelers is not in agreement on this particular point. In his famous account of his travels in France, written on the eve of the Revolution, Arthur Young describes them as "filthy," while Casanova found them "very clean." But whatever their good or bad points, inns were never luxurious. The new restaurants were. Their model, in fact, was the delicate interior decoration of coffeehouses, which, from the early years of the eighteenth century, were discerningly and luxuriously furnished and decorated,

---

[4] Because of the bouillon or "magisterial restorative" (*restaurant*) served in them. The first restaurants served meals at any hour, unlike today when such service is so difficult to come by in an establishment of any quality.

in the taste of the day, both in France and in Italy; indeed, certain of them, or what remains of them, are veritable museums today.

The first restaurants were distinguished by the fact that they were comfortable and quiet. Diderot writes Sophie Volland why he has willingly made it his habit to eat in a restaurant: "You ask if I have taken a liking to restaurants? Yes, really, an immeasurable liking. Meals in them are a bit dear,[5] but they are served at whatever hour one pleases. The beautiful hostess never comes over to talk with her customers, she is too upright and decent for that, but her customers come over to speak with her as long as they please, and she is a good conversationalist. One eats alone, each one has his own private dining room to occupy his attention; she comes on her own account to see if you need anything. This is marvelous, and it seems to me that everyone has nothing but praise for them."

It will be noted that in the beginning a private dining room would appear to have been neither a luxury nor a place for licentious behavior, as later became the case; it was simply a place where one could dine in peace. One of the advantages of the new restaurants was this tranquil atmosphere, for inns were very noisy. What is more, when we examine engravings of the period, we are struck by the ample space between tables, even in the main dining room of restaurants. When we think of how rare it is today to find, in Paris especially, a restaurant that is neither overcrowded nor noisy, the fact that decadence has set in is immediately obvious.

In his *XXVIIIth Meditation*, Brillat-Savarin has left us a detailed description of the "dining salon" of a restaurant in the last years of the eighteenth century. The back of the room was occupied by travelers in a hurry and by large families, who wished to be served quickly, pay, and leave. This was what was later to be called the "brasserie side" of a restaurant. The middle of the room was occupied by the *table d'hôte*, the name now given to the table for regular customers. The remainder of the room was at the disposal of customers who wished to have a leisurely, elegant meal.

The menu from which the diners were invited to make their choice was extremely varied. A restaurant owner, it was said,

---

[5] The bill for a meal, paid for "à la carte," was indeed rather high. Fixed-price menus were soon to be introduced, and regular customers were given a discount.

should present them with a choice of at least a dozen soups, twenty-four hors-d'oeuvre, fifteen or twenty beef entrées, twenty mutton entrées, thirty poultry and game entrées, sixteen to twenty veal dishes, twelve pâtés, twenty-four fish dishes, fifteen roasts, fifty side dishes, and fifty desserts.

As I have said, the advent of restaurants permitted Grand Cuisine, developed in the private mansions of the aristocracy and the great financiers of the eighteenth century, to survive and continue to evolve. In that century, the spearhead of progress was situated in the kitchens of Monsieur de la Popelinière or the Prince de Dombes. In the nineteenth century gastronomical history was written by restaurants: Magny, the Café Anglais, the Maison Dorée, Larue. In the first half or the first third of the nineteenth century, certain private individuals or official figures still admittedly had illustrious tables. Among the most remarkable were those, it is said, of Barras, Talleyrand, Cambacérès, the Rothschilds. But already the names of certain great *restaurateurs* were in no way inferior to them, either as concerns the legends surrounding them or their contribution to the progress of cuisine. The most celebrated of them in this period were the brothers Véry, whose specialty was entrées with truffles, the owner-chefs of the Quatre Frères Provençaux, who introduced Paris to *brandade de morue* (salt cod pounded with oil, garlic, and cream), Baleine, the chef of the famous Rocher de Cancale, in the rue Montorgueil, known principally for the freshness, the goodness, and the beauty of his fish, and Beauvilliers, who founded a restaurant around 1780 and wrote an *Art du cuisinier* (*The Art of the Chef*) that is still followed today—when this is possible!

Beauvilliers was the ideal of the modern *restaurateur*, as active in his kitchen as in the dining room. He could remember the names and faces of all his customers twenty years later, even if they had come to his establishment only once; he would hurry over to each table, recommending or advising against this or that dish, suggesting a wine, giving everyone, each day, the impression that the restaurant had been opened for the sole purpose of receiving only him. He inaugurates the series of great chefs who from the Empire to our day have caused the perfecting of gastronomy to stem from the admiration of the public rather than exclusively from the liberality of a few lofty patrons, as in the past. Like the painter and the poet, the chef was no longer obliged to depend solely on the protection of the mighty to make his voice heard. His success henceforth was to depend on the opinion of anyone and everyone, on the money of his customers, and hence on a new guild that places gastronomical art, like all the other arts, beneath its surveillance: the guild of critics. Like the politician, the writer, the musician, the practitioner of the plastic arts, the chef comes in the nineteenth century to depend on the three mechanisms underlying democratic society: the law of supply and demand, universal suffrage, and freedom of the press.

CHAPTER EIGHT

THE BIRTH
OF THE
INTERNATIONALE

In gastronomy as in numerous other realms, history is indissociable from geography. The reader has doubtless been struck by the fact that beginning with the middle of the seventeenth century the author of the present book seems to have dealt exclusively with French cuisine, and doubtless he has attributed this predominance to the fact that the author is French.

But even though the last two chapters have been concerned almost entirely with French cuisine, the cause for this is not some sort of culinary nationalism. The author is, certainly, sensitive to the fact that gastronomy is one of the domains in which chauvinism and even parochialism make themselves felt in the most naïve and sometimes the most intolerant way. As Montaigne long ago pointed out, everyone is attached to the food habits of his childhood and finds himself inclined to consider foreign foods and ways of preparing them absurd and even disgusting. A Frenchman today is shocked by the mixture of the sweet and the salt to be found in certain present-day German dishes or in the classic mint sauce, made of mint added to unrefined sugar or white granulated sugar and diluted in vinegar, that sometimes accompanies lamb in English cuisine. This Frenchman has forgotten that barely two or three centuries ago, sugar, as we have seen, entered into numerous salted meat or fish dishes in French cuisine or, more precisely, in the medieval European tradition.[1] Similarly, a Frenchman today would consider it barbarous to be served watered wine in a carafe, and adding water to the wine in your glass is quite likely to make you the butt of gibes from the other guests at table. Yet—and here again it is Montaigne who tells us so—this was the usual practice in the sixteenth century, and doubtless remained so for a long time, indeed, until very recently among peasants. In Montaigne's day, drinking one's wine straight was considered to be, and in fact was, a German custom. The author of the *Essays* cites it as an exotic bit of behavior that the intelligent man should not laugh at when he travels abroad on the mere ground that it is different from his own habit. In point of fact, it could be said, to settle the debate, if a rational criterium can be said to apply in the realm of habit, which is

---

[1] Cookbooks dating from the end of the seventeenth century still contain recipes for fish with fruit preserves sprinkled with cinnamon.

by definition irrational, that today little local wines without a bouquet lend themselves to and even gain by being diluted with a little water, though obviously such a thing is out of the question in
the case of great Burgundies, great Bordeaux, and cooked wine.

To come back to what we were saying, if the two preceding
chapters have been devoted to French cuisine, this is due to the
fact that this cuisine was unquestionably the area in which a his-
toric change took place in the eighteenth century. This change
was to bear definite fruit at the beginning of the nineteenth century, after which revisions, reforms, improvements, and degeneres-
cences were to take place within a given framework, but there
was no longer to be any radical revolution.[2] In reality, this French
cuisine whose historical development I have traced, is what I will
refer to, following convention, as *international* cuisine. I in no
way mean by that (happily!) that French cuisine as such invaded
the entire world, for an equivalent movement in the opposite direction also took place and a certain number of recipes from all
over the world have been incorporated into French cuisine.

To be more explicit, I shall say that there exists not so much an
international cuisine as an international *culinary art*. I mean by
"Venetian cuisine," "Irish cuisine," and so on, a *corpus* of fixed
recipes, possessing essential ties to a given region and its resources.
I mean by "international cuisine" not a corpus of recipes, but a
body of *methods*, of *principles* amenable to *variations*, depending
on different local and financial possibilities, just as this body of
methods and principles is conducive to variations within a given
country, depending on seasonal possibilities. The expression "international cuisine" takes on a pejorative connotation when it
designates a certain false grand cuisine also known as "hotel cuisine," a cuisine that retains the outward features and, above all, the
vocabulary of the Grand Cuisine of the nineteenth century, but
that limits itself to drowning various foods in all-purpose sauces
with pretentious names and to engaging in certain types of spectacular presentation for the mere sake of display.

Hence, the expression "international cuisine" has two precisely
opposite meanings: on the one hand, it refers pejoratively to a

---

2 Does the "New French Cuisine" that has appeared since 1970 deserve to be
considered a revolution? We shall take up this question in the conclusion of this
book.

rootless, anonymous cuisine, against which it is a healthy reaction to demand the return to local dishes with the tang of the soil, and, on the other hand, it designates Grand Cuisine, with the potentiality of becoming internationalized because the chefs who know it are men who understand its basic principles, and, since they are possessed of an inventive spirit, men who tirelessly seek to exploit these bases to create new dishes.[3] This cuisine is also international in the sense that it has the capacity to integrate, to adapt, to rethink, I will say almost to rewrite the recipes of all countries and all regions, or at least those that are amenable to such treatment.

The entire problem lies precisely therein. A certain number of recipes, reexamined in the light of the principles that they embody, can be internationalized. Indian curry, Valencian paella, sauerkraut, koulibiaka, red cabbage with chestnuts *à la limousine*, Italian *fritto misto* are capable of being internationalized, and they have proved it. Very often these preparations, once they are refined and improved, are better as dishes in international Grand Cuisine than as regional dishes. In other instances, transposition is absolutely impossible. In these cases, the native tang of local products or techniques of cooking linked to a certain type of dwelling, or heat source, or fuel, or even odors in the air and climatic characteristics cause any attempt to "improve" a recipe, by making it obey the canons of gastronomic art, to end up merely depriving it of all personality. The more primitive a dish is, the more tasty it is. It does not belong to the domain of art, but rather that of ethnology or a mixture of biology and ethnology. Gastronomical art is able, when necessary and possible, to find the equivalents of certain products or of certain ingredients and use them to replace other products and other ingredients that cannot be obtained in certain places. It also knows the cases in which it is necessary to forbear to do so. Certain books on Chinese cuisine for the use of Westerners indicate equivalents of this sort.

To be still more precise, I will say that, in my opinion, there are no *national cuisines:* there is international cuisine, which must remain extremely flexible, and *regional* cuisine. The basic unit in gastronomy is the region, not the nation. A *pauchouse mâconnaise*

---

[3] In the jet age, moreover, it is the great chefs themselves who have begun to travel, to open branches, and to train disciples all over the world.

is as difficult, if not impossible, to make in Marseille as in Sicily. *Cacciucco livornese* no longer has the same scent when it is made a hundred kilometers from the sea, in Florence, a region of inland and peasant cuisine, as when it is made right on the coast of Versilia, at Livorno or Viareggio. There is as much difference between Piedmontese cuisine and Calabrian cuisine as between this latter and Flemish cuisine. Certain regional dishes can travel, but others are refractory to any change of place. We must go to them; they cannot come to us.

In its attempt to assimilate the greatest number of regional dishes possible, international cuisine must be very attentive to the methods of cooking and the sources of the elements that give them their scent and flavor. If this condition is respected, it can absorb a very great number of ideas, because it alone is capable of comprehending the *creative principle* behind this or that local knack of preparing a dish and of applying consciously what was executed unconsciously and mechanically. For international cuisine has curiosity as its motivating force, unlike regional cuisine, which for its part is *obliged* to remain routine and exclusive, finding its salvation purely and simply in the refusal to take into consideration any other register of flavors than its own. But a good chef who wants to export North African couscous, for instance, will pay close attention not so much to the juxtaposition of the elements that make up the recipe—vegetables (including chick-peas), a hot sauce, wheat groats, etc.—as to two fundamental traits of this dish. Couscous is first and foremost the couscous itself, that is to say, the art of "rolling" the groats in such a way that it is as free from stickiness as possible and as free-flowing as sand. The grains of a proper couscous must scatter on the table when one blows on them, at least before they have been wet with bouillon. The second fundamental factor is the aroma of the meat. The only meat that must be used for it is the most tasty mutton; couscous with chicken must be avoided, because modern European chicken has no taste, and *méchoui* or roast mutton must also be avoided, for couscous is a stew, or, more precisely, a "soup," in the ancient meaning of the word. *Méchoui* makes no sense unless it is cooked whole in the open air, roasted above wood coals in which aromatic herbs are

"Preparing fish." Detail of a Japanese color print by Utagawa Toyokuni (1767–1825), beginning of the nineteenth century. Bibliothèque nationale, Paris.

burned. This cooking in the open air is essential to give the surface of the roast the dryness responsible for its unique flavor. The couscous "with *méchoui*" offered on the menu of certain restaurants is therefore the perfect example of the sort of *bad* international cuisine that *transports the picturesqueness* of a regional dish without *transposing its principles*, because they have not been understood.

When such comprehension exists, on the other hand, real Grand Cuisine can sometimes give the diversity of local registers an interpretation that is at once faithful and new. Contrary to received opinion, erudite cuisine from its very inception introduced cosmopolitanism into the art of eating well. As early as the beginning of the nineteenth century, Brillat-Savarin, speaking of Parisian cuisine, could write: "Among these diverse parts constituting the dinner of a gourmet, the principal parts, such as butchered meat, poultry, fruits, come from France; others, such as beefsteak, welch-rabbet [*sic*], punch, and so on, imitate English cuisine; and still other parts are from all over: from Germany come sauerkraut, hamburger, Black Forest filets; from Spain, *olla podrida*, chick-peas, dry raisins from Málaga, the peppered hams of Jerica, and cordials; from Italy, macaroni, Parmesan, Bologna sausages, polenta, ices, liqueurs; from Russia, dried meats, smoked eels, caviar; from Holland, cod, cheeses, peck herring, curaçao, anisette; from Asia, Indian rice, sago, *karrik*, soy sauce, the wine of Shiraz, coffee; from Africa, the wine of the Cape; finally, from America, potatoes, sweet potatoes, pineapple, chocolate, vanilla, sugar, etc. . . . which is sufficient proof of the statement that we have made elsewhere, namely, 'that a meal such as one can eat in Paris is a cosmopolitan whole in which every part of the world makes its appearance by way of its products.' "

Let us complete Brillat-Savarin's statement by declaring that it is obviously not only in Paris that gastronomical cosmopolitanism is practicable or practiced.

In point of fact, this cosmopolitanism embraces three very distinct categories of foods: "specialties" such as salt-cured meats, smoked fish, the countless sorts of sausages and hams, etc., which are already prepared and travel well; foreign or exotic products, among which Brillat-Savarin cites at this early date soy sauce, coffee (whose use had not yet spread to all classes), and sago, a starch extracted from the pith of the palm tree, and most spices (the *kar-rik* here cited by Brillat-Savarin is, in fact, our curry, an essentially composite, variable condiment); and, finally, *dishes* or recipes, such as *olla podrida*, a sort of *potée* or, sometimes, a stew. It is amusing to note that Brillat-Savarin goes back to the Spanish word, since *olla podrida* had been introduced into France as early as the seventeenth century and the name been gallicized to *oille* or *grand-ouille*, the taste for which is due to the influence of Queen Marie-Thérèse, the Spanish wife of Louis XIV. Outside of *oille*, Spanish cuisine had little success during the reign of Louis XIII and Louis XIV, and even less, later, despite the close family and political ties that developed between Paris and Madrid.[4] The Maréchal de Gramont has the following to say about the dinner that he attended on October 19, 1659, at the home of the Admiral of Castille: "The feast was superb and magnificent in the Spanish manner, that is, execrable, and no one was able to eat it. I saw seven hundred dishes served: everything in them was full of saffron and gilded; then I saw them carried off just as they had come in."

The excessive use of saffron is, of course, only a Spanish variation of the medieval abuse of spices, still being perpetuated in this era. As for the "gilding," this too was an old medieval custom, consisting of giving a gold color to various things, usually little birds, thanks to a liquid with an egg yolk base in which they were dipped or with which they were smeared with the aid of a brush. This procedure is quite in keeping with the medieval spirit, wherein culinary ornamentation consists of hiding the food, of creating surprise effects.

To open a parenthesis here, decoration and the disposition of food to please the eye is a chapter in the history of gastronomy that deserves mention. We can distinguish three tendencies in this domain. There is, first, the total absence of frills or of special care; this is characteristic of regional cooking, both inland and on the edge of the sea, in which what one sees is what one eats, a cuisine still called, for this very reason, "straightforward" or "honest" and other synonymous adjectives. Second, there is what we might call

---

[4] And despite the effort of Pierre de Lune, who in 1662 followed his *Nouveau et Parfait Maître d'hôtel royal* with an appendix entitled *Le Cuisinier à l'espagnole* (*The Spanish-style Chef*). He also gives English, German, Italian, and even Portuguese recipes.

PRECEDING PAGES:
"The art of the table." Detail of the painting Belshazzar's Feast, *Flemish School, beginning of the seventeenth century. Musée des Beaux-Arts, Besançon.*

not decoration but disguise: certain fancy presentations in the waning years of antiquity and in the Middle Ages, for instance, which in cuisine last, as we have seen, until the middle of the seventeenth century.[5] Third, we have what might be called architecture rather than gastronomical decoration; this school is distinguished by what were once called *pièces montées*, which are seldom seen today except sometimes as pastry creations. These decorative pieces, sometimes representing human figures or scenes, were often partly composed of nonedible elements. They decorated the table at the first service, which, let us remember, included pastry since meat pies were included. These complicated constructions, often inspired by the finest designs of ornamentists in plaster or stucco, were the reigning fashion principally during the first half of the nineteenth century, to the point that one of those responsible for some of the most brilliant creations, Carême, wrote ironically: "The fine arts are five in number, namely: painting, sculpture, poetry, music, and architecture, the principal branch of this latter being pastry."

Finally, from the middle of the nineteenth century on and in the twentieth century in particular, the aim of the decorative aspect at table has been to set off and blend together the natural colors of the ingredients and sauces. This method consists either of contrasting vivid colors, for example, the yellow of egg yolks and the green of asparagus in poached eggs *Ninon*, or the dark red of tomato broth and the black of truffles in turbot *à la parisienne*, or, on the contrary, of creating subtle monotones, for example in young pullet *à la Néva*, in which everything is the very pale, creamy yellow color of the *gelée* it is molded in, barely highlighted by discreet decorations of truffles and pistachio nuts, or the

---

[5] With a certain improvement in taste, nonetheless. See the documents cited in the note at the end of this chapter.

bright red overall color of bottom round of lamb *à la byzantine*, or the pure whiteness of a chicken sautéed with mushrooms and cream. The variety of salads and the return to the use of herbs, used *au naturel*, also permit countless combinations of colors in modern hors-d'oeuvre. Chinese chefs have achieved an extraordinary degree of subtlety in the use of natural colors in cuisine, going so far as to replace black mushrooms with white ones in order to have in a soup only ingredients of a delicate white.

To return now to gastronomical cosmopolitanism, the ready-made specialties of which I spoke earlier are more a branch of commerce than a branch of cuisine. Exotic foods sometimes soon cease to be so: Brillat-Savarin's list included chick-peas, which have none of the characteristics of a luxury product, but which nonetheless were still capable of astonishing Théophile Gautier when he traveled to Spain around 1840. Today too we have seen certain foreign fruits or vegetables, the avocado, for instance, pass from the category of a rare food, and an expensive one, in Europe to that of a common hors-d'oeuvre and a product that since 1960 can be found in the most modest grocery stores and in the most popular markets.

In short, that cuisine that from the beginning of the nineteenth century came to be known as Grand Cuisine, the invariable expression after Carême, is international by vocation. It consists, certainly, of knowing how to make various dishes but even more of knowing *the conditions allowing them to be made*. It suffices to leaf through the great treatises on cuisine of the last hundred and fifty years to note that they have adapted the principal ideas, but not necessarily the exact *recipes*, of various regional cuisines. The fact, for example, that a master such as Escoffier worked in England for the greater part of his career resulted in the introduction of twenty-seven sauces of English origin into the list of those considered as forming part of Grand Cuisine, twenty-one of them hot, among them cranberry sauce, oyster sauce, reform sauce, and six cold sauces, among them Cambridge sauce, Cumberland sauce, mint sauce, and horseradish sauce. It is significant that none of these sauces, by reason notably of the unjust discredit into which English cuisine had fallen, had been adapted in England from traditional sources, that is to say, by direct and unconscious "osmosis." It had taken the conscious will of a professional chef.

An intelligent chef in the nineteenth century played on a worldwide keyboard, adopting methods from the cuisine of the Near East, so rich in original techniques, from the cuisine of central Europe, from Russian cuisine, from the Jewish cuisines of various countries of Europe or of various provinces of France (Alsace, in particular), from America, to which Brillat-Savarin claims he introduced scrambled eggs, that dish that was to have such a glorious destiny in that part of the world. Brillat-Savarin also recounts the adventure of another French political émigré who made a fortune in London during the French Revolution and the Empire by going into the richest households and making salad dressing, that thing that is so simple and yet so difficult, not to make but to explain how to make. Driving his tilbury himself, transporting all the ingredients in it, this émigré made the rounds of his customers at mealtime and turned out on the spot whatever salad dressing was desired.

Hence the difference between international cuisine and regional cuisines is not, as those who do not know are too often inclined to believe, the difference between the complicated and the simple. Certain phases of international cuisine, certain sauces, certain methods of cooking of Grand Cuisine are sometimes extremely simple, whereas certain regional dishes are neither simple nor complicated but merely impossible outside the local conditions of the land or the maritime region that make them what they are.

We must in all fairness recognize, however, that, on the whole, Grand Cuisine is a cuisine restricted to professionals. That is why, as we already have seen, it has developed and renewed itself in great restaurants down through the nineteenth and twentieth centuries. But it is capable of being adapted to a more modest and more simplified scale, as was the case in numerous cookbooks. At the end of the nineteenth century, for example, a book such as Reboul's *La Cuisinière provençale*, one which in fact goes beyond the framework indicated in the title, was a work intended for the housewife but one which nonetheless applied the fundamental methods of Grand Cuisine with regard to essential points. "Bourgeois" cuisine thus finds its place between the international cuisine of the professionals and the countless varieties of regional cuisine, benefiting from the know-how of the former while at the same time relying on the heritage of the latter.

This is not meant to suggest that "grand" cuisine and regional cuisine are diametrical opposites. Nor can it be said that there is absolutely no such thing as national cuisines, a "French cuisine," an "Italian cuisine," a "Spanish cuisine," and so on . . . Today's French cuisine, for example, has two separate and distinct sources: the various regional cuisines on the one hand and the cuisine practiced by professionals—the one born in the eighteenth century—on the other. The second naturally influenced the first, and today there are practical manuals, Ginette Mathiot's *La Cuisine pour tous*,[6] for example, in which we find both a simplified initiation into Grand Cuisine and a sampler of regional dishes ranging from *potage champenois* (soup from Champagne) to *poule à la comtoise* (hen, Franche-Comté style). The most humble family recipe, such as that for fricassee of chicken, benefits from the distant lessons of a Carême or an Escoffier. The minuteness of the various steps for making this dish that is nevertheless very simple, the spirit that inspires it are much further removed from the typical preparations, even characteristically peasant ones, of the nineteenth century, than they are from the preparations of any of the masters of the nineteenth century. It is not the time spent in preparation nor the amount of money that make the difference here, but rather the conception, and this is as true of simple recipes as it is of complex ones. We thus see how the cuisine of professionals influences popular cuisine, by way of details that are often apparently insignificant, such as the recommendation to sear the chicken parts in butter without browning them, and to mix bouillon with the white wine, or the indication of the precise moment at which the sauce should be thickened with egg yolks or the lemon juice added.

Conversely, certain recipes created directly in Grand Cuisine often evolve in the course of history under the pressure of a certain sort of popular good sense. Thus at the beginning of the nineteenth century the recipe for chicken Marengo (also used sometimes for veal) called for cooking these meats in hot oil till done. Chef Dunand, who had invented or was said to have invented the recipe for Napoleon I, added crayfish as well. Little by little the

---

[6] Paris, Albin Michel, 1955, reprinted in a Livre de Poche edition. This work, while vastly simplified, nonetheless contains 1,243 recipes.

crayfish went by the board, for they really served no purpose in this dish. Later on, since cooking the chicken or veal in oil till done turned out to be too heavy, it came to be merely rapidly browned in the oil, then moistened with a little white wine. The recipe given by Pellaprat in the twentieth century has been even further improved, in that bouillon, which serves to moisten the meat, is added at the same time as the white wine. Little remains of Dunand's original conception, which was really nothing but a chicken *à la provençale* fried in oil with tomatoes and garlic; a "sauté" has been turned into a "stew," since instead of being cooked dry, the chicken or the veal are cooked in their sauce. In short "Marengo" was a fried dish in the beginning and it is today a stew. The popular talent for stews, which are lighter and more aromatic, has little by little—and rightly—pared away what was wrong with a "professional" recipe. (What I mean here by a "professional" recipe is not a refined one but a "creation," as contrasted with a traditionally transmitted recipe.)

Of the seven major types of cooking: boiling, deep frying, baking, grilling, braising, cooking in a sauce or stewing, and cooking in a frying pan or "sautéing," it is culinary art that often determines the one that is most appropriate for a given recipe and sets it off best, a recipe that cooks have stubbornly followed even though the method of cooking was inappropriate. How many times has it happened that someone has perceived that meats and vegetables that previously have been boiled before braising them, sautéing them, or roasting them could simply be braised, thus keeping all of their flavor intact?

In short, in keeping with the advice of Cussy, a gastronome of the nineteenth century: "Gourmets who read me, be content with the cuisine of Picardy, but educate it!"

NOTE

Two documents on the art of serving and decorating the table

To illustrate the above remarks on the role of visual pleasure and the proper use of colors in the art of the table, we can find no better means than to cite two documents, one from the seventeenth century, the other from the beginning of the nineteenth.

The table and the arrangements of silver and dishes on it are tableaux, the dining room is a décor, a banquet can become a theatrical show. It is curious to note that it is chefs themselves and not the maîtres d'hôtel who are most concerned with the presentation of the dishes that they "send in" to the room where they will be eaten. We are surprised to read in classic recipes great numbers of suggestions on the subject, and to note the time that carrying them out requires, especially when we think of the few seconds that suffice to destroy these scrupulously prepared but ephemeral culinary compositions. Sometimes complex patterns made of herbs and condiments molded into an aspic bear witness to a veritable art of edible tapestry or embroidery.[7]

Here is our first text. It is a passage from *L'Art de bien traiter* (1674) in which the author describes the way to serve an *ambigu extraordinaire*, that is to say, a meal in which the dessert is already laid out and therefore does not have to be brought in.

"This meal," he writes, "is a divided *ambigu;* for, outside of the ordinary viands that are on the table, the dessert, the wine, and the lights are also on view everywhere in the banquet hall itself, on the furniture, on the mantlepieces, and other places that are most convenient, and so perfectly arranged that there is no tableau, painting, or spectacle whose richness and composition can bear the slightest comparison with them. This manner charms the eye, and as a foretaste of the good things that are to be found there, it seems at first that one's eyes are about to devour these delicious dishes: the pleasure of seeing them is greater than that of touching them, and it is an inconceivable satisfaction, during the entire repast, to have such pleasing objects present which excite the appetite even more in that they are made expressly to awaken it.

"As everything that surprises in this domain is more touching and more beautiful than what is vulgar and common, so this unusual way of serving must arouse more admiration than is the usual habit among us. In order to occasion this surprise, one must follow what is practiced among all reasonable people, having nothing to do with the *hoi polloi* and the mob: the guests must not enter the dining room until the moment that the food is brought to the

---

[7] In today's cookbooks, it is true, such pictorial compositions can be preserved by means of color photographs.

table. And in order to permit this, there are always places ready, immaculate ones, to receive the guests, who speak, chat, and amuse themselves together as they wait for the host to come and invite them to proceed to the place where the banquet is to take place.

"To begin to execute this design, and supposing that in the dining room there is some large piece of furniture ordinarily decorated with vases, urns, artistically fashioned pots, one will put in the middle of it a great basin of five or six plates of different fruits in a pyramid, decorated with a quantity of flowers of the season. If the repast calls for a more magnificent preparation, one will place two of them on the aforesaid piece of furniture, one at either end, and decorate them with dry sweetmeats or pastries; one will fill the space between and the empty spaces on both sides with pots of flowers, baskets, porcelains, or with lights and girandoles if the late hour prevents us from seeing such rare and splendid objects.

"If there are hams, venison pies, or other large-sized pieces, one will place them on pedestal tables on either side of the piece of furniture. If there are several large pieces of furniture in the room, they must be decorated in the same manner. Put lights about everywhere in profusion, flat mirrors and other well-conceived fancies, all of them so magnificently arranged that they will make an agreeable spectacle for the eyes of the guests. For I maintain that the beauty of a repast is infinitely greater in the evening, in the light of candelabra, than during the day, and even that one eats better then, this being a time when affairs are a bit more relaxed, when importunate intruders are fewer, and it seems a time naturally destined to the discovery of the sweetest pleasures of life. I for my part do not mince my words and I tell you the truth as I know it, as I think it. I am for beautiful silence and repose, and although I am not a child of shadows, I am nonetheless fond of them, and their darkness pleases me when the fire and the light, like so many domestic suns, enhance them. Finally, their time is the time of pleasures; I am at my ease then; it is often the source of the most charming and most secret understandings. Fine evenings are my joy and I prefer them to elegant debauchery on the brightest of days.

"A quantity of crystal bottles, flagons, or vials, filled with the most exquisite wines and liqueurs, more or less depending on the spaces available and the size of the fireplace, will take the place of porcelains and constitute all the ornamentation on either side of it. One will place, if that be possible, pots of flowers between the bottles or behind them; and on the corners of the aforesaid fireplace one will put torches or girandoles; and above all, a large one in the middle of it, along its whole length, so as to light the entire room.

"When the time comes to serve the dessert, it will be close at hand. These agreeable objects, after having diverted the eye, will thus crown the pleasure of the senses, and this fête will see itself brought to a happy conclusion, to the glory of its author and the contentment of the assembled guests."

Here now is another *ambigu*, prepared almost two centuries later by Carême, as recounted by Lady Morgan, a guest at dinner of Monsieur and Madame de Rothschild, in their château in Boulogne. The reader will note the simultaneous use of the colors of the porcelain and the dinner service, the sauces, the creams, and the fruits or vegetables, and finally the effects produced by the "architecture" in spun sugar:

"The atmosphere was stifling despite the venetian blinds and the porticos; the heat of the apartments was unbearable. It had proved impossible to serve dinner in the château. The dining room had been moved outdoors and set out amid orange trees, in a pretty oblong pavilion in white marble, where the air was cooled by little nearby fountains giving off jets of pure, bright water. The middle of the table, served *en ambigu*, was covered with a dessert of an admirable elegance. A limpid day lingered on in the thousand rays of a setting sun: the silver table service shone all the more brightly; porcelains more precious than gold and silver because of their perfect workmanship retraced family scenes. All the details of the service were evidence of a knowledge of the refinements of life, of an exquisite simplicity.

"The entrées were placed in a circle around this handsome dessert. The table arrangement and the dinner, everything, revealed Carême's hand. It was his brilliant variety, his perfect sense of proportion. No more English spices, no more black gravy: on the contrary, delicate flavors and the perfume of truffles; it might well have been the month of January. This service gave rise to universal satisfaction, and at certain moments we heaped praise on various delicious dishes. The vegetables still had their natural colors, the mayonnaise seemed to have been made of snow, like the heart of Madame de Sévigné; the *plombière*, with its sweet freshness and the taste of its fruits, replaced our insipid English soufflé.

"I state categorically that it has taken less genius to compose certain dramas than to execute this beautiful and elegant dinner. If it were the custom to crown the masters of the table as one does actors, Carême's laurel wreath would be in my eyes as precious as the pretty garlands of the Pastas[8] and the Sontags. His dinner was a perfect specimen of the art today, and I fully appreciate its value . . .

"I was seated next to Monsieur de Rothschild: after the soup, I had already sagely hinted that I was not unworthy of a table served by Carême, that I recognized the eminent merit of the man who had been the first to combat *spiced, burned cuisine;* and although I had been accused of favoring the red bonnets [of the French revolutionaries], all my best wishes went to *white bonnets.*

"Monsieur de Rothschild said to me with a smile: 'Carême pays you the honors you deserve too; he has enjoyed your writings; look.' And I read my name on a column of sugar close by me. I blushed suddenly, like Sterne's accusing spirit. This memory was very flattering, however. The column was a piece of the most ingenious architecture; my name was inscribed on it in spun sugar."

---

[8] A famous singer.

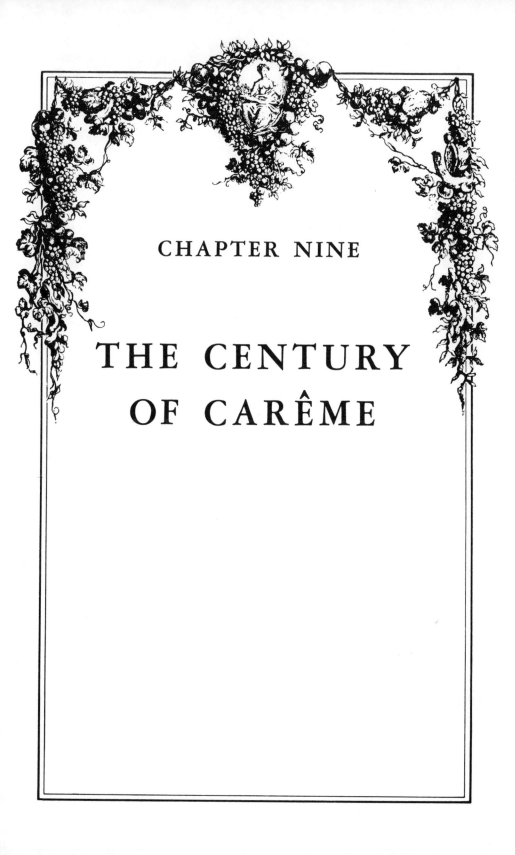

CHAPTER NINE

THE CENTURY
OF CARÊME

It is difficult to espouse, without hesitation, the notion of a gastronomical golden age, for opinions of the contemporaries of any culinary epoch are divided as to the state of the art at a given moment in its overall history. It is surprising to find, for example, an opinion such as the following being put forth in the Second Empire, a period generally considered to be possessed of a rare fecundity in the domain of great gastronomy: "A good dinner is a rare thing today. Gastronomy is like poetry: it is in a period of complete decadence . . . Contemporary cuisine presents a pitiful spectacle [. . .] Today's generation eats without knowing how to eat . . . It is proving itself the enemy of that grand cuisine that was the glory of France . . . The chefs are the cause of this indifference that we are taxed with; they have confused everything, spoiled everything, exhausted everything."[1] The author of this discouraged diatribe attributes the decadence that he believes he discerns to insouciance, to fatuity, to cupidity, to the lack of conviction, and so on, all of them eternal defects naturally capable of reappearing at any and every moment. Carême himself, according to whom cuisine existed only in the embryonic state before the nineteenth century, already speaks of the degenerescence of the art as early as 1820 or thereabouts.[2] "Cuisine grew under the Empire, that is beyond doubt," he writes. "I think that at that time it did improve health.[3] This direction seems to me to be the wrong one. The meanness, the luxury of the two revolutions that followed 1815 have effaced among us those pleasing specialties of the society of the Ancien Régime that attracted rich and elegant Europe to Paris. All that is over and done with; where we are headed I do not know; perhaps the clever pilots who are guiding us know." Thus, according to him, the history of Grand Cuisine lasted a bare ten years . . .

Opinions this contradictory and this unrealistic induce us to be

---

1 *Courrier de Paris*, March 27, 1858.

2 Cuisine, which according to him did not exist before him, would thus have begun to decline after him and around him. Chefs share with philosophers and painters the unquestioned conviction that their time is the only one that is worth anything, and it is summed up, once and for all, in a single man: the one who is speaking.

3 Another fixed idea.

circumspect, both in our censure and in our praise. It is beyond question, however, that our verdict on the nineteenth century will not err if it is highly favorable. It is first of all—and, as we have seen, this is a very important index—an eminently productive century in the domain of gastronomical *literature*. This literature is divided into three branches: the original books of the creators themselves, who experience the need to draw up the complete inventory of their experience, to extend it and renew it; then after these works written by and for professionals come works written for the general public, families, and amateur cooks; and, finally, the nineteenth century also sees the appearance of a veritable flood of books due, so to speak, to the same sort of diners and enlightened gastronomes as the public to whom they are addressed: memoirs, precepts, polemics, and so on . . . All these authors accuse each other of invincible ignorance, which is always a good sign.

It is in the first category, that of professional literature, that we must place, first and foremost, the abundant written texts of Carême himself. But this body of works was preceded by Viard's *Cuisinier impérial* (*The Imperial Chef*) (1806), by Beauvilliers' *L'Art du cuisinier* (*The Art of the Chef*) (1814), and the very important *L'Art de conserver* (*The Art of Preserving Food*) (1810), by Appert, the inventor of methods of home food-preserving that were to remain the only known ones until the advent of modern industrial canning.

In the next years, under the Second Empire, professional gastronomy produced an abundant bibliography, due first of all to Gouffé and then to Urbain Dubois and Émile Bernard, whose *Cuisine classique* (*Classic Cuisine*) (1856), revised for the second edition which appeared in 1864, is perhaps the most complete and most *realistic* summa of the century. We also owe to Urbain Dubois a work entitled *La Cuisine de tous les pays* (*The Cuisine of All Countries*) (1868), which amply demonstrates, as we said in the last chapter, that Grand Cuisine is by vocation an *open* cuisine, as opposed to the *closed* cuisine originating in a parochial regional spirit. The first is fated to create, to seek the new, whereas the duty of the second is to preserve what the centuries have produced for better and for worse.

Let us also cite, among the monumental works, Joseph Favre's *Dictionnaire universel de cuisine* (*Universal Dictionary of Cui-*

sine) in four volumes (1883–89), and finally *La Grande Cuisine illustrée* (*Grand Cuisine Illustrated*), of Salles and Montagnié (1900).

In the second category the list is superabundant; many are called but few are chosen. A few "best-sellers" stand out amid this profusion. In England there were Reynolds' *The Complete Art of Cookery* (1848), an interesting book in that it contains not a single continental recipe, and Eliza Acton's *Modern Cookery*, a great midcentury success which devotes barely fifteen pages out of 650 to foreign cuisine and to Jewish cuisine. Such books prove that the Grand Cuisine of French origin, even though well represented in England in the nineteenth and twentieth centuries by Soyer, Escoffier, and Boulestin in particular, was, in fact, practiced only within a small fraction of the wealthiest class, in certain great clubs and luxury hotels. Eliza Acton's book was soon supplanted by those of Isabella Beeton, which usually had first appeared in the form of articles in women's magazines. In this regard let us not forget that in England and in France as well as in other principal European countries, the nineteenth century was the era in which publications for women first saw the light of day, and they often had press runs and an influence equal to those they have had in the twentieth century. Hence, most of these cookbooks are at the same time manuals of household management.

Women's publications constitute an important sector within gastronomical literature, and in the press in general we see the figure of the gastronomical columnist being born, increasing, and multiplying.

The need to incorporate the lessons of Grand Cuisine within everyday cooking, within the limits of financial resources that were obviously much more restricted than those available to the great chefs in restaurants or in lordly households, piqued people's imaginations and encouraged ingenuity. In 1891, Pellegrino Artusi published a synthesis of Italian cuisine, with special emphasis on Florentine cooking, *La Scienza in cucina e l'arte di mangiar bene* (*Science in the Kitchen and the Art of Eating Well*), a book that is both exemplary because of the care that Artusi took not to leave any detail of execution unexplained and to write sincerely for people determined to *carry out* the recipes therein, and a delight to read because of the purity of its language and the elegance of its style. In each of these respects it is comparable to J. B. Reboul's *La Cuisinière provençale*, which appeared in France in 1893. In his preface, Artusi declares that he is mistrustful "of cooks that deal with culinary art, which books are for the most part misleading and incomprehensible." He offers instead, he says, recipes that have been "tried and tested again and again by myself, addressed to ladies of quality, to good housewives, and to all those who in no way aspire to become cooks only for show." In 1896, Scheibenbogen's *Cuisine Austro-hongroise* (*Austro-Hungarian Cuisine*) appeared. As for France, the year 1823 saw the appearance of Catherine's *Manuel de cuisine bourgeoise* (*Manual of Bourgeois Cooking*), among the first of a long series which was also to include, for example, Mique Grandchamp's *Le Cuisinier à la bonne franquette* (*The Straightforward Cook*) (1883), *Le Traité de cuisine bourgeoise* (*Treatise on Bourgeois Cooking*) and *Les Éléments culinaires* (*Principles of Cooking*) (1893 and 1894) by Colombié, and also works on various regional and foreign cuisines, in particular A. Suzanne's *La Cuisine anglaise* (*English Cooking*) (1840), Gay's *La Cuisine anglo-américaine* (*Anglo-American Cooking*) (1913), and L. Monod's *La Cuisine florentine* (*Florentine Cooking*) (1914), all these titles constituting clear proof that all through the nineteenth century there existed a vast intermingling of various cuisines and multiple reciprocal influences. (The nineteenth century in gastronomy might be said to have extended down to World War One.) The internationalization that we spoke of in the preceding chapter takes the form in each country of a greater knowledge of and a greater curiosity concerning cuisines previously little known or undeservedly scorned.[4]

---

[4] An exceptional case is that of Spanish cuisine, which all through the nineteenth century and the greater part of the twentieth has resisted the penetration of international cuisine with a French base. In these final years of the twentieth century the truth of this statement can be verified by personal experience (Spain is the last of the large European countries in which cuisine *really* varies from province to province) and by consulting one of the latest all-inclusive works to be printed on the subject, Candido's *La Cocina española* (*Spanish Cooking*) (1976). Candido, a celebrated Segovia *restaurateur*, is really the author or the inspiration only of the first section, that devoted to the cuisine of Old Castile. The other sections, each of which has a different author and compiler, cover the other provinces. This is proof that it is impossible, even today, to write a treatise on Spanish cuisine that is not primarily based on and composed of original regional creations, even though there are certain recipes (the *recetario general*) that are common to the whole of the Spanish peninsula.

"Title page with engraving by Jubin, 1814." Bibliothèque nationale, Paris.

L'ART
DU CUISINIER,

PAR A. BEAUVILLIERS,

Ancien Officier de Monsieur, comte de Provence, attaché
aux Extraordinaires des Maisons royales, et actuellement
Restaurateur, rue de Richelieu, n° 26, à la grande Taverne
de Londres.

TOME PREMIER.

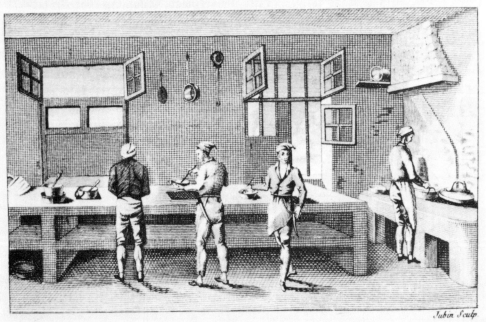

Jabin Sculp.

A PARIS,

CHEZ PILET, IMPRIMEUR-LIBRAIRE, RUE CHRISTINE, N° 5.

IL SE VEND AUSSI

CHEZ { COLNET, LIBRAIRE, QUAI DES PETITS-AUGUSTINS,
{ ET LENOIR, LIBRAIRE, RUE DE RICHELIEU, N° 35.

1814

As for the third branch of gastronomical literature, the one that is created and enriched by amateurs, gourmets, professional critics, and chroniclers of all sorts, it really dates from the beginning of the nineteenth century. As we have seen, amateurs had started to turn their hand to cuisine in the previous century. For the early years of the nineteenth century they do more; they comment, philosophize, and sometimes even compose verses, as does Berchoux in his work entitled *La Gastronomie* (1800), a poem in four cantos, remarkable for its platitude, of which only one verse has come down to posterity, the famous:

> *Qui me délivrera des Grecs et des Romains?*
> (*Who will deliver me from the Greeks and the Romans?*)

La Physiologie du goût is undoubtedly the most successful text written to date by a gastronome, even though Baudelaire was to call this charming book a "false masterpiece," claiming that Brillat-Savarin did not expatiate enough on wine in it. This is true, moreover. But that does not make *La Physiologie du goût* any the less appealing, especially in view of the fact that it is really a historical document, a book written for amateurs by an amateur who does not go into the technical details of cuisine despite the deliberately humorous pedantic titles that he tacks on certain of his chapters.[5] Brillat-Savarin has, in fact, left us a collection of recollections and anecdotes that restores for us the entire atmosphere of lively appreciation of good food at the crossroads of the eighteenth and nineteenth centuries.

Let us also cite *L'Art culinaire*, by the Marquis de Cussy, who is not a writer at all, but whose pages are nonetheless a diverting account of the early years of the Age of Louis XIV. What is interesting about all this outpouring is that witty and often very cultivated people amused themselves by writing about cuisine, that artists and writers such as Rossini and Alexandre Dumas *père* were eager to encourage the art of gastronomy by exalting the figure of

---

[5] The feigned solemnity of style, with a sly wink at the reader, here makes gastronomical criticism a notable branch of the heroicomic genre.

"Session of the jury of gourmet tasters." Frontispiece of L'Almanach des gourmands (The Gourmets' Almanac), *by Grimod de La Reynière, 1804. Engraving by Maradan after Dunant. Bibliothèque nationale, Paris.*

the connoisseur. And let us not forget that Dumas *père* is the author of a *Grand Dictionnaire de cuisine* (published posthumously,
1873) which is chiefly a great *literary* dictionary of cuisine, expressing the dreams of the food-lover rather than the dexterity of
the professional practitioner, the reason for which we have not
classed his work in the category of technical writings, though we
definitely place it in that of texts that should be read. As for Rossini, the method of preparing filet of beef that bears his name
reminds us even today that he was a militant connoisseur. An intimate of the Rothschild household at the time when Carême was
practicing his art there, he had conversations and exchanges of
views with him. Though apparently a simple dish, *tournedos Rossini* has the whole of Grand Cuisine behind it: it is first necessary
to pour over fried croutons a melted meat glaze, already a difficult
basic element to prepare; then place on top of the tournedos a
whole slice of foie gras with truffles, and then make a sauce with
Madeira and a *demi-glace* with essence of truffles. What *restaurateur*, even a relatively honest one, can make this *demi-glace* with
essence of truffles today? The recipe bears the imprint of Carême
from first to last.

The ancestor of all professional "tasters" and gastronomical
writers was unquestionably Alexandre-Balthasar-Laurent Grimod
de La Reynière, Esquire (1758–1838), a barrister before the Paris
Parlement (under the Ancien Régime), a member of the Academy
of the Arcades in Rome, an independent associate of the Museum
of Paris, the editor of the drama section of the *Journal de Neu-
châtel*, and heaven only knows what else. Grimod de La Reynière
was the first modern gourmet and the first organized parasite.
Unlike the spongers in the classical tradition (born in the days of
Greece and Rome and eloquently described from antiquity on),
who exercised their art only at the expense of private individuals,
modern parasites exercise theirs at the expense of society as a
whole. La Reynière contrived not only to satisfy his penchant for
good food with practically no cost to himself, but also to make a
profession of it and earn money from it. He was, in fact, the first
to have the idea of creating a "tasting jury," the ancestor of all the
academies of gastronomes of later days. This jury met either at the
celebrated Rocher de Cancale described by Balzac, where the im-
posing Baleine was the reigning genius, or at La Reynière's own

"Marie-Antoine Carême (1784–1833)." Engraved portrait by Fontaine, frontispiece of L'Art de la cuisine française au XIXe siècle (The Art of French Cuisine in the Nineteenth Century), *volume III, 1835. Bibliothèque des Arts décoratifs, Paris.*

home, where purveyors, caterers, and pastry cooks sent round the products of their shops or of their art. These products then received "legitimations," a sort of certificate of approval or disapproval not unlike those still awarded today by wine-tasters. Grimod de La Reynière was naturally accused of partiality and even of corruption. The "gastronomical press releases" regularly sent him by the *rôtisseurs* and caterers of Paris seem to have inclined the jury and its president toward such indulgence and universal praise that ordinary customers soon disregarded the verdicts handed down. This was unfortunately not the last time that a group of this sort tended to award honors that bore no relationship whatsoever to the experience of the common mortal who paid cash for the product so honored.

Grimod de La Reynière conceived another idea that was to have a rosy future: he was the founder both of gastronomical journalism and of guides that served the same purpose. He was the first to direct the publication of periodical brochures aimed at informing the food-loving general public, exciting it, and distracting it. They were put out under the title *L'Almanach des gourmands* (*The Gourmets' Almanac*), of which eight issues saw the light of day from 1803 to 1812. In addition to various anecdotes and bits of advice that readers of the time apparently found sparklingly witty, though today any given page of it does not seem worth a single phrase of Brillat-Savarin's, Grimod de La Reynière provided in his *Almanach* a "nutritive itinerary," in which he passed in review the *restaurateurs* and the food establishments of the capital, handing out both bad grades and compliments. Since this critical itinerary was revised each year, it was in this era that purveyors and chefs learned to live in the state of anguish that in our day descends upon the French restaurant industry in the weeks that precede the appearance of the Guide Michelin[6] each year. But as I have said, the probity of the editor-author of the *Almanach* was questioned by *officiers de bouche* who could not hold up under the alternate praise and censure doled out by Grimod (depending on how promptly the products to be "legitimated" were delivered to him, according to his detractors), and the *Almanach des gourmands* was to cease to appear following an unpleasant lawsuit.

---

[6] And its rivals. Often they are superior to the Michelin, but as they are not as old they are not as influential.

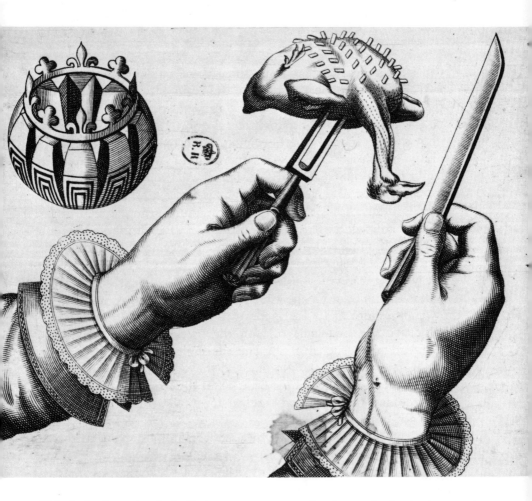

"Method of carving larks." Anonymous engraving from the beginning of the nineteenth century. Bibliothèque nationale, Paris.

It has often been said of Grimod de La Reynière that he contributed more than any other gastronome to the flowering of cuisine that was *understood*. He was called "the Corneille of French gastronomy." It may well be that he was an animating spirit, that he created the climate in which "transcendent" cuisine could become the object of the sort of maniacal attention and exaggerated praise that it needs in order to believe in itself and make others believe in it, that is to say, to exist. But—it is Carême who writes the words—"La Reynière had nothing to do with the rapid progress

that modern cuisine has made since the renaissance of the art."
Like all gastronomical critics, his function was to stimulate the
public's imagination, to invent a culinary rhetoric, thus creating in
people's minds that gustatory anticipation that transforms each
dish: a mere food in the beginning, it becomes a discourse on a
plate, a condition failing which the army of prodigal gastronomes
could not be mobilized. In his *Manuel des amphytrions* (*Manual
for Hosts*), La Reynière lays down, as the rule, the new style of
serving meals that is the one we know, thus putting an end to the
old style of successive buffets consisting of several dishes placed on
the table simultaneously. "The method of serving dish by dish," he
writes, "is the refinement of the art of living well. It is the way to
eat hot, long, and copiously, since each dish is then a single center
that is the focus of all appetites."

Another idea of La Reynière's was to make absolute silence and
discretion the inviolable rule on the part of the personnel, the
maître d'hôtel, and even the chef during sessions of the jury at
the Rocher de Cancale. No one had the right to enter the dining
room unless summoned by a little handbell, except of course when
the cooking of a dish had reached the point where it had to be
brought in immediately.

Lastly, Grimod de La Reynière left behind an aphorism that is
fairly profound and that many people will recognize as hitting
home: "Cheese is the biscuit of drunkards." Since it was the custom in that era to dip one's biscuit in one's wine for dessert,
drunkards, who have little taste for sweet things, were in the habit
of eating their cheese with their red wine. Hence the association
of cheese with red wine, though many cheeses are in fact better
with white wine.

This professional gourmandise comes into existence in the same
period that the figure of the modern chef emerges from protohis-
toric times. At once a creator and an arbiter, an Apollo Musagetes
and a thundering Jupiter, an inspired magus and a capricious star,
he was a little later to have no equivalent save the equally impossible figure of the great couturier.

Despite the fine collection of megalomaniacal chefs with which
our era has blessed us, it is hard for us today to realize the sort of
aura that surrounded Marie-Antoine Carême in his own lifetime.
(The surname Antonin is one he invented for himself.) It is

doubtful whether any other chef, either before him or after him, has ever enjoyed such prestige. Even today the memory of Carême among chefs remains that of a brilliant star, an unparalleled comet. In the eyes of all witnesses, and the witnesses of the witnesses, to guests and the friends of guests, to disciples and the successors of disciples, Carême possessed an indefinable elegance, charm, dissatisfaction, inner tension, secretiveness, pride, creative élan, and capacity for hard work—that certain something that is more than "class," that all those who saw him did not hesitate to recognize as genius. The word was used to describe him from the very moment that he first appeared on the scene, and invariably the emperors and kings who employed him—and found it a difficult experience, for he was very sensitive—felt him to be not only the superior practitioner, but also the man for whom a profession is not simply a profession, and for whom art is not an end in itself but a means of being oneself.

On several occasions, Carême was offered the most lucrative and flattering positions: head chef in the kitchens of George IV in London; of those of Tsar Alexandre I in Saint Petersburg, whose table he had directed in Paris in 1815; in the households of slightly lesser personages, in England, in France, in Austria. He almost always refused either to enter anyone's employ or to remain in it, though never for financial reasons—he was as highly paid as anyone could be—but rather because he judged the conditions in which he was asked to exercise his talent to be unfavorable, either by reason of the psychological climate or the lack of training of the collaborators put at his disposal, or out of a fear that those who would be at table would not be proper connoisseurs. Curiously enough, the greatest chef of the era that ushered in the golden age of restaurants is the exception that proves the rule: he practiced his art only in the households of private individuals.

The one in which he felt most at ease, and met with the greatest understanding, based at once on respect and the absence of unseemly familiarities, the one in which he remained the longest and spent the last years of his active life was the château of Boulogne, belonging to the Baron and Baronne de Rothschild, frequented by Rossini and the scene of the dinner party so well described by Lady Morgan, whose account of it we cited at the end of the preceding chapter.

One detail should be added to her account. At the end of this
open-air dinner, Carême came to take coffee in the garden, and as
she conversed with him Lady Morgan was struck by his good
manners and his cultivation. This is astonishing, for Carême had
been born at the end of the Ancien Régime into a very poor family which had brought into the world no fewer than twenty-five
children (the number of those who lived after birth is not
specified). Carême was twelve years old when his father, after
having offered him a good meal in an eating house in the *barrière*
(the equivalent of today's bistro in an outlying district), announced to him as he paid the bill that these were the last sous that
he would be spending on him. This *paterfamilias* thereupon took
his leave, abandoning his son in the street after having urged him
repeatedly to take advantage of a social universe that offered to an
enterprising soul far more possibilities than he himself could guar-
antee him.

If Carême's story had taken place in the Middle Ages, no one
would believe it. But since it is relatively close to our own time
and since the documents that relate it are irreproachable, we must
accept as true what would otherwise pass for a fable: this little
twelve-year-old boy abandoned in the street finds (should we say
by chance?) a job in a cheap restaurant as kitchen boy and becomes the greatest chef of his time and perhaps the most original
one of all time.

His most striking trait was how rapidly he learned things. This
rapidity may well be the distinguishing trait of genius. And it is
perhaps given only to those who learn *in order to transform*, who
transform what they learn in the process of learning it. The comparison of Carême with Raphael is not my doing: it is common
currency, and this was so even in his own time. At the age of
twenty his habits of thought had already reached full maturity.

Like all creators, he was a stealer of ideas—a stealer, I emphasize,
not a plagiarist. He was passionately attached to all the masters
who had something to say to him, Avice for pastry, Laguipière for
sauces—it is only the weak who are afraid of being influenced,
Goethe said—but none of their conceptions was ever followed by
him down to the last detail, and he always rendered them affec-
tionate and generous homage. His prosopopoeia of Laguipière, the

sauce chef par excellence, is superior to the one of Fabricius penned by Rousseau.

For he astonished us for another reason, one that would tax our credulity if the texts were not there before us: Carême the plebeian, who was probably illiterate when his father did him the favor of abandoning him, was a writer. Had he not been as prolific as Chateaubriand (in fact, he and Chateaubriand are the two most prolific writers of the First Empire), had he written only one book, here again no one would believe that he was the author of it. It would be necessary to invent a bookseller's "plot" to explain it, with a ghost writer as the key figure. The ideas, the recipes, it would be said, were perhaps Carême's, but the style betrays a former pupil of the Jesuit fathers, a reader of Plutarch, an admirer of Mirabeau and of Bernardin de Saint-Pierre.

But unfortunately—or fortunately—Carême's works are so compact and so personal, the style so profoundly imprinted with the defects and the qualities of the era—a purity of language side by side with high-flown rhetoric—that science can prove that an attribution of them to anyone else save their signer is a false one. It thus must be accepted as fact that between the ages of twelve and twenty, Carême not only assimilated and reformed the gastronomy of the Western world but at the same time passed from illiteracy to literary mastery.

He felt the need to write, and wrote down everything that he cooked. After coming back from the market in the morning, he would write or rewrite the menus, the recipes that he would be supervising or executing in the course of the day. When the Baron de Rothschild, on acquiring the château of Ferrières, proposed that Carême consider retiring there in ten years' time, the latter declined this tactful offer; he wanted, he said, to finish his literary *oeuvre* in the solitude of a little place in Paris.

"I also told him,"[7] Carême writes, "that my books had created an income for me that far exceeded my needs. I will increase this income, for I have not yet finished my task; I have still a book to publish on the entire state of my profession in our era."

And a short time before this, after the King of England had

---

[7] The Baron de Rothschild.

tried to persuade him to come back to London, Carême wrote: "I refused with regret and gratitude. My one thought now is to profit from the days that Heaven may still allot me to finish the books that exist in my mind. These have been my lifelong thought."

These books are indeed numerous and voluminous. We see here *Le Pâtissier royal parisien* (*The Royal Parisian Pastry Cook*), in two octavo volumes, illustrated with forty-one plates by the author, for Antonin Carême also knew how to draw! And here is *Le Pâtissier pittoresque* (*The Artistic Pastry Chef*), an octavo volume illustrated with 128 plates, again by the author; there follow *Le Maître d'hôtel français* (*The French Maître d'Hôtel*), a comparison of old- and new-style cuisine from the point of view of the menus to be served according to the four seasons in Paris, Saint Petersburg, London, and Vienna, two octavo volumes; *Le Cuisinier parisien* (*The Parisian Chef*), one volume; and finally his monumental work, the one he alludes to in his conversations with the King of England and the Baron de Rothschild, *L'Art de la cuisine française au XIXe siècle* (*The Art of French Cuisine in the Nineteenth Century*), in five octavo volumes, only three of which were finished in his lifetime; volumes four and five, put into fair-copy form by his disciple Plumerey, were published after his death.

And these are only the works of Carême's devoted to pastry, to supervising the table, to the art of the maître d'hôtel, and to cuisine. For Carême was passionately interested not only in architecture in spun sugar but also in real architecture. He is the author of a work entitled *Recueil d'architecture* (*An Anthology of Architecture*) and another entitled *Projets d'architecture* (*Architectural Projects*), this latter consisting mainly of plans for buildings for Saint Petersburg. Tsar Alexandre permitted the book to be dedicated to him, and as a token of gratitude to the author he offered Carême a magnificent ring studded with diamonds.

From time immemorial, of course, the role of head chef had been held in high regard, as can be explained by the complexity of the task of knowing not only how to prepare food but also how to organize a kitchen. Even today we cannot help being astonished when we see the head chef of a great restaurant taking note of the orders called to him through the window by the maîtres d'hôtel, cooking the meals for twenty or thirty tables simultaneously and keeping in mind the preparation time and the probable moment that each of the dishes ordered will be consumed, in addition to which each guest at each table will almost always have ordered something different from what the friends with whom he is dining have. Hence, the chef must keep track of sixty or eighty different menus in his head and prepare them within the limits determined on the one hand by the speed of mastication of the customers and on the other by the preparation time required by his art. It is therefore understandable why these various abilities, which go far beyond the minor talent necessary to cook a nice little dish for one's family or friends, have always inspired in those who were witness to them the sort of admiration inspired by an orchestra conductor or a surgeon. In the fifteenth century, at the court of the dukes of Burgundy, La Marche, the author of the well-known chronicle of life in Dijon, reported that in the huge kitchen of the ducal palace, with seven gigantic fireplaces, the cook sat on a raised seat from which he could survey the army of kitchen boys, scullions, roast cooks, soup cooks, and so on, holding in his hand a big wooden spoon for tasting the soups and sauces as they passed by. On great occasions, the cook himself came to serve the duke, torch in hand. This was the case when the first fresh herring arrived or the first truffle of the season was served.

"Why," La Marche wonders, "is it the cook who is present at his master's repast and not the kitchen equerry? What is the procedure for naming a head cook? Who must replace him when he is absent—the roast cook or the soup cook?" He then answers: "When the office of master cook is vacant at the court of the prince, the maîtres d'hôtel call in the kitchen equerries and all those who serve in the kitchen, one by one; and it is by their solemn vote, attested to under oath, that the head cook is named." As to which cook replaces him, the answer is: "Neither; the one who replaces him will be chosen by vote." It will be noted that self-management and election of the director by the workers thus existed at the court of the dukes of Burgundy, at least in the kitchens.

Carême has left us a description of a kitchen at the crucial moment. "Let the reader imagine that he is in a great kitchen such as that of Foreign Relations on the occasion of a great dinner [i.e., the kitchen at Prince Talleyrand's, one of the households through which Carême passed], watching some twenty cooks at their various pressing occupations, going and coming, acting quickly in this stifling abyss. Look at the *voie* [a cubic meter] of coal set ablaze on straw pallets for the cooking of the entrées, then another *voie* on the stoves for the soups, the sauces, the stews, the fried foods, and the double boiler. Add to that a quarter of a *voie* of blazing wood in front of which four spits are turning, one with a piece of sirloin weighing from forty-five to sixty pounds, the other a quarter of veal weighing from thirty-five to forty-five pounds, the two others for poultry and game. In this brazier everyone acts promptly; not a whisper is to be heard; the chef alone has the right to be heard, and when he speaks everyone obeys. Finally, to cap all our sufferings, for about half an hour the doors and casement windows are shut so that drafts will not make the food cold. And this is how we spend the finest days of our lives. But honor commands," Carême adds. "One must obey, even when one's physical strength fails. It is coal that is killing us, though."

The coal-burning stove, made of cast iron, had indeed replaced the "soup stove" of the eighteenth century. But as a result of bad ventilation—which is still faulty in certain badly installed kitchens in our day—cooks began to breathe in an abnormal quantity of carbon monoxide. Later, the famous chef Soyer did a great deal to further cooking with gas in London, though of course people were suspicious of it at first, as always happens with any change of equipment or fuel in the kitchen, for such changes are always suspected of changing the flavor of food for the worse.

But Carême lived at the height of the coal-burning era and died before he was fifty, burned out, as Laurent Tailhade has put it, "by the flame of his genius and the coal of the spits."

Let us review Antonin Carême's biography and career chronologically, and then we shall quote a few of his recipes that best reflect his style. He was born in Paris on June 8, 1784, and died, also in Paris, on January 12, 1833. After having vegetated for some time as a cook's helper, he had the good fortune to enter the service of Bailly, the celebrated *pâtissier* in the rue Vivienne, one of whose customers was Talleyrand. In the course of his training there, young Carême adopted the habit of working, during his rare moments of leisure, at the Cabinet des Estampes, the national print museum, copying motifs that could be used in *pièces montées*

made of pastry. He then worked in Talleyrand's kitchens, under
the orders of Boucher, the head chef of the Prince of Benevento.[8]
During the Empire he also worked under the celebrated sauce
chef Laguipière, who later met his death during Napoleon's retreat
from Russia; Carême's *Le Cuisinier parisien* is dedicated to Laguipière's memory. "It was above all in this period of my life that I
devoted myself to serious studies," Carême writes in his memoirs
. . . "I had the excellent habit of noting down each evening, on
returning to my quarters, the modifications that I had made in my
work, where each day brought a number of changes. Pen in hand,
I consigned to paper the reasons that had determined my decisions.
This sort of intimate account will always be a cause of progress."

Carême personally executed 196 sorts of French soup and 103
foreign ones, the Marquis de Cussy informs us. In the realm of
pastry his influence was such that even he, modest as he was, could
write: "When in order to forget envious men I cause my eye to
wander in Paris, I note with joy the increase in the number of pastry shops and the improvement in them. Nothing of all that
existed before my labors and my books. As I predicted, pastry-
makers have become very skillful and very meticulous." While
still in his youth, Carême invented *gros nougats, grosses me-
ringues, croquantes, poupelins,* and *solilemmes,* or at least perfected them, for according to him pastry-making had reached its
apogee at the time of the treaty of Utrecht[9] and it was only its
presentation that he felt the need to renew. Let us add that he
brought puff pastry to its supreme degree of refinement; he had
begun his career as a *tourte*-maker at Bailly's.

Another of the domains in which he manifested his genius was
that of cold entrées, above all meatless ones, his name seemingly
having predestined him to do so.[10] "It is in Lenten cuisine that the
skill of the cook can make a splendid show; it was at the Élysée
Impérial and through the examples of the famous Laguipière and
Robert that I was initiated into the work of this refined branch
. . . For two years Laguipière and I redid this great *meatless*
cuisine; we gave the Church back fine meatless cooking." Is it

---

[8] The title awarded Talleyrand by Napoleon I.
[9] 1715.
[10] *Carême* means "Lent" in French. (*Translator's note*)

not legitimate on our part to write that Carême is a real Cha-teaubriand of cuisine, the author of a gastronomical *Genius of Christianity?*

Carême was likewise the inventor of "cold" cuisine, that new art that before him had been rudimentary but was now transformed, the object of which was to preserve all the flavor of dishes already cooked. This art, which seems so natural to us today, is in fact a very recent one. On the occasion of the marriage of Prince Jérôme and the Princess of Württemberg, Carême and Riquette (one of the chefs of the time in whom our man recognized an equal) were put in charge of the cold dishes: galantines, head cheese, jellied veal loin, jellied beef, aspics of rooster crests and kidneys, salmis of young red partridge chaud-froid, cold salmon steaks, galantine of eel in Montpellier butter, borders of tender green ravigote sauce, of jellied truffles—all inventions, innovations.

Montpellier butter, today unjustly forgotten, must be made as follows according to Carême's recipe: "Wash well in cool water a large handful of chervil, about 20 sprigs of tarragon, and the same amount of *pimprenelle*,[11] plus a pinch of chives. These herbs having been drained, blanch them in boiling water with salt so as to preserve their bright green color; put them in a large saucepan and after boiling 5 or 6 minutes remove this ravigote with a skimmer and set it to cool in cold water. Put 8 eggs on to boil in the water in which the ravigote has been blanched, then press it in order to extract the water from it. Grind it thoroughly in a mortar; add to it 20 fine anchovies, skinned and well washed, 2 dessert-spoonfuls of fine capers, 6 pickles, the yolks of the hard-boiled eggs, and a small clove of garlic. Grind this mixture in a mortar for a good 10 minutes; mix in 8 ounces of fine butter, a pinch of pepper, some fine salt. Incorporate into it a glassful of good Aix olive oil and a quarter of a glassful of tarragon vinegar: this should give you a soft, velvety butter with an exquisite taste.

"To make it more appetizing still, mix in a little essence of the green of spinach in order to color it a nice pistachio green. One must be careful to mix only a little of this green in at a time, so that the butter is a pale green. Taste for seasoning; then put it through a fine sieve, crushing it with a wooden spoon; after that

---

11 *Poterium sanguisorba;* in English, salad burnet; in Italian, *pimpinella.*

put it in a little terrine on ice to make it firm and use immediately.

"The seasoning of this delicious butter requires knowledge that only practice can provide; for it is necessary to have an exquisite sense of taste to make it perfectly, so that none of these seasonings composing it dominates the others. It is easy, however, to tone down an excess of vinegar by adding a little oil, and to remedy the insipid taste of the oil by mixing in vinegar and salt."

In 1814 and 1815, Carême directed, as we have already mentioned, the table of Tsar Alexandre in Paris, and later this same table during the Congress of Aix-la-Chapelle. His manner so pleased the Tsar that he tried to hire him permanently and bring him to Saint Petersburg. Again it was literature that kept Carême from accepting. "I could not make up my mind to leave the research and the writing that I had begun in Paris," he writes.

He nonetheless accepted employment, with Lord Stewart, the English ambassador in Vienna, and then he decided to go to Saint Petersburg, by boat from Honfleur. He had barely arrived in the imperial capital when he decided to return to the West, for he had realized that the position of chef to the Tsar, in a country where corruption and petty theft were traditional, "was debased, as a consequence of abuses, by a humiliating surveillance. A vain effort was made to get me to stay; my colleagues could not understand how I could leave Saint Petersburg without profiting from the offers that were made me." The colleagues he refers to were his old friend Riquette, Benoist, and Talon, who at the time reigned over the best tables in Saint Petersburg. On his return to the West, Carême entered first the service of the Princesse Bagration, then that of George IV in London, where he could not get used to the climate, and finally that of the Baron and Baronne de Rothschild, as we have said. What is more, we have omitted the countless temporary though flattering positions he held at various times and have said nothing of the fact that during a very great part of his career, Carême spent most of his time organizing special occasions. He was often entrusted, for example, with the preparations for a great official banquet, of the sort known then as *extraordinaires*, to which he might easily devote several months.

At the end of the year 1832, he began to feel the first pains of the illness that was to be the death of him: "They are pains in the right side, which are often unbearable after a taxing service. I fell;

"Six set pieces and two braised hams (designed by the author)." Plates from two works by Carême: Le Pâtissier royal parisien (The Royal Parisian Pastry Cook), *1854, and* L'Art de la cuisine française au XIXe siècle (The Art of French Cuisine in the Nineteenth Century), *volume III, 1835. Bibliothèque des Arts décoratifs, Paris.*

I am staying in bed; my strength is draining away. One of my old friends, Monsieur Magonty, is taking my place. The good family of Monsieur le Baron can see that it was on account of my health that I told him that I would abandon my work forthwith . . ."

He did, in fact, do so, as we have said, on January 12, 1833, having spent the last two days of his life dictating the final recipes of his career to his daughter on his deathbed.

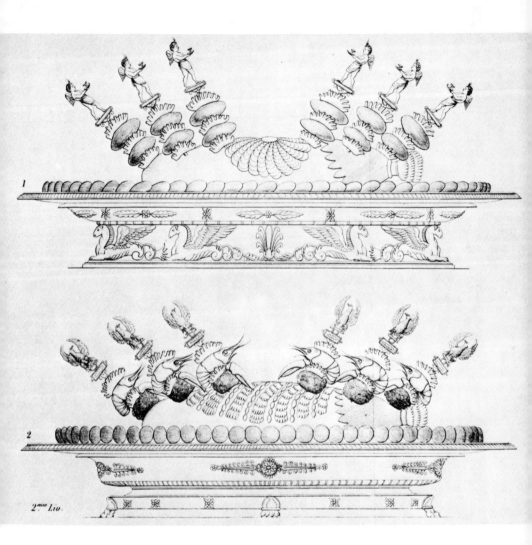

Carême's cuisine always has several stages. It is only rarely that the first food or ingredient mentioned determines the appearance of the final dish. Every recipe requires the use of the strainer, of silk, of the sieve to put ingredients through, to extract, to concentrate, to reduce. Any and every dish, moreover, depends on the prior preparation of other products of the chef's art: purées, essences, quintessences, the composition of which is presumed to have already been mastered and is often described as something exquisite, and at the same time as readily available as a bit of celery

or a minced onion. Hence, Carême's cuisine is not a cuisine for
amateurs. Half the terms he employs are addressed to professional
chefs who have a kitchen staff at their disposal. With Carême
transcendent cuisine becomes more than chemistry: it is an alge-
bra.

Like classic art, the result of Carême's art is always very simple
and immediately obvious. What is complicated is the process for
arriving at this result, a process whose aim is not to superimpose
flavors but, quite the contrary, to isolate them and set them in re-
lief. Grand Cuisine with him is not what it is too often presumed
to be, and what in fact it is in the myriad caricatures of it that pop
up everywhere: a barbarous accumulation of heterogeneous products put together in haphazard proportions. It is, rather, one dominant note that the final preparation preserves. Carême introduced
into cuisine what in painting are called "values"; that is to say, he
was the first to put across the fact that flavors and odors must be
judged not in the absolute but according to their mutual rela-
tionships.

～

Before concluding this chapter, I shall now give a "sampler" of
a few of Carême's recipes that are particularly representative of
his style but, at the same time, chosen from among his simplest
creations:

"Lady Morgan English fish soup: Having removed the filets
from an average-sized brill, a sole, and a small eel, cut the bones
and the trimmings of the filets into pieces and put them in a
medium-sized pan, adding a bottle of champagne, the pulp of a
lemon, the parings of a pound of truffles, 2 onions, a carrot, a
stalk of celery, and 2 leeks, the whole finely chopped, and then
half a bay leaf, a small pinch of grated nutmeg and cayenne
pepper, 2 cloves, 2 well-rinsed anchovies, and a little salt; simmer
this seasoning for an hour, put it through a silk sieve, and then
pour it into a good veal stock.

"Sauté the filets of brill, sole, and eel now; then shape them into little scallops. Make a quenelle forcemeat with a large whiting, mixing into it a crayfish butter to replace the fine butter you ordinarily put into it; make little quenelles of this mixture, forming them in coffee spoons and poaching them in consommé; then cut the prepared truffles (cooked in consommé) with a root slicer measuring an inch in diameter, and after that cut them into scallops 2 lines thick. When it is time to serve, drain the quenelles and place them in the soup tureen with the scallops of fish which you drain on a napkin, along with the truffles and 20 mushrooms blanched a pure white, 24 oysters, a like number of shrimp tails and the tails of the crayfish that have been used to make the butter for the quenelle mixture.

"You must clarify the broth of the soup by mixing with it the trimmings of the fish filets and the liquid they have been cooked in, as well as the consommé of quenelles, truffles, and oyster meat. At the moment of serving, you pour it boiling-hot into the soup tureen, which has been garnished as we have described above.

"This splendid, tasty soup suits the taste of those who appreciate culinary science. I served it for the first time at Boulogne, near Paris, in the household of Monsieur le Baron de Rothschild, the very day that I had the honor of being presented to the celebrated Lady Morgan."

"*Champagne sauce:* After having dressed 2 average-sized soles, cut them in scallops and put them in a stewpot with half a bottle of champagne, 2 baskets of mushrooms, 2 onions, some diced carrots, 2 shallots, a small garlic clove, a seasoned bouquet, a little mignonnette, and some mace. Simmer and reduce over a slow fire for 30 to 40 minutes; then press this essence through a sieve; add to it 2 large soup-spoonfuls of *sauce allemande* and 4 baskets of lightly simmered mushrooms and their stock; reduce in the usual manner; add a glass of champagne, and when the sauce is properly reduced, pour it into a double boiler.

"At the moment of serving, mix in a little glaze and Isigny butter.

"This sauce suits turbot, fresh cod, sole, and in general fish cooked in salted water or grilled.

"I served this sauce for the first time in 1815, at the Élysée Bourbon."

LE DESSERT.

LE GARDE-MANGER, U FROID.

LE GLACIER.

LA ROTISSERIE.

PRECEDING PAGES:
"The kitchens of Les Tuileries in 1866. The dessert kitchen, the ice cream and sherbet kitchen, the pantry, the rôtisserie." Lithograph after sketches by M. Moullin. Bibliothèque nationale, Paris.

"*Quarter of salt-meadow lamb gastronome:* After having dressed it as for the spit, garnish it with lardons of breast, tongue *à l'écarlate,* and truffles prepared *idem;* season them with pepper, grated nutmeg, and a little salt; trim off the ends of the lardons that extend beyond the meat; then truss the quarter of salt-meadow lamb and braise it, adding the truffle trimmings and a few thin slices of lean ham; baste and turn it in its cooking liquid, making sure that it simmers for 3 hours, after which you untruss it, glaze it in the usual manner, place it on a bed of minced truffles *à la périgueux,* and serve it."

"*Potato croquettes:* Cook 2 platefuls of potatoes with a little white consommé, a little butter, salt, pepper, grated nutmeg, and a pinch of granulated sugar so as to tone down the slight acridness that this leguminous plant has. Simmer them with a fire above and below, being careful to add very little liquid. When they are done, mash them in the pan, put them through a horsehair sieve, and then crush them in a mortar along with 2 egg yolks and a little very thick cream. When this mixture is cold, form little balls of it of the size and shape of a plover's egg; roll them in very fine bread crumbs, after which you soak them in 4 eggs beaten into an omelette, drain them with a fork, and roll them straightway in bread crumbs into which you have mixed a little grated Parmesan cheese. Shape them nicely and at the moment of serving put them on a false brass bottom, which must have the same shape as the frying pan, containing frying oil heated to the proper temperature; put the croquettes in it and take them out when they have taken on a fine light-yellow color; drain them on a napkin and arrange them on a plate.

"One can also prepare this same mixture with potatoes baked in ashes, using only the heart of them, except that in this case you must add a bit more cream; the remainder of the procedure is the same."

❦

The only changes that the conceptions so brilliantly perfected by Carême underwent during the nineteenth century had to do with his complicated decorations. The time spent in making *pièces montées* was cut down. Décor became simpler: bases of dishes carved out of solid lard, platters trimmed with noddle dough, cleverly decorated dishes, "tiers" made of fine white bread disappeared. This aspect of Carême's preoccupations is perhaps the only facet of his genius that seems a bit archaic to us today. But the basic principles of cuisine, interpreted, translated into a more accessible language, were not to undergo any important change for some time, despite what people have claimed.

Following in Carême's footsteps, several masters of international cuisine were to invent new dishes, to create a recognizable personal style, but they did not change the basic principles of cuisine. No master after Carême, however, had a purity, an unselfishness as great as his, and none was consumed to the same degree by the passion for surpassing himself. A number of them yielded to the temptation to commercialize their glory, to industrialize their talent, to take in the naïve amateur, to orchestrate their publicity, to enrich themselves at the expense of their art rather than enrich that art itself. It remains to be seen whether Carême's cuisine was not a beautiful madness, a cuisine almost impossible to execute outside of a context in which the probity and genius of the cook and the affluence and enlightened taste of the diner made possible the man who has rightly been called "the king of chefs and the chef of kings."

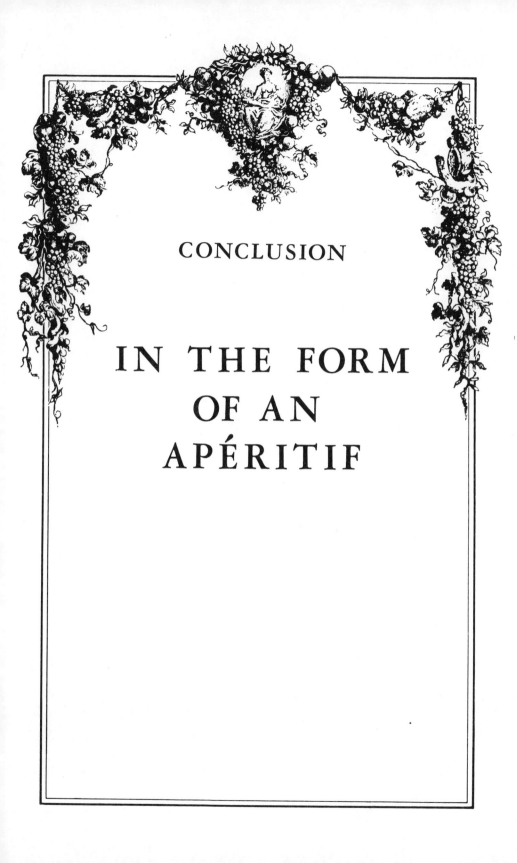

CONCLUSION

IN THE FORM
OF AN
APÉRITIF

N ow that we have arrived at the middle of the nineteenth century, there is no further reason to continue this attempt to resurrect the lost gastronomical *atmosphère* of times past, for from this date onward we are at home with texts, tastes, customs. Cuisine in every country has, of course, evolved in the last century and a half; so too have natural products changed (more than anything else, perhaps), and likewise the tastes and demands of consumers several times. Each and every detail of a recipe that is a hundred years old or from a place a thousand kilometers away from his birthplace may not always be clear to today's reader, for terms in cuisine shift meaning. But as far as essentials are concerned, after 1850 we find ourselves already in the world that is still ours. Hence the curiosity that has guided me in this book has no further object. What I wanted to know was what was hidden behind the words; when I read the account of a repast at the court of the dukes of Burgundy or in a thatched cottage described by Rousseau, I wanted to know *Wie es eigentlich gewesen ist:* how was it really? As it draws closer to us, the curtain of time past becomes more and more transparent until eventually it disappears and the spectacle is understood without any need for keys or translations. My mission is thus finished, if not accomplished. For as I have already said in the Prologue, and repeat here, I had neither the ambition nor the pretention of being exhaustive, of covering all times and all countries. I have tried to put together not an encyclopedia but an anthology. Encyclopedias exist, but they do not bring the sensation of things past back to life. I have tried to bring back to the surface a few examples of this sensation.

I have, nonetheless, also tried to draw useful lessons for us from what people in other times have felt. That is the object of this conclusion. For even though I have no reason to enter into a detailed discussion of the century that we are living in, since my primary goal was the search for the past, I can still isolate its principal traits. I realize, in fact, that in cuisine, as elsewhere, the past can serve to make the present understandable, and I also realize that in many respects if not in all, the present, unbeknown to those who live it, is frequently the repetition of the past.

Since the middle of the nineteenth century, erudite or professional cuisine, soon followed and imitated from afar by private cuisine insofar as the resources of the household permitted, has gone through phases and obeyed tendencies that can be reduced to a few fundamental cases.

Two phases are:

1) the phase of complication of preparation and increasing heaviness, accompanied by effects of sheer mass and accumulation where quantities are concerned. Decorative, deceptive presentations;

2) the phase of simplification of preparation and increasing lightness, and the reduction of quantities. Plain, straightforward, "honest" presentations.

Alongside these two phases, two tendencies may be distinguished: the tendency toward internationalization of cuisine and the tendency toward a return to regional cuisines.

To these two phases and two tendencies, two accents are added:

1) the accent upon seasonings, spices, very definite flavors, strong tastes, penetrating aromas that carry the odor of the dish to the far corners of the room;

2) the accent on the natural food, its freshness, its authenticity. Hence, mixtures in which natural flavors and odors cancel each other out are banished, as are added spices (beginning with salt), which destroy them by brutally overwhelming them. Subtle, imperceptible, or nonexistent aromas.

And finally we find again, since the middle and even the beginning of the nineteenth century, the conflict between two values: the valuing of tradition and the valuing of invention.

It is amusing to follow the alternation of these two factors through successive generations of gastronomical guides and even the names of restaurants, emphasizing as they do the qualities that their owners pride themselves on possessing or those that they are said to possess. When "tradition" is the predominant value, every owner boasts of cooking "as in the good old days," and baptizes his establishment The Real Burgundy or Grandmother's Kitchen or L'Antico Fattore (The Old Farmer's). When, on the contrary, it is invention that is the predominant value, gastronomical critics have kind words to say only about the *creations* of cooks, personal originality, and "specialties" that appear in no cookbook.

Of the eight characteristics that determine the evolution of cuisine that I have just mentioned, certain of them are very obviously antithetical and naturally mutually exclusive, whereas others, as is immediately evident, can well go hand in hand and reinforce each other. This is what recent history, prolonging past history, demonstrates.

The battle between complication and simplicity, between heaviness and lightness, between an emphasis on everything that *surrounds* a particular food (sauces, spices, garnishes) and a respect for the natural truth of the food itself, is in fact a constant one, as is the alternation throughout the history of cuisine of the two phases that I have outlined. The battle and the alternation between the cuisine of creation and the cuisine of tradition, linked to a region and its soil, are also eternal. In the first chapter of this book we have seen how the art historian C. F. von Rumohr, writing behind the mask of his chef, Joseph König, crosses swords with Apicius, the author of the principal work on Roman cuisine, across a distance of fifteen hundred years. In his *Geist des Kochkunst* (1822), Rumohr attacks Apicius as the propagator of what he stigmatizes as "destructive cuisine." Why destructive? Because it reduces everything to stews, jellies, forcemeats, pâtés, and purées and drowns everything in heavy complicated sauces and, finally, mercilessly assaults natural foods, grinding them down, mixing them, and seasoning them until they are unrecognizable, either to the eye or to the palate. The German historian distinguishes in cuisine the same three styles as in his works on painting: the severe style, the agreeable style, and the hypocritical style. He, for his part, favors the agreeable style as opposed to the hypocritical style (that of Apicius). It is striking to realize that this polemic by the German writer might just as well have been unleashed against his contemporary Carême, or, more precisely, against Carême's dull-witted followers, and to see that the advocates of the "New French Cuisine" of the years since 1965 have unwittingly used the same arguments in favor of a return to the truth of natural foods. Cuisine, according to this school, must follow and prolong nature, reap the benefit of it rather than combat it. But the school of "New French Cuisine" has very rapidly fallen, in its turn, into a new academicism, wherein the cult of "lightness" and "invention" has driven a host of imitators in the direction of a cuisine that is at once extravagant and dull, giving rise to a uniform international style that is still more forbidding than the old "hotel cuisine." This school, moreover, has very soon come to violate its own principles, spreading as it does the use of raw salmon, foie gras, caviar, truffles, and crayfish everywhere, and thus calling for ingredients that are exceptional, rare, or impossible to come by in the countries in which they are consumed (crayfish, for instance, are now practically nonexistent in France) so as to give personality to dishes that no longer had any of their own. It is amusing to see the liege lords of "New French Cuisine" haughtily excommunicate *tournedos Rossini*, a nineteenth-century recipe consisting of preparing a filet of beef with foie gras and truffles, as being a dish that is too artificially complicated, when these same liege lords call for foie gras and truffles everywhere and, at that, use them indiscriminately instead of organically incorporating them within a coherent preparation that has the continuity and the transitions of a truly erudite cuisine.

In reality, this New French Cuisine illustrates several aspects of the classic cases enumerated earlier. It claims to be a struggle of invention against tradition and of lightness against heaviness. But in fact it is merely reacting against another erudite cuisine, another "invention," another academicism, rather than against true tradition, which is rooted in the soil. To praise invention exclusively is to force the majority of chefs, incapable one and all of inventing, in the direction of neglecting traditions. Hence, on the one hand, they abandon all tradition and, on the other, they do not really create anything. Can anyone imagine what would become of Chinese cuisine if all Chinese cooks found themselves obliged to serve nothing but original creations? When a cuisine is based on centuries of experiments, of skill, of little accumulated knacks and secrets, it is madness to demand that every practitioner of the art start over from zero. Such practitioners forget tradition, which thus is lost, and, with half a dozen exceptions that turn up in every generation, they create nothing but hollow words on a menu. As for "lightness," if it can be attained only by association with tastelessness, what merit does it have?

We have met this reaction against a cuisine overloaded with spices, fats, and sauces many times, however, in the preceding pages. Medieval cuisine was one in which the strength of spices, sugars, and acids and their mixture overwhelmed other tastes, and the "gastronomical revolution" of the seventeenth and eighteenth centuries was first of all a search for delicate flavors to replace this heavy artillery of the Middle Ages, though in the nineteenth century it engendered in its turn excesses similar to those it had eliminated.

Another characteristic of cuisine in the last hundred years, but above all since the middle of the nineteenth century, has been its internationalization or, rather, its spread throughout the world, its universalization. "International cuisine" has become a pejorative term. The expression means, in fact, that we find everywhere the same cuisine, in general a cuisine of French origin that has become conventional and dull. "Universalization" is just as ugly a word but it means exactly the contrary: namely, the fact that one finds more and more frequently, in numerous countries, the most diverse and even the most local national cuisines, very far from their geographical origins. This sudden multiplication of cuisines has been due to several causes: first of all, the forced migrations that in our time of persecution, wars, and crises have led entire peoples to bring their culinary customs with them to their countries of adoption and open restaurants and food shops; second, the prodigious development of tourism and the discovery on the spot, by countless travelers, of certain "typical" dishes or even the entire palette of a foreign cuisine; and finally, the desire to remedy either the poverty of one's own national cuisine or the tastelessness of international *"haute cuisine"* by importing foreign dishes with a distinctive flavor that in most cases are dishes of popular and regional origin, the food of peasants and seafarers. This is true of Neapolitan pizza, lasagna alla bolognese, bouillabaisse, paella, couscous, mussels *à la marinière*, Indian curry, goulash, sauerkraut, Welsh rarebit, Brazilian *feijoada*, Mexican *mole*, several dishes from North Africa, *escabeche*, American southern-fried chicken, English roast beef, *waterzooï*, Turkish-style eggplant, *aïoli*, and a hundred other regional "specialties." It is the ties with the soil, with the natural foods forthcoming from this soil, and with the ancestral skills that go into the making and cooking of them that, as I have already indicated in the first chapter, make most of these dishes ones that, as the expression goes, "travel badly." At times a dish, although relatively simple, degenerates because it is thus cut off from its roots; at other times, it is an entire cuisine that shrinks and becomes impoverished when it is exported because it is basically too rich and too complex. This is the case with Chinese cuisine. The number of Chinese restaurants in Europe and North America is infinitely greater than the number of competent Chinese cooks available on all five continents; such cooks, parodoxically, cannot even be found in those cities of the West where there are a large Chinese population and vast Chinatowns. It is not the restaurant but the Chinese cook, therefore, to whom food-lovers are faithful throughout all his peregrinations from one establishment to the other. Another reason why cuisine "travels badly" has to do with the health laws that in certain countries forbid the importation of certain products. In the United States, the Food and Drug Administration is extremely strict, confiscating at customs even the humblest sausage that the traveler has intended to offer to his friends. Hence, it is impossible to get a decent *cassoulet* in New York, for the flavor of this dish comes above all from the very special sausage products of the Southwest of France. For the same reason, the link with a particular geographical location, it is impossible to get a decent *cocido madrileño* in New York.

Despite this inevitable loss when transported, regional cuisines have been paradoxically saved because of the worldwide spread of cuisine. The fight to defend them has gone hand in hand with the tendency toward cosmopolitan nomenclature and with the fight for a return to natural foods, to the vegetables, poultry, bread, and wines of the prechemical and preindustrial era. Digestion begins in the kitchen, an old proverb has it. No—it begins in the garden, in the fields, in the poultry yard. In this domain, as in many others, nature is admittedly a luxury, but happily it is a luxury that is becoming more and more within the reach of all classes. People's appreciation of natural flavor and perfect freshness has assured, for instance, the international success of Japanese cuisine. Who could have guessed around 1950 that this cuisine would one day go far beyond its own borders, to the point of passing on to Europeans a taste for raw fish and inspiring them to create recipes in which chad and salmon come directly from the sea to the diner's plate without ever passing by way of a saucepan or an oven? Let us not drift into the excesses of overgeneralization, but let us risk a hypothesis nonetheless: the predominant characteristic of contemporary gastronomy, in these closing years of the twentieth century appears to me to be obvious: for better and for worse, this predominant characteristic is the return to nature.

PHOTOGRAPHIC SOURCES

Alinari-Giraudon, pp. 34, 35
Bibliothèque Nationale, Paris, pp. 84–85, 101, 104, 105, 107, 109, 121, 122, 123, 130–31, 133, 136–37, 143, 159, 161, 162–63, 179, 201, 243, 256–57, 260–61
Bulloz, pp. 30 (*both pictures*), 96–97, 128–29, 220–21
J. L. Charmet, Pauvert, pp. 174, 175, 181, 192, 193, 195, 217, 237, 239, 241, 254, 255
Chuzeville, p. 37
Giraudon, pp. 31, 67, 70–71, 98, 124–25, 156–57, 184–85, 202–3
Herbert Pattusch, p. 100
Roger Viollet, pp. 16–17, 21
Leonard von Matt, pp. 42–43, 44, 45, 72–73

INDEX